THE SERMON ON THE MOUNT

AN EXPOSITION

Books by Dr. Boice . . .

Witness and Revelation in the Gospel of John

Philippians: An Expositional Commentary

The Sermon on the Mount

How to Live the Christian Life (originally, *How to Really Live It Up*)

Ordinary Men Called by God (originally, *How God Can Use Nobodies*)

The Last and Future World

The Gospel of John: An Expositional Commentary (5 volumes in one)

"Galatians" in the Expositor's Bible Commentary

Can You Run Away From God?

Our Sovereign God, editor

Our Savior God: Studies on Man, Christ and the Atonement, editor

Foundations of the Christian Faith (4 volumes in one)

The Foundation of Biblical Authority, editor

The Epistles of John

Does Inerrancy Matter?

Making God's Word Plain, editor

Genesis: An Expositional Commentary (3 volumes)

The Parables of Jesus

The Christ of Christmas

The Christ of the Open Tomb

Standing on the Rock

The Minor Prophets: An Expositional Commentary (2 volumes)

Christ's Call to Discipleship

Daniel: An Expositional Commentary (available in 1989)

Ephesians: An Expositional Commentary (available in 1989)

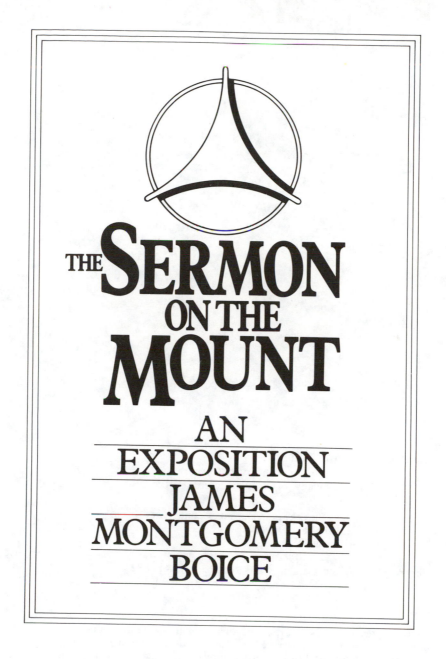

THE SERMON ON THE MOUNT

AN EXPOSITION

JAMES MONTGOMERY BOICE

Ministry Resources Library

Zondervan Publishing House • Grand Rapids, MI

MINISTRY RESOURCES LIBRARY is an imprint of Zondervan
Publishing House, 1415 Lake Drive, S.E.,
Grand Rapids, Michigan 49506

Library of Congress Catalog Card Number: 72 - 83882

ISBN 0-310-21511-0

Printed in the United States of America

91 92 93 94 / CH / 21 20 19 18 17

To Him
*who came not to destroy the law
but to fulfill it*

Contents

Preface

Preface

The Sermon on the Mount is found in the fifth, sixth, and seventh chapters of Matthew's gospel, and it is the purpose of this volume to examine each of those chapters in detail. Before we get on with that, however, it may be well to state at the outset the basic principle underlying these studies: that in dealing with the Sermon on the Mount we are dealing with the need for a new life rather than with a legalistic system of morality.

I believe that the failure to see this truth has led to nearly all the great misunderstandings of the Sermon on the Mount. This was true of the way the Sermon on the Mount was handled by leaders of the Social Gospel movement which flourished at the beginning of this century. Under the leadership of such men as Washington Gladden and Walter Rauschenbusch, the Social Gospel movement focused the Church's attention upon the corporate aspects of twentieth-century life and the need for achieving social justice. In this crusade the Sermon on the Mount was regarded as the battle plan of the churches, and the phrase "the kingdom of God" was erected as the banner. All that was needed for the realization of Christ's kingdom, they said, as a widespread understanding of the Sermon on the Mount and a vigorous application of it to our culture.

It must be said in favor of the leaders of this movement that they were aware of the crying social needs of our society at a time when a defense of the working man or the poor man was not popular. Their efforts have certainly borne fruit in the gradually awakening social conscience of the Christian churches today. But for all their virtues, the Social Gospel movement to which they gave birth had one great and ultimately fatal defect. It was aware of Christ's ethic, but it tried to preach the ethic to those who were not possessed of Christ's life. Consequently, the attempt to actualize Christ's standard of human conduct universally was doomed to disheartening failure. Shaken by the hard realities of two world wars, this form of the Social Gospel movement quickly became outmoded.

The churches now turn to wealth, mass movements, and politics to effect by force what they cannot effect by merely moralistic preaching.

At the other extreme from the Social Gospel's approach to the Sermon on the Mount are three other misunderstandings, all of which are attempts to reject it entirely and to concentrate on the so-called "legitimate" aspects of the Church's proclamation. These errors also stem from a failure to see that Jesus Christ was calling for a new life rather than a legalistic system.

The first of these attempts is found in a type of evangelistic preaching that has identified the Sermon on the Mount with legalism. To this way of thinking the Sermon on the Mount is essentially a carry-over from the law of the Old Testament although a better interpretation of it and, as such, is opposed to the Gospel of salvation by faith in Jesus Christ and to His atoning work on Calvary.

This misunderstanding of the Sermon on the Mount betrays great insensitivity to Christ's teachings. It is true that in Matthew's gospel Jesus Christ is pictured as a second lawgiver, like Moses, but the point of the comparison lies mostly in the area of contrast. Six times in chapter five Jesus is quoted as saying, "Ye have heard that it was said . . . but I say unto you . . ." (verses 21f., 27f., 31f., 33f., 38f., 43f.), implying His greater and independent authority, and the chapter itself closes with a most un-Mosaic statement devastating to all attempts to exalt human righteousness as a means of salvation: "Be ye, therefore, perfect, even as your Father, who is in heaven, is perfect" (5:48). That is not legalism. It is not the Old Testament law restated. It is a condemnation of all attempts to please God by legalism in order that the way may be cleared for a man to come to God by faith in Jesus Christ and to receive a new life capable of that which He requires. To identify the Sermon on the Mount with legalism is to miss the entire flavor of what our Lord is saying. Christ's ethics go beyond the law of Moses in order that we may be brought to the feet of the Gospel.

There is also an objection to the Sermon on the Mount rising from the feeling that the standards set down are impossible and are, therefore, not to be taken seriously by Christians. This line of argument at least recognizes the terribly high standards that are found here, but it does not recognize that Christians are called precisely to an impossible standard or that the Holy Spirit has been given to them to help them achieve that standard.

Moreover, to reject the Sermon on the Mount in this way is also to take an unjustifiably high-handed approach to the Bible. That is the error of liberalism, which feels at liberty to accept one part of Scripture while it rejects another. Neither this view of the Sermon on the Mount nor liberalism entirely subjects itself to the Bible. The only difference is that liberalism holds to the ethic (or part of it) while rejecting the Gospel, whereas this type of conservatism holds to the Gospel while rejecting the ethic. If the Bible says that *"all* Scripture is . . . profitable for doctrine, for reproof, for correction, for instruction in righteousness"* (2 Tim. 3:16), it means the Sermon on the Mount too. And Jesus must have had it in mind when He told His disciples, "Go, ye, therefore, and teach all nations, . . . teaching them to observe *all* things whatsoever I have commanded you" (Matt. 28:19, 20).

The fourth misunderstanding of the Sermon on the Mount is the view of some forms of early dispensationalism, a movement of Scriptural interpretation that had a tremendous influence in the first part of this century and has left an abiding influence upon many conservatives through the justified success of the popular Scofield Bible.

According to this system of Bible interpretation the Sermon on the Mount was an official proclamation by Jesus of the ethical principles on which His messianic kingdom would be founded. In these three chapters the Lord Jesus Christ speaks as Israel's king. Hence, the ethics of the Sermon are to be applied not to our age, the age of the Church, but to the future age of Christ's rule. Dr. I. M. Haldeman, one of the dispensationalists, wrote, "The Sermon on the Mount must be taken in its wholeness and in its literalness. This sermon . . . cannot be taken in its plain import and be applied to Christians universally . . . It has been tried in spots, but . . . it has always been like planting a beautiful flower in stony ground or in a dry and withering atmosphere." * Similarly, the early edition of the Scofield Bible says, "For these reasons the Sermon on the Mount in its primary application gives neither the privilege nor the duty of the Church."

I have no quarrel with some types of dispensationalism. I am not a dispensationalist myself. But if others find it helpful to divide biblical history into periods in which God seems to have been particularly interested in demonstrating certain truths — such as the

* I. M. Haldeman, *The Kingdom of God* (New York: F. E. Fitch, 1931), p. 149.

inability of man to govern himself by conscience, human government, law, or anything else — I will not object to it. I am for any system that actually helps a person to read and assimilate the Bible. I am delighted to say that the Scofield Bible was a great influence upon my own early study of the Scriptures. Moreover, I have the deepest respect for these gifted teachers. They were deeply spiritual men. They were steeped in the Bible — far more, for instance, than most Bible teachers today, myself included. And yet, I am convinced that in their approach to the Sermon on the Mount the leaders of dispensationalism were wrong.

It is no great discredit to them to say that. There has never been a system of Bible interpretation that has been right in every point, and the early leaders of dispensationalism would have been the first to admit their own fallibility.

Why were they wrong? They were wrong for at least three reasons. First, their view is without real proof from the Scriptures. The dispensationalists say that the ethics of these chapters are reserved for Christ's messianic kingdom, which is yet to come. But surely this view is nowhere to be found in Christ's teaching. In fact, the reverse is true. Christ actually emphasizes the lasting validity of His words rather than indicating that their present import be postponed. The Sermon is filled with present tense imperatives: "rejoice," "swear not," "go," "give," "take heed." Jesus said, "Till heaven and earth pass, one jot or one tittle shall in no way pass from the law, till all be fulfilled" (5:18). He nowhere indicated that His words were to be disregarded either then or now.

Second, it is apparent from careful study of the Sermon on the Mount that it is just such a world as ours that Christ had in view when He spoke the words of the Sermon. According to the dispensationalists the words should be applied to an age in which the Lord's earthly rule is established and in which justice is enforced and righteousness required. But if this were so, what could be the possible meaning of a verse such as Matthew 5:44: "But I say unto you, Love your enemies, bless them that curse you, do good to them that hate you, and pray for them who despitefully use you, and persecute you"? In the kingdom age no one will have liberty to practice these things — to persecute others or use them despitefully. Hence, a statement like this one would be meaningless.

The world of the Sermon on the Mount is a real and sinful world — a world of tax collectors, unjust officials, hypocrites, thieves, of those who are weak or poor, and false prophets. It is a statement of how those who are born again by faith in Christ are to live in spite of it.

The third — and in some ways the most significant — objection to this error of some forms of dispensationalism is the interesting fact that even the dispensationalists could not be entirely consistent in this interpretation of the Gospel. It is a great tribute to their own walk with the Lord that in many instances their spiritual sensitivity to what the Sermon on the Mount has to say won out over their doctrinal theory. Thus, the great expositor, Arno C. Gaebelein, wrote in his commentary on Matthew that while the Sermon on the Mount should be assigned to the messianic age, this fact *"never* excludes application to us who are His heavenly people, members of His body, who will share the heavenly throne in the heavenly Jerusalem with Him." * I am pleased to see that the New Scofield Bible, while keeping the general scheme of dispensationalism in its valuable notes, nevertheless omits the previous statement about the Sermon's being "neither the privilege nor the duty of the Church" and says, instead, "Although the law, as expressed in the Sermon on the Mount, cannot save sinners (Rom. 3:20), and the redeemed of the present age are not under law (Rom. 6:14), nevertheless both the Mosaic law and the Sermon on the Mount are a part of Holy Scripture which is inspired by God and therefore 'profitable for doctrine, for reproof, for correction, for instruction in righteousness' (2 Tim. 3:16) for the redeemed of all ages." Perhaps the case against all the various objections to the Sermon on the Mount may rest with that one statement from Scripture.

Why, then, should we in our day study the Sermon on the Mount? There are at least four reasons.

First, the Sermon on the Mount shows us the absolute necessity of the new birth. Show me a man who claims that he is living up to the standards of the Sermon on the Mount, and I will show you a man who either has never read it, does not understand what it is teaching, or is lying. The Sermon on the Mount does not encourage righteousness in man apart from Christ; it condemns him for falling short of God's righteousness, and it drives him in desperation to the cross. Paul says that the law was our schoolmaster to bring us unto Christ, that we may be justified by faith

* Arno C. Gaebelein, *The Gospel of Matthew* (New York: Loizeaux Brothers, 1961), p. 110.

(Gal. 3:24). And if that was true of the Old Testament law, which was largely external, how much more true it is of this Sermon. The Sermon on the Mount calls for a pure righteousness that flows from a regenerated heart.

Second, the Sermon on the Mount should be studied because, like all Scripture, it points us to the Lord Jesus Christ. This should be the case even in a literary or historical study, for it is impossible to study any document well without giving attention to its author. It should also be true spiritually. We shall see as we proceed that it is impossible to enter into the deepest understanding of these chapters without realizing that in a very large measure they bring us into the deepest possible contact with the person and nature of our Lord. The preacher of the Sermon on the Mount *is* the Sermon on the Mount, and we are constantly brought into the most intimate contact with Him.

Third, we should study the Sermon on the Mount because it indicates the way to blessing for Christians. The Christian finds happiness, not in accordance with the world's standards, but in accordance with these principles. It is the poor (not the haughty), the meek (not the proud), the merciful (not the cruel), the peacemakers (not the agitators) who are called blessed.

Finally, we study the Sermon on the Mount as Christians because it shows us the way to please our heavenly Father. It is true that we cannot please Him until we first become a member of His family. That comes only with the new birth. But once we are in His family it is a privilege to please Him. We are able to do so when we discover what He wants for us by reading the Scriptures.

Four of the five studies on sex and marriage (Matt. 5:27-32) have already appeared as articles in *Eternity* magazine (Sept.-Dec., 1970) and are reprinted by permission. Most scriptural quotations are from the New Scofield Bible, and are also used by permission. If the translation deviates from the NSB text and is not identified as another standard translation, the rendition is my own.

I wish to thank the session and congregation of the Tenth Presbyterian Church, Philadelphia, who allow me to spend much of my time in writing and Bible study, and Miss Caecilie Foelster, my secretary, who carefully edited the manuscript.

JAMES MONTGOMERY BOICE

Philadelphia, Pa.

Chapter 1

The Secret of Happiness

(Matthew 5:3-12)

Sometimes God gives an unbeliever more insight into the lives of Christians than most Christians have. For instance, someone once said to Hannah Whitall Smith, the author of the very successful book, *The Christian's Secret of a Happy Life,* "You Christians seem to have a religion that makes you miserable. You are like a man with a headache. He does not want to get rid of his head, but it hurts him to keep it. You cannot expect outsiders to seek very earnestly for anything so uncomfortable." * I do not know what you may think of this statement, but I believe that in some instances this unbeliever was right in his assumption. Christians often are quite miserable, even though through the indwelling of the Holy Spirit they may sense that true happiness is their birthright as members of the family of God. And because they are miserable they have little to offer a world that is desperately and often hopelessly searching for happiness.

To such a world and to all unhappy Christians the opening words of the Sermon on the Mount give hope. For Jesus Christ began His first great sermon with the promise of the happiness of heaven. He said, "Blessed are the poor in spirit. . . . Blessed are they that mourn. . . . Blessed are the meek. . . . Blessed are they who hunger and thirst after righteousness. . . . Blessed are the merciful. . . . Blessed are they who are persecuted for righteousness' sake; for theirs is the kingdom of heaven."

In this sermon the word "blessed" means "happy," not in the world's sense, of course, for the happiness of the world is a superficial happiness that depends upon circumstances. The happiness spoken of here does not depend upon circumstances and fills the soul with joy even in the midst of the most depressing events. For this reason the Phillips paraphrase of the New Testament makes this verse say, "How happy are the humble-minded," and *Today's*

* Hannah Whitall Smith, *The Christian's Secret of a Happy Life* (Westwood, N.J.: Fleming H. Revell, 1952), p. 15.

15

English Version, "Happy are those who know they are spiritually poor: the Kingdom of heaven belongs to them."

The New Testament scholar A. M. Hunter writes, "The Beatitudes of Jesus describe the character of the men who, living under God's Fatherly Rule made manifest in Jesus, enjoy . . . happiness even here and now, though its perfection belongs to the heavenly world." *   And he would agree that in this verse and in the other seven beatitudes Jesus Christ gives men the secret of happiness.

MEANING OF BLESSED

The word "blessed" has an interesting background in the English language. In the days of the origin of the English language, when Anglo-Saxon was in use and a number of related dialects were competing for prominence as the common speech, there were more than thirty forms of the Old English word for blessed, among them *bloedsian, bledsian,* and *bletsian.* These words were based on the Old English noun *blod* (meaning "blood"), and they were altered in time to become our words "blest" or "blessed." At this period of the history of the English language a thing was considered blessed when it was set apart to God by a blood ritual, and the word then referred to consecration. In this sense the elements of the communion service were called "the blessed sacrament." We use the word in this way when we speak of the prayer used before meals as a "blessing," for in our prayer we consecrate the food and ourselves to God's service.

In time, the word "blessed" in its earlier forms came to be used as a translation for the Latin word *benedicere* in the Bible and in ecclesiastic speech. And thus a new meaning was added to the word. *Benedicere* (which, in its turn, had been used to translate the Greek word *eulogein)* meant "to speak well of" something or someone, or "to eulogize." It was always used in the Latin Bible for the eulogizing or praising of God. When men sing God's praises they bless Him. Thus, the word is used in this second sense in verses like Luke 1:68: "Blessed be the Lord God of Israel; for he hath visited and redeemed his people." The same sense occurs in the Sermon on the Mount in the verse in which Jesus tells us to love our enemies and "bless them that curse you." By this He meant that we are to speak well of those who do not speak well of us.

A third meaning of blessed arose from the fact that the words

* A. M. Hunter, *Design for Life* (London: SCM Press, 1965), p. 34.

"bless" and "blessed" were similar in spelling and pronunciation to another ancient English word, the word "bliss," and therefore came in time to assimilate its meaning also. We know this because eventually writers began to spell the word "blessed" with an *i* or a *y* instead of with an *e*. And the word "blissed" or "blyssed" was the result. "Bliss" meant happy or joyful. At this final stage of its development "blessed" meant either consecration, praise, or happiness; and "bliss" became a term for spiritual joy. When this happened a new word was called in to express non-religious joy, the word "blithe." And so, in 1746, we find a poet writing to a former friend, "I trust that we shall meet on blither terms."

It is the third use of the word "blessed" that occurs in the Sermon on the Mount. Hence, when Jesus spoke these words He was telling His listeners how they could be deeply, spiritually, and profoundly happy and how they could maintain this happiness even in the midst of life's disappointments and hard times.

PORTRAIT OF CHRIST

We cannot go very far in our study of the Sermon on the Mount without realizing that by its own definition Jesus was Himself most happy. In his study on the Beatitudes Billy Graham has written, "If by happiness we mean serenity, confidence, contentment, peace, joy and soul-satisfaction, then Jesus was supremely 'happy.' We never read of His laughing, though I am sure He did. He was not given to pleasure-seeking, hilariousness, jokes or poking fun at others. . . . His happiness [was not] dependent on outward circumstances. He did not have to have an outward stimulus to make Him happy. He had learned a secret that allowed Him to live above the circumstances of life and fear of the future. He moved with calmness, certainty and serenity through the most trying circumstances — even death! . . . Certainly if anyone had genuine happiness and blessedness, it was Jesus." *

Is it not true that when we turn to the Beatitudes we find them to be a portrait of Jesus? Who is the man who was poor in spirit but who possessed the kingdom of heaven? Jesus! Hence, Paul can say about Him that He "humbled himself and became obedient unto death, even the death of the cross" for which cause "God also hath highly exalted him, and given him a name which is above every name, that at the name of Jesus every knee should bow"

* Billy Graham, *The Secret of Happiness* (Garden City, N.Y.: Doubleday & Company, 1955), pp. v, vi, 3.

(Phil. 2:8-10). Who is the man who mourned and yet was comforted? Certainly, it is Jesus! The 22nd Psalm describes it. It is possible to find verses that identify each statement of character in the Beatitudes with Jesus, to show that He is the meek One, the One who hungered and thirsted after righteousness, the merciful, the pure in heart, the peacemaker, the One persecuted for righteousness' sake, and so on.

PURSUIT OF HAPPINESS

Now, if Jesus was happy in this deep spiritual sense, then it follows that we too can be happy. For Jesus became like us — in all our suffering, in temptation, in disappointment — in order that we may become like Him.

We must realize, however, that if we are to find this happiness we must not look for it in the world's way. The world looks for happiness through money, but there is no real happiness there. A man thinks he will be happy if he can save ten thousand dollars, but when he gets his ten thousand he begins to think in terms of fifty thousand and then a hundred thousand. If his fortune carries him so far, then he wishes he could become a millionaire. After that he starts on his second million, and his third, and his fourth. His frantic pursuit of money indicates that he is searching for something, but that the money itself has failed to supply it. Happiness does not come through fortune. It was a Texas millionaire who said, "I thought money could buy happiness — I have been miserably disillusioned."

Some men try to find happiness through fame, but fame does not guarantee happiness. Voltaire was one of the most famous men in Europe during the eighteenth century. But as he lay dying this noted French infidel is reported to have cried out to his doctor, "I am abandoned by God and man. I will give you half of what I am worth if you will give me six months' life."

Another man thinks he will be happy with power. So he runs for the office of alderman, and wins. Immediately he thinks of being mayor. Once he is mayor he turns his eye to the governor's chair. If he succeeds there, he turns to national politics. Power does not satisfy the heart. One of the world's greatest statesmen once said to Billy Graham, "I am an old man. Life has lost all meaning. I am ready to take a fateful leap into the unknown."

No, if we are to find true happiness, we must not seek it in the world's way. We must look for it in the way outlined by Jesus.

And according to Jesus the way to happiness is found in a poverty of spirit, in a character that is marked by meekness, in a hunger and a thirst for righteousness, in mercy, in purity, and in a desire to make peace. Jesus *lived* these things. Because He lived them, we too can find happiness.

THE SECRET OF HAPPINESS

We are going to be looking at each of these characteristics in the coming studies. But before we look at them in detail we need to look at them as a whole and ask: What, then, is the secret of happiness? What does happiness consist of? In the light of these verses and in the full light of the Word of God we can answer that the secret of happiness consists of at least three things.

First, we must recognize that we shall never get anywhere in our search for happiness until we give up trying to find it by our own efforts and receive it instead as God's free gift. This means that God is the source of all spiritual blessings, and in this as in all things we must look to Him. James presents this simple truth clearly. "Do not err, my beloved brethren. Every good gift and every perfect gift is from above, and cometh down from the Father of lights, with whom is no variableness, neither shadow of turning" (James 1:16, 17). Certainly, the first effect the Beatitudes have on those who understand them is to turn their minds to God our heavenly Father.

Second, we must realize that the blessing of God in an individual life begins with forgiveness of sins. When David wanted to speak of the happiness of the believers in Old Testament times he wrote, "Blessed is he whose transgression is forgiven, whose sin is covered. Blessed is the man unto whom the Lord imputeth not iniquity, and in whose spirit there is no guile" (Ps. 32:1, 2). Paul, years later, quoted these verses as a description of the initial happiness that comes to a man who believes in Jesus.

Sin is a horrible barrier that divides a person from God. Sunday school children sing a song about God's blessings.

> *"There shall be showers of blessing,"*
> *This is the promise of love;*
> *There shall be seasons refreshing,*
> *Sent from the Savior above.*

But for the unsaved man sin is somewhat like a great black umbrella that keeps him from the showers of blessing. Oh, he can walk about under the umbrella hunting for puddles; but they will always be muddy, and he will not be satisfied. Instead of this he must ask God to remove the umbrella — as God has promised to do, for anyone who will trust in Christ's death and resurrection — and thereby place him under the direct flow of happiness.

Finally, we are to study the practical means by which the Lord Jesus Christ will introduce us to the life of true happiness and how we are to avail ourselves of it. The life of the Sermon on the Mount is the life of Jesus. And the life of Jesus is communicated to the Christian by the Spirit of Jesus, the Holy Spirit, who comes to live within him.

In one of his uncirculated manuscripts Dr. Donald Grey Barnhouse referred to this truth as the reason why no believer can find an excuse to fail to live a joyous life. He wrote, "There is, therefore, no excuse for any believer to sink to a low-level Christian life. The fountain is flowing, and there is plenty of water within the reach of every believer. . . . If you submerge a bottle in water what happens? Some of you will say, 'The air bubbles out and the water flows in.' But I have seen a bottle submerged in water and no air came out nor did any water flow in. There was a cork in the bottle, which must first be pulled out. God is like that with us. He has the purpose and the power, but He will not ravish our beings. Love can never be commanded, and He wants us to love Him, so He woos us by creating all the qualities which go with emptiness and frustration. But when we tell Him to go ahead and do His work, out come the obstacles which keep Him from filling our beings, and in comes the power of the Holy Spirit, so that the life at once takes on abounding quality. There is no abounding without the pressure of His power behind it. Nothing can overflow from us until we have first been filled. And we cannot be filled until His power comes in with the enabling." That is the secret of happiness.

Do you know this secret? Many do not. And even Christians often apparently do not know it. Recognize the fact that happiness comes from God. Learn that the first step to God's happiness is the forgiveness of sin. Find it practically through the enabling power of Christ's Spirit. Finding happiness is as simple as that. Men will seek for it through money, fame, power, love, security — in every way but this. Jesus said, "Seek ye first the kingdom of God, and his righteousness, and all these things shall be added unto you" (Matt. 6:33).

Chapter 2

How To Inherit God's Kingdom

(Matthew 5:3)

I do not know much about Sophie Tucker, the actress, but years ago I heard a statement of hers that I have remembered. She was being asked about her early struggles for success and whether or not she had found a certain special happiness in her years of poverty. She answered, "Listen, I've been rich, and I've been poor. And believe me, rich is better." For years I have found this remark interesting. And I remember it now because it seems to be the direct opposite of the first great principle taught by the Lord Jesus Christ about how you and I can find happiness.

In the first verse of the Sermon on the Mount, in the first beatitude, Jesus Christ said, "Blessed are the poor in spirit; for theirs is the kingdom of heaven" (Matt. 5:3). According to Jesus, happiness is related to some sort of poverty, and the heirs of God will be those (and only those) who find it.

POVERTY OF SPIRIT

In all fairness to Sophie Tucker, however, I must admit that when Jesus Christ was talking about poverty of spirit He was not talking about poverty in the same sense that most of us talk about it. He was not talking about the opposite of being materially rich. This is the sense in which many commentators on Matthew's gospel have taken Christ's saying, but this is not its true meaning. There would be some justification for this interpretation if Luke's version of the Beatitudes was all that we possessed in our Bibles, for Luke reports Jesus as saying: "Blessed be you poor; for yours is the kingdom of God" (Luke 6:20). This could be material poverty, but it is not; for Matthew rules out this meaning by quoting Christ's full saying. "Blessed are the poor in spirit." To be poor in spirit is to be poor in the inward man, not in outward circumstances. Consequently, to be poor in spirit is to recognize one's poverty spiritually before God.

If it were true that Matthew 5:3 refers to material poverty, then it would be an unchristian thing for a Christian or any other person to seek to alleviate the burdens of the destitute and the starving. It would mean seeking to abolish that which actually brings them closer to God and to His happiness. If this were the meaning, it would not be right to attempt to relieve those who are starving in war-torn countries. It would not be right to try and provide for the refugees left homeless by natural calamities. There could be no social programs within the Christian churches. There could be no orphanages, no hospitals or inner city missions. None of these things would be Christian if this verse taught that spiritual blessedness was to be derived from material poverty.

Fortunately, the verse does not say that at all. And what is equally important, God does not sanction poverty in any other biblical passage either. It is true that there are verses that teach that sometimes riches can be a bad thing. Christ said that it is often hard for a rich man to enter the kingdom of heaven. A person can be so caught up in the material things of this world that he can miss God's spiritual benefits. That is true. But if it is true that it is hard for a rich man to enter the kingdom of heaven, it is true that it is sometimes difficult for a poor person to enter also, for the poor man can be equally materialistic. No, the first beatitude is not talking about either material riches or material poverty.

It is not talking about the "poor in spirit" in the sense of being poor-spirited, either. A poor-spirited person is a person who lacks drive and enthusiasm for life. There are many Christians who seem to be like this. But this is not endorsed by Christ's teaching. David was the one man in all the Bible who was called a man after God's own heart, and there was not a more ambitious or successful man in all of Israel's history. David was a man who entered vigorously into the affairs of his day. He forged a nation out of diverse and mutually jealous tribes, and he united them successfully enough to be able to drive off all the surrounding nations that desired to conquer Israel. David was not poor-spirited! And yet, he epitomized, perhaps far more than any other character in history, what Jesus meant when He said that His followers were to be poor in spirit before God.

What exactly did Jesus mean? We can see the answer to this

question when we recognize that being poor in spirit is the opposite of being rich in pride. In fact, you might say that being poor in spirit is to be spiritually bankrupt before God. It is the mental state of the man who has recognized something of the righteousness and holiness of God, who has seen into the sin and corruption of his own heart, and has acknowledged his inability to please God. Such a person is poor in spirit. It is to such a person, Jesus said, that the kingdom of heaven belongs. Seen in this way, the first of the eight Beatitudes is one of the strongest statements in the Bible of the great doctrine of justification by faith in Jesus Christ alone, for it is a statement of a person's complete inability to please God by any human effort.

FIRST PRINCIPLES

This first great teaching of the Sermon on the Mount is one that can be spelled out more clearly in a number of related propositions. The first is this: we must recognize as a first principle for understanding the Sermon on the Mount that we cannot fulfill the standards of the Sermon on the Mount by ourselves. The Sermon on the Mount was not given so that a man could say to himself, "Come on, old chap, I guess we'll just have to try harder to pull you up by your bootstraps." This cannot be done. Paradoxically, Jesus teaches that the Sermon on the Mount is only for those who know that they cannot live by it.

Have you ever recognized this same fact about the law of God given in the Old Testament? It was not given by God so that a person might fulfill it, or some of it, and then congratulate himself on how well he is doing. It was given to drive a man to God for God's mercy.

This is clearly demonstrated in the first giving of the law on Mount Sinai. The people of Israel had asked for the law, and God had called Moses up into the mountain to receive it. There, Moses was told that there were to be no other gods before the one true God of Israel. There were to be no idols. There was to be no greed, no adultery, no murder, no breaking of the Sabbath day, and so on. But while the precepts of the law were being given to Moses on the top of Mount Sinai, the people who had come with him out of Egypt were down in the valley doing the very things that God was forbidding. And so, right at the beginning of Israel's history we have a demonstration that the standards of God's righteousness cannot be achieved by sinful human beings.

In time the people of Israel recognized this truth. And those who submitted to it came to God humbly, confessing their sin, and availing themselves of the cleansing God had provided through the sacrifices. Those who would not submit to this truth and who, instead, boasted and wished to boast in their own self-righteousness, sought to whittle the high standards of the law down to the low level of their own performance. They did this by interpreting and reinterpreting it. Under the direction of the scribes a series of supplementary commandments was added to the law which had the effect of lowering its requirements, although they would not acknowledge this. Actually, the rabbis said that they were putting a "hedge" about the Torah. This meant that they were constructing a series of safeguard commandments around the central, God-given commandment, so that anyone who came close to breaking it would be warned before he did so and thus be kept from sinning. In practice, however, this meant only that the individual could tell himself that he had kept the Sabbath if he did not travel more than a Sabbath day's journey, did not cook in his home, did not work in the field, and so on. And it was possible for him to escape entirely the far more important demands upon his mind and conduct that in God's view actually made the day holy.

This was the situation in Jesus' day, and the result was that Jesus confronted the hypocrisy of the religious people directly. Jesus said, "For I say unto you that except your righteousness shall exceed the righteousness of the scribes and Pharisees, ye shall in no case enter into the kingdom of heaven" (Matt. 5:20). And He ended the first great section of the Sermon on the Mount with the categorical statement, "Be ye, therefore, perfect, even as your Father, who is in heaven, is perfect" (Matt. 5:48). In other words, Jesus was saying, "Even though you may have kept the commandments of Rabbi Hillel, Rabbi Jehuda, or Rabbi Jose, that does not necessarily mean that you have kept the commandments of God. And the purpose of those commandments is actually to show you that you have not kept them and that you will never be able to keep them."

Years later the Apostle Paul came along and spelled out this teaching for his churches. He wrote, "Now we know that whatever things the law saith, it saith to them who are under the law, that every mouth may be stopped, and all the world may become guilty before God. Therefore, by the deeds of the law there shall no flesh be justified in his sight; for by the law is the knowledge of sin" (Rom. 3:19, 20). All the verses which I have quoted boil down to this: the one thing that the law cannot do is to make a man righteous before God. Rather, it condemns him. Consequently, if we are ever to understand the ethical teachings of Jesus Christ, we must recognize as a first great principle that we just cannot abide by them. And we must come in faith to the only One who did fulfill them and who alone can fulfill them in those who give their lives to Him.

Let me illustrate the truth in this way. To preach the standards of the Sermon on the Mount to persons who are unregenerate and who do not have Christ's nature within them is a bit like preaching the prophecies about the bliss of the millennium in Isaiah to the animal world. The eleventh chapter of Isaiah says that when Jesus Christ will return to this world to set up a holy kingdom, all things will be made right. Sin will be stopped, and even in nature the wolf will dwell with the lamb. Well, try practicing that today. I have been to the zoo often enough to know that a lamb wandering into a wolf's cage would be dinner with wool on — no matter how many preachers were reading the eleventh chapter of Isaiah to the wolf. If the prophecy is to be fulfilled, it is necessary for the wolf to have a new nature. And so, too, if the law is to be fulfilled in us it is necessary for us to have a new nature. We need to recognize as a first principle of Christian ethics that a new nature, given by the Lord Jesus Christ, is prerequisite.

EMPTY VESSELS

The second great principle suggested by Matthew 5:3 is that there must be an emptying in our lives before there can be a filling. We must become poor in spirit before we can become rich in God's spiritual blessings. The old wine must be poured out of the wineskins before the new wine can be poured in.

Right back at the beginning of the Lord's earthly life Simeon acknowledged this in a prophecy made to Mary and Joseph when they appeared in Jerusalem for the presentation of the infant Jesus at the temple. Simeon said, "Behold, this child is set for the fall and rising again of many in Israel" (Luke 2:34). Notice the order: first the fall, then the rising again. In other words, the emptying comes before the filling, repentance before conversion, a recognition of worthlessness in God's sight before acceptance of His salvation.

This is what all God's children have found. It was known to

St. Augustine. Before his conversion the future Bishop of Hippo
was proud of his intellect and knowledge, and these things actually
held him back from believing. It was only after he had emptied
himself of his pride and his sense of being able to manage his
own life that he found God's perfect wisdom through Scripture.
Luther's experience was similar. When the future German reformer
entered the monastery at a young age his purpose was to earn
his own salvation through piety and good works. Nevertheless, he
experienced an acute sense of failure. It was only after he recognized his own inability to please God and emptied himself of all
attempts to earn his salvation that God touched his heart and
showed him the true meaning of salvation by grace through faith.
Then Luther became the great reformer of the Church. In the
same way a modern hymn-writer has written:

> *But tho' I cannot sing, or tell, or know*
> *The fullness of Thy love, while here below,*
> *My empty vessel I may freely bring:*
> *O Thou, who art of love the living spring,*
> *My vessel fill.*

> *I am an empty vessel — not one thought*
> *Or look of love, I ever to Thee brought;*
> *Yet I may come, and come again to Thee,*
> *With this, the empty sinner's only plea —*
> *Thou lovest me.*

An empty vessel! "*I* am an empty vessel." If you will say that,
then God will fill you with the life of Jesus Christ — supernaturally
— and you will begin to live the standards of the Sermon on the
Mount by the power of the One who gave them and who Himself
lived them perfectly in this world.

CONFRONTED BY GOD

There is only one more observation that needs to be added to
these comments on the first beatitude. I have said that there must
be an emptying of a person before there can be a filling by God.
There must be a true poverty of spirit. But this is unnatural to
man, and, therefore, impossible. We must, therefore, add that
nothing but a direct confrontation with the holy, just, and loving
God will produce it.

You see, it is never possible to create a true poverty of spirit
by looking within or by looking around at other people. The hu-

man heart is corrupt. And because of it you will always latch upon someone who is worse in some respect than yourself. You will find someone who is prouder than you are, and although you may still be quite proud you will congratulate yourself on being humble. You will find someone who has strong fits of temper, and although you too have a temper you will congratulate yourself on being more moderate in your temper than he. So it will go with all the failings that make you less perfect than Jesus Christ and therefore the fit object of His mercy and salvation.

And yet, you need not look to other men for the basis of a self-evaluation. You may look to God as you see Him reflected in the person of the Lord Jesus Christ. There you will learn a true humility, a true sense of need, and the result will be beneficial. You will say as Isaiah did when he saw God, "Woe is me! For I am undone, because I am a man of unclean lips, and I dwell in the midst of a people of unclean lips; for mine eyes have seen the King, the LORD of hosts" (Isa. 6:5). C. S. Lewis once wrote of this experience, "Whenever we find that our religious life is making us feel that we are good — above all, that we are better than someone else — I think we may be sure that we are being acted on, not by God, but by the devil. The real test of being in the presence of God is that you either forget about yourself altogether or see yourself as a small, dirty object. It is better to forget about yourself altogether." *

As we proceed in our studies of the Beatitudes I am sure that both of those things will happen. But one other thing will happen also. We shall see more and more of Jesus, the One who *is* Himself the Sermon on the Mount, and we shall be drawn increasingly closer to Him.

---

* C. S. Lewis, *Mere Christianity* (New York: The MacMillan Company, 1958), pp. 96, 97.

Chapter 3

Life on Wings

(Matthew 5:4)

In one of the great Old Testament Psalms, after a passionate description of the disappointments and bitterness of this life, David cries out, "Oh, that I had wings like a dove! For then would I fly away, and be at rest. Lo, then would I wander far off, and remain in the wilderness. I would hasten my escape from the windy storm and tempest" (Ps. 55:6-8). In these words David voices a wish that is as ancient as fallen humanity and which will endure as long as men live on this planet. It is a cry for freedom, for life on wings. It is uttered by those who yearn for comfort in a life of bitterness, frustration, disappointment, and trials.

All men know the longing for freedom, sometimes intensely, but not all find the solutuion. Fortunately, David found it. For he said, "As for me, I will call upon God, and the LORD shall save me" (v. 16). God was David's solution. God gave him joy. In his joy he recommended a life of trusting to others: "Cast thy burden upon the LORD, and he shall sustain thee; he shall never suffer the righteous to be moved" (v. 22). David had found that the way of escape in life's sorrows does not lie to the north or the south — or to any of the points of the compass — but upward, and that God Himself provides it. He would have said with Isaiah, "They that wait upon the LORD shall renew their strength; they shall mount up with wings like eagles; they shall run, and not be weary; and they shall walk, and not faint" (Isa. 40:31).

I believe that the second of the Lord's Beatitudes is a New Testament expression of this identical lesson, for it speaks of the happiness of the man whom God comforts. Jesus said, "Blessed are

28

they that mourn; for they shall be comforted." And there is no comfort to compare with the comfort given to a man by God.

MOURNING FOR OTHERS

The unusual thing about Christ's statement, however, is that He links the comfort of God to mourning, or to what we would call intense sorrow, and He seems to say that the way to a jubilant heart is through tears. Everything in the world opposes this principle. The world says, "Let us eat, drink, and be merry; for tomorrow we die." The English poet Edward Young wrote, "'Tis impious in a good man to be sad." We sing,

> *What's the use of worrying?*
> *It never was worthwhile.*
> *So pack up your troubles in your old kit bag*
> *And smile, smile, smile.*

But Jesus says that happiness comes through sorrow. And the parallel passage in Luke 6 makes His words even sharper: "Blessed are ye that weep now; for ye shall laugh" (Luke 6:21). Dr. D. Martyn Lloyd-Jones writes, "This saying condemns the apparent laughter, joviality and happiness of the world by pronouncing a woe upon it. But it promises blessing and happiness, joy and peace to those who mourn." *

It is evident, of course, that in this, as in the other Beatitudes, Jesus is dealing with a spiritual principle, a spiritual mourning, and not merely with things seen from a purely human standpoint.

The verse could mean three things. It could refer only to a human sorrow, such as the sorrow we know when faced by death or disappointments. It would be correct when it says that such sorrow can lead to comfort. In his commentary on Matthew's gospel William Barclay reminds his readers of an Arab proverb that says, "All sunshine makes a desert." And it is true that a life of unmixed happiness would be unbearable and withering to the soul. Sorrow gives spice to life. It teaches us to appreciate good things. It increases our sensitivity, particularly to the needs and sorrows of others. Moreover, such sorrow will sometimes drive a man to God. John R. W. Stott, the minister of All Souls Church in London, once conducted a poll of his congregation to find out what actually caused the members of it to become Christians. He

* D. Martyn Lloyd-Jones, *Studies in the Sermon on the Mount* (Grand Rapids: Wm. B. Eerdmans, 1967), Vol. I. p. 53.

was surprised to find that a majority listed as the greatest single human factor a feeling of personal desperation, a sense of being at the end of their resources. The second beatitude could refer to such sorrow. And yet, it is hard to feel that this sense of sorrow lies at the heart of Christ's teaching.

The beatitude also could refer to a mourning for the evil of this world, to what we could call a social conscience. It seems to me that this comes a great deal closer to Christ's meaning, particularly if we link it to a sorrow for the world's sin. The English social reformer, Lord Shaftesbury, probably did more to improve the life of normal men and women in England in the last century than any other person, and yet his career as a social reformer began quite simply. One day as a boy, when he was going along the streets of Harrow, he met a pauper's funeral. The body of the poor man had been placed in a hand-made coffin, shoddy and unembellished, and it was being pushed through the street on a hand-drawn cart. The men who accompanied it were apparently drunk. As they wove their way along the streets they sang their risque drinking songs and told lewd stories. Their way led up a hill to the graveyard, and as they went up the hill the coffin slid off the cart and broke open. The scene that followed was hilarious to the drunken companions. It was disgusting to some onlookers. But to Shaftesbury it seemed an evil that called for the deepest sorrow. He said to himself, "When I grow up I am going to use my life to see that such things will not happen."

The second beatitude can refer to such sorrow. And it does refer to it in part. Christianity is partly caring for other people. And it should produce a sound social conscience. In fact, if it does not, we have some reason to doubt our Christianity. For John said, "By this we do know that we know him, if we keep his commandments. He that saith, I know him, and keepeth not his commandments, is a liar, and the truth is not in him" (1 John 2:3, 4). What were Christ's commandments? Well, there were many. But among them were these: "Love your enemies, bless them that curse you, do good to them that hate you, and pray for them who despitefully use you, and persecute you" (Matt. 5:44); "All things whatever ye would that men should do to you, do ye even so to them; for this is the law and the prophets" (Matt. 7:12). "Give to every man that asketh of thee" (Luke 6:30); "Be ye, therefore, merciful, as your Father also is merciful" (Luke 6:36); "Let your light so shine before men, that they may see your good works, and glorify your Father, who is in heaven" (Matt. 5:16). An awareness of the sin of the world should produce a mourning for its evils in Christ's followers.

It follows from this that the Christian Church should never stand aloof from the great social movements of the day or, worse yet, be critical of them. Christians should be in the vanguard of social reform. And they should be there from a heartfelt love of humanity and from an acute awareness of the horror and destructiveness of man's sin.

I believe that this often has been true in past periods of church history. Lord Shaftesbury was one of the great Christian social reformers, but there were others: Calvin, Oberlin, Wilberforce, Moorehouse. And it would be proper to include in this list most of the pioneers of the modern missionary movement — William Carey, Robert Moffat, David Livingstone, John Paton, and others — all of whom combined an evangelistic zeal with social action. Unfortunately, however, much of the force of their social concern has been lost to the believing church today.

There are reasons for the present dullness of the evangelical church on social issues. For one thing, much of the time, money, and effort of this great body of Christendom has gone into the missionary movement, with striking results. And there is a natural limit both in time and resources to what one body of Christians can do. For another thing, confronted with the rising tide of liberalism at the start of this century, conservatives found much of their efforts taken up quite properly with a defense of Scripture and basic biblical doctrines. Third, major efforts were also made in the area of evangelism. None of these programs was wrong. All were essential. But the involvement of believers in the social ills of this and other nations was important too, and the neglect of these crying ills inevitably gave the impression that the Christians were unaware of them and, in fact, did not mourn for others.

To each of us, therefore, the second beatitude is a call to involvement in the social arena — in the struggle of blacks for true equality, the plight of underpaid workers, pollution of our natural resources, education, ethical problems in politics, medicine, and business, and other contemporary problems — just as Christians were formerly active in the war against slavery, child labor, lack of freedom of the press, and immorality. We should mourn for such things. And we should mourn deeply enough to do something about them.

MOURNING FOR SIN

There is no doubt then that these thoughts are wrapped up in the second beatitude. It speaks to these issues. And yet, I cannot feel that even this point gets quite to the heart of Christ's statements. Jesus was speaking of an individual mourning, but He also spoke of an individual comforting. And the combination seems to suggest that the primary mourning should be for the individual himself and for his own spiritual condition. This is a mourning for sin. And if this is the primary interpretation of the verse, then it is a promise that God Himself will comfort the one who sees his own unworthiness before Him.

This sense of the promise is substantiated by several factors. We already have seen in these studies that the promise of happiness to the poor in spirit is actually a promise to the one who knows himself spiritually bankrupt. It is a statement of the first qualification for a man's justification before God. As a mourning for sin the next one of Christ's beatitudes would naturally flow from it.

Moreoever, because a mourning for sin lies at the heart of Christ's message, it is natural to expect this theme in the first of His great sermons. When Jesus entered the synagogue at Nazareth on the day that He began His formal ministry, He read from the scroll of Isaiah. He read: "The Spirit of the Lord is upon me, because he hath anointed me to preach the gospel to the poor; he hath sent me to heal the brokenhearted, to preach deliverance to the captives, and recovering of sight to the blind, to set at liberty them that are bruised, to preach the acceptable year of the Lord" (Luke 4:18, 19). What was the deliverance Christ preached? It was not a proclamation against slavery, although that rightly followed in the history of the Christian Church. Jesus did not set about to overthrow the slavery of the Roman Empire; He never preached against it. The deliverance He proclaimed was a deliverance from the tyranny of sin. And it was actually because He broke this tyranny over men that He proved so effective later — as His Spirit worked through His disciples and followers — as a corrector of many of the social ills of this world, including physical slavery.

The gospels tell us that Jesus wept twice in His ministry, once for the unbelief of the Jews at the grave of Lazarus and once over the sin and hardness of heart of Jerusalem. Sin was the great problem. And, thus, He asked men to weep for it.

CHRIST'S COMFORT

The promise of the second beatitude is "comfort," comfort to those who sense their sin and mourn for it.

In the first place there is comfort in a deliverance from sin's penalty. The sensitive soul will grieve for his sins and see them as the great offense to God that they are. But he may also experience the comfort that God has provided through Christ's cross. The Bible tells us that we were dead in trespasses and sins, that we merited nothing from God but alienation and eternal death. But Jesus Christ came to step between the wrath of God against sin on the one hand and all who trust in Jesus Christ on the other. He took the blow of God's wrath upon Himself, paying the full penalty for our sin, and God has placed the full righteousness of the Lord Jesus Christ to our account, so that we are seen as being perfectly acceptable before God in Him. The Bible tells us that we have been made "accepted in the Beloved" (Eph. 1:6). There is unspeakable joy in this experience. This is the joy that was foretold by the angels on the evening of Christ's birth, for they said, "Fear not; for, behold, I bring you good tidings of great joy, which shall be to all people. For unto you is born this day in the city of David a Savior, who is Christ the Lord" (Luke 2:10, 11).

Then, too, the deliverance of Jesus Christ also means a deliverance from present sin and from its power. If you are a Christian, Christ lives in you through His Holy Spirit. You are united to Him. And you are united to Him in order to make a victorious, triumphant life possible.

I know that there are some who teach that there is no victory over sin in this world. And I know that, even according to the Bible, sin will always be with us. John says, "If we say that we have no sin, we deceive ourselves, and the truth is not in us" (1 John 1:8). This is true. But in spite of the fact that sin will always be with the Christian so long as he lives, it is simply not true that he needs to be defeated by it. Paul in Galatians says, "Walk in the Spirit, and ye *shall not* fulfill the lust of the flesh" (5:16). The book then goes on to tell what sins we shall not fulfill if we do walk in the Spirit: adultery, fornication, uncleanness, lasciviousness, idolatry, sorcery, hatred, drunkenness, revelings, and the like. According to Galatians the Christian is supposed to have victory over these things.

The presence of sin in our lives is a bit like the presence of carbon monoxide in the exhaust system of an automobile. So long as the car runs, the deadly gas will be present. If it is unchecked, it will bring death to the occupant of the car. But when the car is properly run and properly maintained, the carbon monoxide is contained within the exhaust system so that it does not break forth in death and only a slight smell is present as it is mixed with the burning oil and gas fumes. In the same way, there will always be the smell of sin about us and in what we do. But it need not break out to bring death. The restraining power of Christ through the Holy Spirit will prevent it, and the contamination of death need not spread from us. In this, too, there is great comfort for the Christian.

The final aspect of God's comfort lies in the fact that one day Christ will remove sin and all of its effects from the believer forever. This will mean a deliverance even from sin's presence; and it will mean an end to pride, hate, suffering, sickness, and death. Now we are aware of our sin. The smell of it is about us. But the day is coming when we shall be taken from this world into Christ's presence. In that day there will be no more sin to confess, for we shall be like Him (1 John 3:2). We shall know an unmixed good. We shall be "delivered from the bondage of corruption into the glorious liberty of the children of God" (Rom. 8:21). That will truly be "life on wings." And we shall know that those who mourned for their sin have been comforted.

Chapter 4

God's Gentlemen

(Matthew 5:5)

Some time ago I heard of a person who had been converted to Christianity because, as he said, he needed "an easy religion." I was amused by the incongruity of his statement. An easy religion! If he wanted an easy religion, he should not have become a Christian. As it was, he was a little like a bartender at a Methodist Sunday school picnic or a comedian at a funeral — he had come to the wrong place.

The preceding studies on the Sermon on the Mount should already have made this fact clear. Christ's statements are intended to teach, among other things, that the kind of life He requires actually is impossible for men. And it remains impossible until men first come to Christ acknowledging that they cannot live it and asking Him to live it in them. The poor in spirit are blessed, not the proud. And the comfort Christ promises is for those who first mourn for their sin and for the sin of others. At this point, however, Jesus makes His description of the happy life even more difficult, for He goes on to show that the way of blessing is also through meekness. He says, "Blessed are the meek; for they shall inherit the earth" (Matt. 5:5). According to Jesus it is the meek — not the haughty, forward, arrogant, or aggressive — whom God blesses.

A Difficult Statement

This third beatitude must have been received in shocked silence by Christ's listeners. But they could not have been much different from the people we know today. To most men and women the association of an earthly inheritance with meekness seems incredible. The world associates happiness with worldly possessions, and it believes that the way to gain them is through ability, strength, hard work, self-assurance and, at times, even through self-assertion and conquest. The religious leaders of Christ's day sought happiness through a materialistic and militaristic kingdom. Christ's statement would have been a shock to them. We seek it through homes and their contents, success and the praise of men for it, power and the stature it confers. So it is a shock to us also. Against all these outlooks on life and these ambitions Jesus teaches that meekness must be a characteristic of those who are to share His kingdom.

Moreover, the other biblical writers say this also. James writes that meekness is to characterize our initial response to God's truth: "Wherefore, put away all filthiness and overflowing of wickedness, and receive with *meekness* the engrafted word, which is able to save your souls" (James 1:21). Peter says that Christians are to witness to others in a spirit of meekness: "But sanctify the Lord God in your hearts, and be ready always to give an answer to every man that asketh you a reason of the hope that is in you, with *meekness* and fear" (1 Peter 3:15). Paul lists meekness as one of the fruits of the Spirit: "But the fruit of the Spirit is love, joy, peace, long-suffering, gentleness, goodness, faith, *meekness, self-control*" (Gal. 5:22, 23). Several times Paul speaks of meekness as the spirit of mind in which one was to deal with problems in the early Christian congregations (Gal. 6:1; 1 Cor. 4:21; 2 Cor. 10:1), and in Colossians he writes, "Put on, therefore, as the elect of God, holy and beloved, tender mercies, kindness, humbleness of mind, *meekness,* long-suffering" (Col. 3:12).

Taken together these verses teach that meekness is a characteristic by which God promises to bring blessing in the lives of Christians and through them to others, and that it is not a natural characteristic in man but is the result of the supernatural working of God's Spirit.

WHAT IS MEEKNESS?

Now we shall never get far in understanding Christ's statement until we realize that in the Bible meekness does not mean what most people think it means. It does not mean spiritlessness. It does not mean weakness or indolence or cowardice. Actually, it is compatible with high spirits, courage, and great strength.

The first clue to the biblical meaning of meekness lies in the discovery that the word it translates was one of the great words in Greek ethics. The word is *praus*, and it is defined with great care in Aristotle's work on ethics. For Aristotle the virtues of life were always defined as the mean between an excess of the virtue and a deficiency in it. For instance, courage is a virtue because it is the mean between cowardice (which is a deficiency in courage) and foolhardy actions (which result from too much). Generosity is the mean between stinginess and a profligate waste of one's resources. To Aristotle meekness was also a virtue because it was the mean between excessive anger and the inability to show anger at all. He describes as meek the man "who is angry on the right occasion and with the right people and at the right moment and for the right length of time."

On the basis of this definition it would be possible to translate the beatitude fairly as Barclay does in his excellent commentary on Matthew: "Blessed is the man who is always angry at the right time, and never angry at the wrong time." * And we could look to the example of Jesus Christ for insight into such a controlled and righteous anger.

Barclay adds, "If we ask what the right time and the wrong time are, we may say as a general rule for life that it is never right to be angry for any insult or injury done to ourselves; that is something that no Christian must ever resent; but that it is often right to be angry at injuries done to other people. Selfish anger is always a sin; selfless anger can be one of the great moral dynamics of the world." ** Thus does Aristotle provide part of the picture.

A second sense of the word comes from the fact that *praus* also was used of animals to designate those that had been domesticated. These were animals who had learned to accept control by their masters and who were therefore properly behaved. By extension, the word was then used of persons who also knew how to behave. And the word came to refer to those who were of the upper classes because they were well-mannered, balanced, or polite. This sense of the word "meek" is far better preserved in English by the related word "gentle" from which we get our compounds: gentlefolk, gentlewoman, and gentleman. Gentleness is a soft and loving behavior, the opposite of awkwardness or rudeness. In this sense the Christian is also to be meek. He is to be loving, well-mannered, polite, balanced, and well-behaved. He is to be God's gentleman.

A final sense of the word "meek" comes from the fact that in biblical language the word is used most often to indicate a sub-

* William Barclay, *The Gospel of Matthew* (Philadelphia: The Westminster Press, 1958), Vol. I, p. 91.
** *Ibid.*

servient and trusting attitude before God, and this makes meekness generally a vertical virtue rather than a horizontal one. It is the characteristic that makes a man bow low before God in order that he may stand high before other men; it makes him bold because he knows that his life has been touched by God and that he comes as God's messenger.

I believe that this was the primary sense in which Christ used the word "meek" in this beatitude, because the beatitude itself is quoted from a context in which that thought is prominent. I know that someone will say, "What? I thought Jesus originated the Beatitudes, that He made them up." Well, it is true that He did make most of them up, but not this one. This beatitude actually comes from the thirty-seventh psalm. And it comes at the end of a long list of commands that encourage a person to place his trust in God. The psalmist writes:

> *Trust in the* LORD, and do good; so shalt thou dwell in the land, and verily thou shalt be fed.
> *Delight thyself also in the* LORD, and he shall give thee the desires of thine heart.
> *Commit thy way unto the* LORD; trust also in him, and he shall bring it to pass.
> And he shall bring forth thy righteousness as the light, and thy justice as the noonday.
> *Rest in the* LORD, and wait patiently for him; fret not thyself because of him who prospereth in his way. . . .

He then closes the section by saying:

> For yet a little while, and the wicked shall not be; yea, thou shalt diligently consider his place, and it shall not be.
> But *the meek shall inherit the earth,* and shall delight themselves in the abundance of peace (Ps. 37:3-7, 10, 11).

Who then are the meek according to the thirty-seventh psalm? They are those who trust in the Lord, who delight themselves in the Lord, who commit their way unto the Lord, who rest in the Lord. It is these who are happy, according to Jesus Christ; and it is these who shall inherit the earth.

THE MEEKEST MAN

All of this is illustrated in a remarkable story from the book of Numbers. One sentence embedded in the midst of the story tells us that the main character was, in God's sight, the meekest man who ever lived. The man was Moses. And the sentence says "Now the man Moses was very meek, above all the men who were upon the face of the earth" (Num. 12:3). The story is about a rebellion against Moses led by Miriam, his sister, and Aaron, his brother, the first high priest of Israel.

This is the story. When Moses had fled from Egypt forty years before God used him as the deliverer of His people, he had gone to Midian where he had settled and married Zipporah, the daughter of Reuel, a priest of Midian. Zipporah was of the same stock as the other Israelites and had borne children to Moses. But she had died by the time of the story recounted in the twelfth chapter of Numbers, and Moses was marrying another wife. This new wife was a Cushite, a name given to the inhabitants of ancient Ethiopia. And the point of the story lies in the fact that the Cushite was black. She was not a Semite. And those who were closest to Moses, his sister and brother, felt that the stock of Israel was being compromised by the mixed marriage.

I have noticed in preparing this study that not all of the commentators on Numbers are willing to accept this understanding of the story; in fact, most of them simply ignore the girl's racial characteristics. But we have every reason for believing that this was the case and that the rebellion was based purely on racial prejudice. Some conservative commentators would dismiss this view on the grounds that the people of Israel were later forbidden to marry among the Canaanites, who inhabited the land of Canaan before their conquest under Joshua. But this was later, and it was based in the debased religion and sexual malpractices that characterized the people of the land (Exod. 34:16). At this time there were no such injunctions. Joseph had married an Egyptian girl, Asenath, the daughter of an Egyptian priest. And many persons of other oppressed nations had left Egypt with Israel at the Exodus and presumably were incorporated into the newly emerging nation (Exod. 12:38). It was one of these whom Moses married, and it seemingly was against her racial characteristics and skin color that Miriam and Aaron rebelled. The Bible says, "And Miriam and Aaron spoke against Moses because of the Cushite woman whom he had married; for he had married a woman of Cush. And they said, Hath the LORD indeed spoken only by Moses? Hath he not spoken also by us? And the LORD heard it" (Num. 12:1, 2).

Now if there are still doubts about this interpretation of the story these should be dispelled by the sequel. For God gave a punishment to Miriam, the instigator, that was frighteningly appropriate to her prejudice. The Bible says, "And the LORD spoke suddenly unto Moses, and unto Aaron, and unto Miriam, Come out ye three unto the tabernacle of the congregation. And they three came out. And the LORD came down in the pillar of the cloud, and stood in the door of the tabernacle, and called Aaron and Miriam, and they both came forth. And he said, Hear now my words: If there be a prophet among you, I the LORD will make myself known unto him in a vision, and will speak unto him in a dream. My servant, Moses, is not so, who is faithful in all mine house. With him will I speak mouth to mouth, even plainly, and not in dark speeches. . . . Wherefore, then, were ye not afraid to speak against my servant, Moses? And the anger of the LORD was kindled against them; and he departed. And the cloud departed from off the tabernacle; and, behold, Miriam became leprous, white as snow" (Num. 12:4-10).

In other words, God said to Miriam, "You're brown, this girl is black; and you think white is better. All right, have more of it." So she became a leper, as God used the incident to teach that there was to be no racial prejudice in Israel.

As we come to the end of the story we find that Moses prayed for Miriam, and she was healed. But we ask, "What was the conduct of Moses through the incident? What was the conduct of the man whom God says was the meekest man who ever lived? Did he fight back? Did he seek to defend himself against his accusers?" Not at all. Moses submitted himself to God. That was his meekness. He bowed low before God and was vindicated. Thus, in this response Moses became a forerunner in conduct of Jesus Christ, "Who did no sin, neither was guile found in his mouth; who, when he was reviled, reviled not again; when he suffered, he threatened not, but committed himself to him that judgeth righteously" (1 Peter 2:22, 23). Meekness of this sort will take off its shoes before the burning bush, yet will obey God by walking up to the mightiest ruler of the day and demanding, "Thus saith the LORD God of Israel, Let my people go" (Exod. 5:1).

To Inherit the Earth

The second beatitude goes on to teach that the meek "shall inherit the earth." What does this mean? Well, it is not a promise that the children of God will own oil wells, or blocks of downtown

Manhattan, or orchards in southern California. It is a promise for the future.

Yet there is a sense in which the meek shall inherit the earth now. For the meek man is the man who is satisfied and is therefore content. Paul was such a man. He owned very little, yet he spoke of himself as "possessing all things" (2 Cor. 6:10). He wrote to the contentious Corinthians: "Therefore, let no man glory in men. For all things are yours, whether Paul, or Apollos, or Cephas, or the world, or life, or death, or things present, or things to come; all are yours, and ye are Christ's, and Christ is God's" (1 Cor. 3:21-23). With such a spirit I can cross the Alps, gaze upon the Bay of Naples, visit a museum, cross the wide expanses of the American continent, attend a concert, listen to the teaching of the Bible, or do anything else, and I can know that these things are mine as much as they are anyone's. And I can thank God for the people who maintain them for me.

At the same time I can know that Christ's promise has a future reference also, for it falls in line with Paul's reminder that "the saints shall judge the world" (1 Cor. 6:2). You shall judge the world if you are a Christian, for you are God's heir and a joint-heir with Jesus Christ. There may be sorrow now. There may be suffering. But when Jesus returns, we shall reign with Him (2 Tim. 2:12).

Now you may be saying, "All that is wonderful, but for me it is in the area of fantasy. It is a beautiful thought, but it is not possible. I am not meek, and I shall never become meek by any amount of effort." The answer is that of course it is impossible by your own effort. This characteristic is not in man. But it can be created in a man by Jesus. He said, "Come unto me, all ye that labor and are heavy laden, and I will give you rest. Take my yoke upon you, and learn of me; for I am meek and lowly in heart, and ye shall find rest unto your souls" (Matt. 11:28, 29). Jesus can do what you think is impossible. He can teach you meekness, and you will find rest to your soul.

Chapter 5

Guaranteed Satisfaction

(Matthew 5:6)

Ever since famine drove Joseph's brothers to Egypt in the second millennium B.C. (and probably also before that time) crop failures, and consequent hunger and starvation, have been a chronic problem of mankind. Drought, wars, and plant disease have swept through history, leaving behind a trail of misery and death. Often little could be done to stop them.

Famine came to Rome in 436 B.C., causing thousands of people to throw themselves into the Tiber River and end their lives. Famine struck England in 1005. All Europe suffered in 879, 1016, and 1162. Even in the nineteenth century, with its great advances in technology and commerce, hunger stalked many countries — Russia, China, India, Ireland — and many died. Today, in India, thousands die of malnutrition and its accompanying diseases, and hundreds more perish in the nations of Latin America and the other emerging nations. Hunger, like war and pestilence, has always been a bellicose neighbor to large sectors of the human race.

Unfortunately, the physical hunger of some men is only a pale reflection of a far more serious hunger that affects all mankind. It is a spiritual hunger, which is satisfied only by God through the Lord Jesus Christ. St. Augustine spoke of this hunger when he wrote, "Thou hast made us for thyself, and our hearts are restless until they find their rest in thee" (Confessions, I, 1). Jesus showed how this hunger could be satisfied. He said, "Blessed are they who do hunger and thirst after righteousness; for they shall be filled" (Matt. 5:6). This statement of Jesus Christ's is the fourth beatitude of the Sermon on the Mount. It is God's answer to man's spiritual longing.

GOD'S ANSWER

This beatitude follows in a very definite order upon the first three of Christ's beatitudes, and there is a sense in which it stands at the heart of this short compendium of Christ's teachings.

The first three verses of the Sermon on the Mount have all

pointed to man's need and have shown the type of approach that is necessary if a man is to be made spiritually happy by God. First, the man who comes to God must be "poor in spirit." He must recognize that he is spiritually bankrupt in God's sight and that he has no claim upon Him. Second, he must "mourn." This does not refer simply to the kind of sorrow experienced for the sick or dying. It is sorrow for sin. And it implies that the one who sorrows must come to God for comfort. Third, the man who would experience God's salvation must also be "meek." This refers to his taking a lowly place before God in order that he might receive God's salvation. These beatitudes have all expressed man's need. Now in the fourth beatitude there comes a solution: if a man will hunger and thirst after righteousness, God will fill him with righteousness and will declare him righteous. That man will be justified before God, and he will embark upon the blessed and effective life outlined in the remainder of Christ's sermon.

Does this verse touch your heart as an expression of all that is most precious in the Christian Gospel? Dr. D. Martyn Lloyd-Jones writes of this verse, "This Beatitude again follows logically from the previous ones; it is a statement to which all the others lead. It is the logical conclusion to which they come, and it is something for which we should all be profoundly thankful and grateful to God. I do not know of a better test that anyone can apply to himself or herself in this whole matter of the Christian profession than a verse like this. If this verse is to you one of the most blessed statements of the whole of Scripture, you can be quite certain you are a Christian; if it is not, then you had better examine the foundations again." * The verse is precious because it offers the solution to man's great need by pointing to the offer of God's greater remedy in Christ.

TRUE RIGHTEOUSNESS

The verse is most specific about how one can obtain this happiness, but the reason why so many people are unhappy spiritually is that they will not accept God's remedy. What must man do? First, he must desire *righteousness*. Second, he must desire a perfect (and, therefore, a *divine)* righteousness. Third, he must desire it *intensely*. That is, he must desire it enough to abandon all hope of achieving salvation by his own efforts, and cling instead to the

* D. Martyn Lloyd-Jones, *Studies in the Sermon on the Mount* (Grand Rapids: Wm. B. Eerdmans, 1967), Vol. I, pp. 73, 74.

efforts made for him by God. Each of these points is suggested explicitly in the beatitude.

In the first place, the man who would be happy must come to God seeking righteousness. So many come seeking anything and everything else. Some seek happiness itself. But the verse says that the happy people are those who seek, not happiness primarily, but holiness before God. Some people seek happiness through other things, such as fortune or fame. Some seek it through sex and marriage. The Bible teaches that happiness comes only through righteousness.

A moment's reflection will show why this must be so. God is the source of all good things: fortune, fame, sex, success, happiness, and other things besides. James says, "Every good gift and every perfect gift is from above, and cometh down from the Father of lights, with whom is no variableness, neither shadow of turning" (James 1:17). But God is also holy, and, because He is, He can have no dealings with those who are not holy. Men are sinners. Sin breaks the fellowship that should exist between men and God; it makes all who are sinners God's enemies. The only way that man can enter again into fellowship with God and find the happiness and blessing he longs for is to possess a righteousness and holiness that will commend him to God.

Can this be done? Not by man, certainly. But God can and will do it. The heart of the Gospel of Jesus Christ is that in Him God has obtained our redemption and provided all who believe in Christ with that righteousness. The Bible says that Jesus Christ "is made unto us wisdom, and righteousness, and sanctification, and redemption" (1 Cor. 1:30). And those who hunger and thirst after His righteousness shall be filled.

Moreover, *Christians* must hunger and thirst after righteousness. For that which enters into their becoming a Christian must also characterize their life. Dr. Lloyd-Jones writes, "There are large numbers of people in the Christian Church who seem to spend the whole of their life seeking something which they can never find, seeking for some kind of happiness and blessedness. They go around from meeting to meeting, and convention to convention, always hoping they are going to get this wonderful thing, this experience that is going to fill them with joy, and flood them with some ecstacy. They see that other people have had it, but they themselves do not seem to get it. . . . Now that is not surprising. We are not meant to hunger and thirst after experiences; we are not meant to hunger and thirst after blessedness. If we want to be truly happy and blessed we must hunger and thirst after righteousness. We must not put blessedness or happiness or experience in the first place." *

What is the case in your life? Do you put righteousness first or do you seek after something else, even something quite good in itself? Do not forget that righteousness *must* come first. Jesus said, "Seek ye first the kingdom of God, and his righteousness, and all these things shall be added unto you" (Matt. 6:33).

A PERFECT RIGHTEOUSNESS

The second point of the fourth beatitude is that the one who would know true happiness must desire not merely righteousness but perfect righteousness, and this means desiring the righteousness of God. It is necessary that we see this and see it clearly, for you and I are always ready to settle for something less than God requires, and if it were possible, we should always rush to substitute some of our own goodness for God's.

In order to understand how this point emerges from the text it is necessary to point out a fact of Greek grammar. In the Greek language it is a rule of good grammar that verbs of hungering and thirsting are followed by nouns in the genitive case. This is the case that is expressed by the preposition "of" in English. An example of a genitive would be the last words in the phrases "peace *of mind*," "love *of God*," "object *of faith*," and so on. The Greek would express a feeling of hunger by saying something like this: "I am hungry for *of* food" or "I am thirsty for *of* water."

This particular use of the genitive case has an unusual characteristic on the basis of which it is called a partitive genitive. This means that it has reference only to a part of the object that occurs in the sentence. Thus, when the Greek would say, "I am hungry for *of* food," he would be saying that he was hungry only for part of the food in the world, not all of it. And similarly, when he would say that he would like some water, the genitive would indicate that he did not want all the water the world has to offer, but only some of it. In more modern times the same grammatical structure appears in French. When seated at the table, you would never say, "Passez *le* pain, s'il vous plait" — that would mean pass all the bread there is. Instead you say, "Passez *du* pain," for that means, "I would like some of the bread, please."

* *Ibid.*, p. 76.

The significance of this point for interpreting the fourth beatitude lies in the fact that the normal Greek usage is entirely abandoned in this verse. Instead of the word "righteousness" occurring in the genitive, as it should, it occurs in the accusative. And the meaning is that the one who hungers and thirsts as Christ intends him to hunger and thirst must hunger, not after a partial or imperfect righteousness (either his own or God's), but after the whole thing. He must long for a perfect righteousness, and this means, therefore, a righteousness equal to and identical with God's.

Of course, this is exactly what most people will not do. Most men and women have a desire for some degree of righteousness. Their self-esteem demands at least that. Thieves will have some code of honor among themselves, however debased. A murderer will strive for some small spark of nobility. A good man will take great pride in his philanthropy or good deeds. But the problem comes from the fact that few (and none unless God has prodded them) seek for the perfect goodness which comes only from Him. If I were to rephrase the verse in order to recapture this flavor of the language, I would say, "O how happy is the man who knows enough not to be satisfied with any partial goodness with which to please God, who is not satisfied with any human goodness. He alone is happy who seeks for the divine righteousness, because God will certainly provide it."

HUNGER AND THIRST

The third point of advice in Christ's statement about how to discover God's righteousness is that a man must desire it intensely. In Christ's words, he must "hunger and thirst after righteousness" if he is to be filled. How quickly these words pierce to the spiritual heart of a man! And how quickly do they separate real spiritual hunger from mere sentimentality and vaguely religious feeling!

Since there is almost nothing in our experience today to suggest the force of Christ's words, we must put ourselves in the shoes of His listeners if we are to fully understand them. Today almost none of us knows hunger. And few of us have ever known more than a momentary thirst. But it was not that way for Christ's contemporaries. In the ancient world men often knew hunger. Wages were low, if they existed at all. Unless men were of the aristocracy they seldom grew fat on the fruit of honest labor. Many starved. Moreover, in a desert country where the sun was scorching and sand and wind storms were frequent, thirst was man's constant companion. To such a world hunger meant the hunger of a starving man, and thirst, that of a man who would die without water.

It was against this background that Christ's words were spoken. And they were, in effect, "So you think that you would like to be pleasing to God, that you would like to taste of His goodness. Well, how much do you want it? Do you want it as much as a starving man wants food or a parched man wants water? You must want it that desperately in order to be filled. For it is only when you are really desperate that you will turn to me and away from your own attempts to earn that goodness."

Several years ago an article appeared in *Eternity* magazine by Dr. E. M. Blaiklock on the significance of water in the Bible, part of which is quite relevant here. The article was one in a series of articles on Bible imagery, and in one part of it Dr. Blaiklock referred by way of illustration to a book by Major V. Gilbert called *The Last Crusade,* an account of part of the British liberation of Palestine in World War I. Dr. Blaiklock wrote of the book: "Driving up from Beersheba, a combined force of British, Australians and New Zealanders were pressing on the rear of the Turkish retreat over arid desert. The attack out-distanced its water-carrying camel train. Water bottles were empty. The sun blazed pitilessly out of a sky where the vultures wheeled expectantly.

" 'Our heads ached,' writes Gilbert, 'and our eyes became bloodshot and dim in the blinding glare. . . . Our tongues began to swell . . . our lips turned a purplish black and burst . . .' Those who dropped out of the column were never seen again, but the desperate force battled on to Sheria. There were wells at Sheria, and had they been unable to take the place by nightfall, thousands were doomed to die of thirst. 'We fought that day,' writes Gilbert, 'as men fight for their lives. . . . We entered Sheria station on the heels of the retreating Turks. The first objects which met our view were the great stone cisterns full of cold, clear, drinking water. In the still night air the sound of water running into the tanks could be distinctly heard, maddening in its nearness; yet not a man murmured when orders were given for the battalions to fall in, two deep, facing the cisterns.'

"He describes the stern priorities: the wounded, those on guard duty, then company by company. It took four hours before the last man had his drink of water, and in all that time they had been standing 20 feet from a low stone wall, on the other side of which were thousands of gallons of water.

" 'I believe,' Major Gilbert concludes, 'that we all learned our first real Bible lesson on that march from Beersheba to Sheria wells.' If such were our thirst for God, for righteousness, for His will in our life, a consuming, all-embracing, preoccupying desire, how rich in the fruits of the Spirit would we be." *

CHRIST, OUR SATISFACTION

The conclusion of this study is that where there is this desire for righteousness there will be filling. And the filling will be Christ Himself.

In this first sermon, given early in His three-year ministry, Jesus said, "Blessed are they who do hunger and thirst after righteousness; for they shall be filled," but He did not elaborate further on the filling. Later, when His teachings began to make their impact on the small circle of His listeners, He did. He said to the woman of Samaria, "If thou knewest the gift of God, and who it is that saith to thee, Give me to drink, thou wouldest have asked of him, and he would have given thee living water. . . . Whosoever drinketh of this water shall thirst again; but whosoever drinketh of the water that I shall give him shall never thirst, but the water that I shall give him shall be in him a well of water springing up into everlasting life" (John 4:10, 13, 14). To the disciples who had witnessed the miracle of the multiplication of the loaves in Galilee He added, "I am the bread of life; he that cometh to me shall never hunger, and he that believeth on me shall never thirst" (John 6:35).

Have you drunk deeply at that spring and fed on that bread? Or are you still feeding on things that do not satisfy? When the prodigal son left home he expected to find complete satisfaction. He wanted to live; and life to him meant money, clothes, food, companionship, and gay times. Instead of these things he found poverty, rags, hunger, loneliness, and misery. When he was hungry he turned to feeding swine. It was only when he was finally starving that he turned back to his father. In his father's company he found all he had thought to find in the world. His father clothed him, fed him, welcomed him, and rejoiced in his return.

How sad if you should turn from the One who guarantees satisfaction in life to things that will never satisfy for long! How blessed for you to return to the Father through the way in which He has told you to come, through the Lord Jesus Christ!

* *Eternity*, August 1966, pp. 27, 28.

Chapter 6

Three Virtues

(Matthew 5:7-9)

Some time ago I was speaking with one of my friends about the relationship of Christian teaching to Christian conduct. The conversation had begun when he had told me of his desire to write an article on "Doctrine and Devotion" showing the theological relationship between the two. When I heard what he meant by the terms I agreed with his thesis wholeheartedly and added that I would be glad to cooperate on the project if time should permit. For I was convinced that the relationship that he wished to prove theologically also can be shown biblically in the composition of the biblical documents.

Most New Testament scholars would agree that the Book of Romans is probably the most explicitly doctrinal book in the Bible, for it seeks to set forth the meaning of the Gospel of Jesus Christ in terms of man's enslavement to sin and God's total emancipation of him through Christ. It is significant, however, that the outcome of this statement is not a call to admire the doctrine itself but rather to live a holy life through the power of the living and reigning Christ. Thus Paul writes, referring explicitly to the lengthy doctrinal section, "I beseech you therefore, brethren, by the mercies of God, that ye present your bodies a living sacrifice, holy, acceptable unto God, which is your reasonable service. And be not conformed to this world, but be ye transformed by the renewing of your mind, that ye may prove what is that good, and acceptable, and perfect, will of God" (Rom. 12:1, 2). Similarly, the great passage in Philippians 2:5-11 regarding the doctrine of Christ is

49

given so that we might show forth "the mind of Christ" in our conduct. And the great chapter on the resurrection in 1 Corinthians concludes, "Therefore, my beloved brethren, be ye steadfast, unmovable, always abounding in the work of the Lord, forasmuch as ye know that your labor is not in vain in the Lord" (1 Cor. 15: 58). According to the Word of God, Christian doctrine must always express itself in a new outlook on life and changed behavior. What you believe must always affect your conduct.

A Turning Point

It is the same in the Sermon on the Mount and even, in a general way, in the Beatitudes. We have already noticed in our study of the first four beatitudes that the order in which they occur is intentional. In one respect all of the Beatitudes describe the character of the Christian man. The man who possesses this divine and divinely given character (and only he) is instructed to live as the rest of the sermon indicates. Thus, an application follows verse 12. In another respect, however, even the Beatitudes contain this development. For if it is true that the first three beatitudes show how a man must stand in his relation as a sinner to God — spiritually bankrupt, sorry for sin, and meekly humble — and if it is true that the fourth beatitude contains the promise of God's provision of righteousness for the man who so comes to God, then it is logical to expect that the remaining beatitudes will reveal the transformed character of the one who now has been touched by Christ's Spirit and is being progressively remade in Christ's image.

This, in fact, is precisely what we do find. For with the fifth, sixth, and seventh beatitudes a turning point is reached and the character of the Christian man, particularly in regard to others, is delineated. Jesus said, "Blessed are the merciful; for they shall obtain mercy. Blessed are the pure in heart; for they shall see God. Blessed are the peacemakers; for they shall be called the sons of God" (Matt. 5:7-9). According to Jesus the man who has tasted God's righteousness is to show mercy to others; he is to be pure in heart; he is to be a peacemaker.

The points to be made about each of these qualities are so similar in their general outline that we can really treat all three in one message. The salient points are these: 1) all three qualities are essentially divine qualities; 2) we can understand them (if we do understand them) only because we have first seen them exhibited by Christ; and 3) because we have experienced them in Christ we are on this account to exhibit them to others. The conclusion is that we shall be able to do this only as our lives are yielded to Him.

THE QUALITY OF MERCY

The first of these three practical beatitudes, then, deals with mercy. What is mercy? When Shakespeare defined mercy in the well-known speech by Portia in *The Merchant of Venice* —

> *The quality of mercy is not strain'd.*
> *It droppeth as the gentle rain from heaven*
> *Upon the place beneath. It is twice blessed:*
> *It blesses him that gives and him that takes.*
> *'Tis mightiest in the mightiest; it becomes*
> *The throned monarch better than his crown —*

he covered some of its qualities: impartiality, gentleness, abundance. But this is not the full definition. And it is only the Bible that gives the word "mercy" its true scope and spiritual significance. In some ways mercy may be compared with grace; that is, it is undeserved. But it is not grace itself. And in the pastoral letters Paul even adds mercy to his normal Christian greeting — grace and peace — thereby implying a distinction between them. "Grace, mercy, and peace, from God, our Father, and Jesus Christ, our Lord" (1 Tim. 1:2; cf. 2 Tim. 1:2; Titus 1:4).

What makes mercy different from grace? Primarily it is the quality of helplessness or misery on the part of those who receive mercy. Grace is love when love is undeserved. Mercy is grace in action. Mercy is love reaching out to help those who are helpless and who need salvation. Mercy identifies with the miserable in their misery.

We cannot state the definition of mercy, however, without thinking at once of the cross of Jesus Christ. For it was here that God acted out of grace in mercy to fallen, sinful man. In fact, God's act was so complete at the cross that there is a sense in which mercy can be seen by a sinful man there only. In his sinful, fallen state man could do nothing to save himself, so God stepped forward to do everything that needed to be done. Dr. Barnhouse has written, "When Jesus Christ died on the cross, all of the work of God for man's salvation passed out of the realm of prophecy and became historical fact. God has now had mercy upon us. For anyone to pray, 'God have mercy on me,' is the equivalent of asking Him to repeat the sacrifice of Christ. All the mercy that God ever will have on man, He has already had when Christ died. This is the totality of mercy. There *could* not be any more. . . . [God can now] act toward us in grace because He has already had all mercy upon us. The fountain is now opened and flowing, and it flows freely." * We speak of this mercy when we say:

> *He saw me ruined in the fall,*
> *He loved me notwithstanding all;*
> *He saved me from my lost estate —*
> *His loving-kindness (mercy), O how great!*

And we correctly sing:

> *Mercy there was great, and grace was free,*
> *Pardon there was multiplied to me,*
> *There my burdened soul found liberty —*
> *At Calvary.*

Paul wrote of it, "But God, who is rich in mercy, for his great love with which he loved us, even when we were dead in sins, hath made us alive together with Christ (by grace ye are saved), and hath raised us up together, and made us sit together in heavenly places in Christ Jesus; that in the ages to come he might show the exceeding riches of his grace in his kindness toward us through Christ Jesus" (Eph. 2:4-7). Because we have experienced this mercy from God we in our turn are to show mercy to others.

WHICH COMES FIRST?

We cannot go on from this point, however, without first calling attention to the fact that this beatitude has been a problem to some persons because it seems to imply that receiving mercy from God depends upon our showing mercy to others. The beatitude reads, "Blessed are the merciful; *for they shall obtain* mercy." This seems to imply that we must act first in showing mercy.

Does it mean this? Obviously not, unless this statement of Jesus Christ is to be accepted as contradicting all Scripture, including His own clear testimony, or unless we are to abolish the doctrine of grace entirely and with it all hope of salvation. If we are to be dealt with on these terms, no man would ever see heaven. No one would ever receive God's mercy. Actually, of course, it is the other way around. For what Jesus actually was saying was that we are to show mercy because we have received mercy and are confident

* Donald Grey Barnhouse, *God's Discipline* (Grand Rapids: Wm. B. Eerdmans, 1964), p. 4.

that we will continue to receive it. Conversely, if we do not show mercy to others, we show that we either understand little of that mercy by which we have been saved or else have never actually received it.

PURITY OF HEART

The next beatitude says, "Blessed are the pure in heart; for they shall see God." Again the same general principles apply. We are to purify ourselves, as John says in the first of his epistles (1 John 3:3), but we are enabled to do so only because we first have been made pure by God and have come to see true purity in the Lord Jesus Christ.

The verse actually says that we are to be pure in *heart,* and this gets quickly to the core of the problem, because the heart of man is impure. What is the heart? In the Bible the heart is the center of the personality; it involves the mind, the will, and the emotions. Three verses from the book of Romans make this complex definition clear. In Romans 1:21 Paul speaks of men who are without God saying, "Because, when they knew God, they glorified him not as God, neither were thankful, but became vain in their imaginations, and their foolish heart was darkened." Here Paul is thinking primarily of the clouding of men's minds by sin. In Romans 2:5 he says, "After thy hardness and impenitent heart [thou art treasuring] up unto thyself wrath against the day of wrath and revelation of the righteous judgment of God." Here the emphasis falls mainly on man's implacable will. Finally, in Romans 5:5 he writes, "And hope maketh not ashamed, because the love of God is shed abroad in our hearts by the Holy Spirit who is given unto us." In this verse the heart is the seat of the emotions. A reference to the heart of man is therefore a reference to the center of man's personality, and it is this that is the source of man's problems. Jeremiah said, "The heart is deceitful above all things, and desperately wicked" (Jer. 17:9). Jesus said, "Out of the abundance of the heart the mouth speaketh" (Matt. 12:34). And He added, "Out of the heart proceed evil thoughts, murders, adulteries, fornications, thefts, false witness, blasphemies" (Matt. 15:19). That is the state of your heart and mine as God sees it. And if that is the case, we may well ask, "How can a man be pure in heart?"

The answer is that only God can make him pure. You can begin by trying to cleanse your own heart; but whether you turn to ethics, religion, asceticism, fetishes, or whatever it may be, you will find that your heart is as corrupt at the end as at the beginning. Only God can cleanse your heart from its impurities. David knew this and prayed, "Create in me a clean heart, O God, and renew a right spirit within me" (Ps. 51:10). God does that for all who believe on Jesus Christ. He does it judicially in the moment of our belief. He does it practically during the moments of our earthly life as we yield to the gentle urging of His Holy Spirit. He will do it finally and completely in the moment of our death as we are then purified from all evil and brought without spot into His holy presence.

Because of this assurance we strive now to please Him, to yield to Him, allowing Him to make us increasingly pure. As we do, we come increasingly to see Him as He fills our being and makes Himself known to us. We take our place with those countless others who endured "as seeing him who is invisible."

PEACEMAKERS FOR CHRIST

From our study of the preceding two beatitudes it is now evident that only those who have first tasted peace with God at the cross of Christ can become peacemakers. But simply because they have known God's peace they *must* be peacemakers.

Among other things they must be peacemakers in the home. Dr. Barnhouse wrote, "Every minister knows that adjustments must be made by two people who have stopped living in single liberty to take up life with each other. At the time of their wedding, a man and woman are like two planets which have been going around the sun at different speeds and in different orbits. Now they must travel in the same orbit at the same speed. For if they pursue the same path at different speeds, sooner of later there will be a planetary crash.

"How can such collisions be avoided? Each must pursue the things that make for peace. I know of a home where the wife asked the husband to repair an electric light over the kitchen sink, and he promised to do so. Next day she again asked him to fix the light and again he promised, but with some irritation. Two or three days later she asked again, and he shouted at her to stop nagging him. Finally, the matter became a source of great tension between them. The proper functioning of the light was very necessary to her work at the sink, but if she had called an electrician to do the job, the husband might have exploded. Yet having promised to do the work, he should have done it; and his failure showed lack of understanding of his wife's problems. To her it revealed a great flaw in the man she loved: evidently he did not have a proper sense of responsibility and integrity.

"The way to avoid such difficulties in the adjustment of husband and wife is to have prayer together every day, asking the Lord to keep both in the way of grace. It is also good for each to be willing to face weaknesses in self and to ask the other, 'Is there something that I do that annoys you?' And when the answer is given in love, it is a small matter for love to remove the annoyance." *

In the same way we may work constantly as God's peacemakers in all areas of our lives — in the community, at church, in the office, school, or store, and on the international scene if we have contact with that. You must think of it in terms of your boss or your teacher. If you are on the management level in your business, you must think of it in terms of your employees. You must think of it in terms of all persons with whom you come in contact. And if your old nature cries out that it wants to be first, that it is being taken advantage of and consequently cannot have things exactly its own way, then you must look upward to the Lord Jesus Christ, yielding to Him and asking Him to crucify your old nature for you with all its affections and lusts. You can do it, Christ working in you. And thus we can all grow together into a more perfect reproduction of His gracious life and character.

* Donald Grey Barnhouse, *God's Glory* (Grand Rapids: Wm. B. Eerdmans, 1964), p. 23.

Chapter 7

Persecuted for Christ

(Matthew 5:10-12)

The Bible says, in many different passages, that true disciples of Jesus Christ will be persecuted. It is inevitable, a natural consequence of exhibiting true Christian character. And yet, any honest assessment of the Christian church in America must point up that although the country itself is far from being Christian and is ungodly, nevertheless there is very little persecution of Christians today. Undoubtedly there is racial persecution for some. There is persecution in politics and sometimes, I suppose, in business. But there is very little persecution for most Christians, at least openly. What is wrong? Is it possible that the Bible is wrong? Or are Christians today simply not showing forth the type of righteous character that Jesus said results in persecution?

Once, on the Bible Study Hour, I asked Dr. Harold Voelkel, a missionary for many years in Korea, about persecution in this country as contrasted with the terrible persecution of Christians that he had observed overseas. He answered, "Well, I see no persecution here at all." For most Christians this is true, and this is true in spite of the clear implication of the Beatitudes that persecution will come to one who lives as Christ has indicated. Jesus said, "Blessed are they who are persecuted for righteousness' sake; for theirs is the kingdom of heaven. Blessed are ye, when men shall revile you, and persecute you, and shall say all manner of evil against you falsely, for my sake. Rejoice, and be exceedingly glad; for great is your reward in heaven; for so persecuted they the prophets who were before you" (Matt. 5:10-12).

PERSECUTION INEVITABLE

Some person will object that those verses do not actually teach that persecution is inevitable. I agree that they do not teach that you as a Christian as the result of everything you do, will be reviled and suffer every day for righteousness' sake. On the other hand, the verses do conclude the list of statements that delineate the Christian's character, and the natural implication is that the one who lives like this will be persecuted. It is an amazing and provocative statement. And yet, it is as much a description of the Christian as the words: poor in spirit, they that mourn, the meek, the pure in heart, and the peacemakers.

Moreover, this is exactly the way in which the disciples of the Lord received the statement. Peter, who heard the Lord give this sermon, later quotes the beatitude twice in his first epistle: once in 3:14 ("But and if ye suffer for righteousness' sake, happy are ye"), and once in 4:14 ("If ye be reproached for the name of Christ, happy are ye; for the Spirit of glory and of God resteth upon you; on their part he is evil spoken of, but on your part he is glorified"). And it is this epistle that most stresses the inevitability of suffering. Peter writes, "Beloved, think it not strange concerning the fiery trial which is to test you, as though some strange thing happened unto you, but rejoice, inasmuch as ye are partakers of Christ's sufferings" (4:12, 13).

Paul, who had himself endured much persecution, says the same. To Timothy he wrote, "Yea, and all that will live godly in Christ Jesus shall suffer persecution" (2 Tim. 3:12). In Philippians he says, "For unto you it is given in the behalf of Christ, not only to believe on him but also to suffer for his sake" (1:29). He wrote to the Christians at Thessalonica, after a period of persecution in that Macedonian city, "No man should be moved by these afflictions; for ye yourselves know that we are appointed to these things. For verily, when we were with you, we told you before that we should suffer tribulation, even as it came to pass, and ye know" (1 Thess. 3:3, 4).

All these writers would have agreed in an instant that even in the most tolerant country the cross would never cease to be a symbol for derision and intense hostility, and they would have urged that the absence of persecution (as well as its presence) should drive a believer quickly to his knees.

FOR RIGHTEOUSNESS' SAKE

Now at no point in the entire list of beatitudes is it more necessary to be careful to indicate exactly what is meant by Christ's statement, for there is no beatitude which has been more often misunderstood and misapplied than this one. For what is the Christian persecuted? That is the heart of the teaching. The answer lies in the phrase "for righteousness' sake," and in the parallel phrase in the following verse, "for my sake." It does not say, "Blessed are they that are persecuted," as though the Lord Jesus Christ was sanctifying any persecution that might occur at any time and at any point in history. It says, "Blessed are they that are persecuted for righteousness' sake." ˙This means, "Blessed are they who are persecuted because, by God's grace, they are determined to live as I live."

This means that there is no promise of happiness for those who are persecuted for being a nuisance, for Christians who have shown themselves to be objectionable, difficult, foolish, and insulting to their non-Christian friends. This is not the thing about which Christ was speaking.

A humorous example of this non-sanctified type of persecution is given by Joseph Bayly in an imaginary story about Christian witnessing called *The Gospel Blimp*. It is a satire, of course. It is wildly exaggerated. But, unfortunately, in many of the attitudes represented it is all too true of much so-called Christian activity. The believers in an imaginary town conceive the idea of witnessing by means of a blimp which is to fly over the town trailing gospel signs and dropping tracts and leaflets called "bombs." It is a silly idea; no one is ever converted by it. But for a while at least the town is tolerant. Tolerance changes to hostility, however, when the promoters of the project add sound equipment to the blimp and begin bombarding their neighbors with gospel services broadcast from the air. At this point, according to Bayly, the "persecution" begins. And the town newspaper prints an editorial that reads:

> For some weeks now our metropolis has been treated to the spectacle of a blimp with an advertising sign attached at the rear. This sign does not plug cigarettes, or a bottled beverage, but the religious beliefs of a particular group in our midst. The people of our city are notably broad-minded, and they have good-naturedly submitted to this attempt to proselyte. But last night a new refinement (some would say debasement) was introduced. We refer, or course, to the air-borne sound truck, that invader of our privacy, that raucous destroyer of communal peace. . . . *

* Joseph Bayly, *The Gospel Blimp* (Grand Rapids: Zondervan, 1966), p. 32.

That night the sound equipment of the blimp is sabotaged, and the Christians call it persecution.

Well, it is not persecution. That is Mr. Bayly's point. It is a provoked response to an unjustified invasion of privacy. And, similarly, it is not persecution today when Christians are snubbed for pushing tracts onto people who do not want them, insulting them in the midst of a religious argument, poking into their affairs when they are not invited, and so on. Christ was speaking of the persecution of those who are abused for the sake of His righteousness.

Moreover, the beatitude does not mean, "Blessed are those who are persecuted for wrongdoing." This should almost go without saying. But it cannot be left unsaid for the simple reason that most persons (including Christians) will always attempt to justify a wrong act by loud cries of unjustified persecution or prejudice. Peter wrote, "Let none of you suffer as a murderer, or as a thief, or as an evildoer, or as a busybody in other men's matters" (1 Peter 4:15), for he knew that Jesus was speaking of a persecution for the sake of righteousness.

Then, too, it is not a persecution for being fanatical. When the Jewish court in Jerusalem tried Michael Rohan for attempting to burn down the Mosque of Al Aqsa in the temple enclosure of the city, it was not persecuting him. His act was a fanatical act, and it was not performed for the cause of Christ's righteousness or for the sake of conformity to Him.

Finally, the persecution about which Jesus spoke is not persecution evoked by following a cause, even — and you must understand me rightly here — for following Christianity. Dr. D. Martyn Lloyd-Jones has written correctly on this point, "I say that there is a difference between being persecuted for righteousness' sake and being persecuted for a cause. I know that the two things often become one, and many of the great martyrs and confessors were at one and the same time suffering for righteousness' sake and for a cause. But it does not follow that the two are always identical. . . . I think that in the last twenty years there have been men, some of them very well known, who have suffered, and have even been put into prisons and concentration camps, for religion. But they have not been suffering for righteousness' sake. . . . This is not the thing about which our Lord is talking." *

Well, then, if the verse does not mean being persecuted for

* D. Martyn Lloyd-Jones, *Studies in the Sermon on the Mount* (Grand Rapids: Wm. B. Eerdmans, 1967), Vol. I, pp. 131, 132.

being objectionable, or doing wrong, or being fanatical, or endorsing a cause, what does it mean? What does it mean to be persecuted for righteousness' sake, for Christ's sake? Simply put, it means to be persecuted for being like the Lord Jesus Christ Himself. Jesus said that those who are persecuted for being like Him will be happy. And what is more, those who are like Him will always be persecuted.

When Jesus came into the world in His righteousness He exposed the evil of the world, and men hated Him for it. Before He came men could get away with hypocrisy, lying, dishonesty, selfishness, greed, and a long list of other vices. They could excuse themselves by pointing out that other men were like themselves and that they were better in some of these respects than others. After He came, all these vices were revealed for what they were, just as the filth of a sewer is revealed by thrusting a strong light into one of its openings. Men hated the exposure of their inner hearts and natures, and they killed Christ for exposing them. In a similar way, they will hate any exposure of their evil nature that comes from the evidences of the righteousness of Christ in His followers. That is why Jesus said, "The servant is not greater than his lord. If they have persecuted me, they will also persecute you; if they have kept my saying, they will keep yours also. . . . If I had not come and spoken unto them, they had not had sin; but now they have no cloak for their sin. He that hateth me hateth my Father also" (John 15:20-23).

Is there anything in your conduct that reveals Christ's righteousness? Is Jesus Christ seen in your character? It is true that we live in a country that has adopted many Christian values, tolerance being among them, and so has risen to a level where persecutions are not likely to be what they were in the early Christian centuries. But it is also true that much of our Christianity has sunk to a level where it is hardly noticed. The world has become tolerant of us. But we have become far more tolerant of the world. There is sometimes precious little true Christian character visible.

Have you ever put the principles of Christ's righteousness into action in your home, your job, or your business? You might reply, "I am up against a situation in my factory that is so rotten and has been going on for so long that if I did the righteous thing I'd be fired." A man came to Tertullian once with the same problem. His business interests had been conflicting with his loyalty to Jesus Christ. He told of the problem. He ended by saying, "What can

I do? I must live." "Must you?" asked Tertullian. Even in Tertullian's day the believer's choice between righteousness and a livelihood was to be righteous.

HAPPINESS THROUGH PERSECUTION

Now this beatitude not only describes the nature of the Christian's persecution, persecution for the sake of righteousness, it also promises happiness to the one who is so persecuted. How can persecution add to a Christian's happiness? Let me suggest two ways in which it is possible.

First, persecution is evidence that the believer is united to Jesus Christ. Jesus said, "If ye were of the world, the world would love its own; but because ye are not of the world, but I have chosen you out of the world, therefore the world hateth you" (John 15: 19). If we are persecuted for Christ's sake, we can be happy in this proof that we are His and are united to Him forever. Second, if we are persecuted for righteousness' sake, we can be certain that the Holy Spirit has been at work in our hearts, turning us from our sin and our sinful ways to Christ's way, and is making progress in molding us into His sinless image. We can be happy in that. If you have known examples in your life of the persecution about which we have been talking — by taking an honest path at work, by refusing to compromise on quality or service, by remaining pure when friends and acquaintances are profligate — you can rejoice at this evidence of God's gracious and supernatural working.

THE LITTLE PEOPLE

This brings us to the end of our exposition of this eighth and last beatitude. We should add a word now for those who are not and who never will be great martyrs for the sake of the Lord Jesus Christ. That includes most of us. What about us? Well, we may be certain that God sees the little martyrs as well as the great ones, and that He is as pleased — sometimes more pleased — with the small sacrifices and small insults patiently borne for His sake as He is with the far more spectacular persecutions.

Think of the persecutions of Job — not the loss of his family and possessions by a series of calamities caused by Satan, this was not persecution — but the persecution he suffered from his friends who accused him of sinning greatly because of his sudden and tragic losses. What historian would ever have mentioned Job?

None! No ancient historian would have thought twice about him. You can be certain that if Job had risen to wealth in New York City and had later died in poverty in Harlem, his name would not even have made the obituary columns of the New York newspapers. Yet the struggles of Job in his persecutions were viewed by God and angels.

It may take more grace and it may be a greater victory for a man to spend forty years of his life at the same desk in the same office watching other men being promoted over him because he will not do some of the things that are demanded of officers in his company than it would take for a John Hus to be burned at the stake for his testimony. And it may be more of a victory for a housewife to stay at home, raising her family in the things of the Lord while her nit-picking neighbors laugh at her for being hum-drum and unglamorous, than it would be for a Joan of Arc to die at Rouen.

We may all take comfort in this, and turn to Christ for the victory. If we have not known persecution, even in little ways, let us search our hearts before Him. And let us ask for that righteousness of character that will either repel men or draw them to our blessed Savior.

Chapter 8

How To Rejoice in Persecutions

(Matthew 5:12)

The most striking part of Christ's eighth and last beatitude is the command that the Christian is to rejoice in persecutions: "Rejoice, and be exceedingly glad; for great is your reward in heaven; for so persecuted they the prophets who were before you." How puzzling! For these questions immediately arise in the mind of any thoughtful reader: "How are we to rejoice in persecutions? How does one rejoice when unjustly insulted, scorned, or condemned?" These are valid questions, and the answer is well worth pondering. How does a Christian rejoice in persecutions?

I am convinced that the only valid answer to that question is — by knowledge.

KNOWLEDGE

In order to understand this it is necessary to recognize that some battles in the Christian life can be won in no other way than by knowledge — not by reason, not by feelings, but by knowledge.

A young man goes to college and meets a girl with whom he falls in love and whom he would like to marry but who is not a Christian. He wants to marry her, but he should not. The Holy Spirit within him is telling him so. As a result a terrific battle is in progress. How is he to win it? Well, it is certain that he will never win it by trusting his feelings, for his feelings are what have created the problem in the first place. He will not win it by reason, for the human mind is subtle, and he will always find ten reasons why he should marry her for every one why he should not. Neither can he win the battle by trusting his conscience. The human conscience can be bent to do almost anything we want it to do; in this case

63

it can even be bent to immorality. There is only one way in which the young man will win the victory in this situation, and that is by clinging to the knowledge of God's will that he has received from Scripture. He must say, "Lord, I do not want to give this particular girl up. I can think of a dozen reasons why I do not need to give her up. I can even make my conscience tell me that I should not give her up. But I know that I must. And because of that I will do it." The young man must make an intellectual decision. And this means that, apart from any other factor, he must determine simply to walk in the way that he *knows* God would have him to go.

It is exactly the same when a Christian is in the midst of persecution. And what is more, almost every verse in the Bible that refers to persecution implies this. If you are enduring persecution, perhaps from your friends or your family, you dare not trust your feelings. There are times when Christians feel on top of the world even when they are suffering. But this is not always true. It is just as probable, perhaps more so, that the Christian will feel sad and dejected, as Elijah did under the juniper tree. If you trust your feelings, you will rejoice at best only at times and then only partially.

Neither can you trust your reason, for the reasoning power of a Christian is often that which is most shaken in the midst of persecution. Have you ever noticed how the Apostle Paul described his mental state in the midst of his many persecutions? He writes about it in 2 Corinthians, telling us that confusion of his reason was at least part of the problem. He says, "We are troubled on every side, yet not distressed; we are *perplexed,* but not in despair; persecuted, but not forsaken; cast down, but not destroyed" (2 Cor. 4:8, 9). Along with being troubled, persecuted, and cast down, Paul also says that he was often perplexed. And hence he had learned that he could not trust even his own great powers of reason in the midst of troubles and persecutions.

If we cannot trust our feelings and if we cannot trust our reason, what can we Christians trust in order that we might rejoice in persecutions? We can only trust the knowledge that we have of God's purposes in persecution and His control of suffering. And this is a knowledge gained only through Scripture. The victory is intellectual. It is only knowledge that will calm the Christian's troubled heart and allow the supernatural joy of God's Spirit to triumph in the midst of his suffering.

IDENTITY WITH CHRIST

What are the things that a Christian can know that allow him to rejoice in persecutions? There are at least five. The first one is this: the Christian must know that through persecutions God is demonstrating his *identity with Christ*. This is the point of all the verses that teach that if we suffer with Christ we also shall be glorified with Him. And it is behind Christ's observation in our text, "For so persecuted they the prophets who were before you."

We can see an example of this in what it means to be an American today in areas of the Near East where America's present foreign policy is disliked and sometimes hated. Several years ago I was present in one of the Near Eastern countries in the company of two friends. One of them was another American with whom I had journeyed around the better part of the Mediterranean. The other was a Christian pastor who was born and raised in that country. We Americans thought very little of things we were doing as we toured the sights, but some of those things, although innocent in themselves, worried him. There were places where he did not want us to linger, objects we were not to photograph, subjects that he did not want us to speak about in public. In answer to our confused questions he explained that at the moment anti-American feeling was running high and that an innocent act, however well motivated, might be dangerously misconstrued. He said that this strong feeling was not directed so much against us personally as against our nation.

In just the same way the world always will be bitterly opposed to Jesus Christ and to His foreign policy, and it will hate His ambassadors. To the citizens of "His country," however, the persecution will merely be evidence of their identification with Him. They will know that it places them in the great company of those who have been similarly persecuted, and the persecution itself will be a matter of honor.

It was this knowledge that gave joy to the first Christians ever to be persecuted. They were Peter and John, and perhaps some of the other apostles, and they were beaten for the sake of their testimony in Jerusalem. We read, however, that after they were beaten, "They departed from the presence of the council, rejoicing that they were counted worthy to suffer shame for his name. And daily in the temple, and in every house, they ceased not to teach and preach Jesus Christ" (Acts 5:41, 42). Persecution is evidence of the believer's identification with his Lord.

PURIFICATION

The second part of a Christian's knowledge that will help him to rejoice in persecution is the knowledge that God often uses persecution to *perfect the believer*. In the great wisdom of God, persecution is often the means by which the Christian is helped along the road to practical holiness and thereby made a little more like Jesus.

Peter knew this. He had known it personally, and he had seen it in the lives of his converts. Hence, when he wrote his first letter to those in Asia who were experiencing persecution, he wrote this about it: "In this ye greatly rejoice, though now for a season, if need be, ye are in heaviness through manifold trials, that the trial of your faith, being much more precious than of gold that perisheth, though it be tried with fire, might be found unto praise and honor and glory at the appearing of Jesus Christ, whom, having not seen, ye love; in whom, though now ye see him not, yet believing, ye rejoice with joy unspeakable and full of glory" (1 Peter 1:6-8). Peter was saying that for the Christian, persecution (and also suffering in general) is the crucible in which God the refiner purifies us and removes the dross from our lives.

Let me give you another illustration. Dr. Billy Graham tells of a friend of his who went through the depression in the 1920's, losing a job, a fortune, a wife, and a home. But he was a believer in Jesus Christ, and he tenaciously held to his faith even though he was naturally depressed and cast down by circumstances. One day in the midst of his depression he stopped to watch some men doing stonework on a huge church in the city. One was busy chiseling a triangular piece of stone. "What are you going to do with that?" he asked. The workman stopped and pointed to a little opening near the top of the spire. "See that little opening up there near the spire?" he said. "Well, I'm shaping this down here so that it will fit in up there." The friend said that tears filled his eyes as he walked away from the workman, for it seemed that God had spoken to him personally through the workman telling him that God was shaping him for heaven through his ordeal.

Peter said, "But the God of all grace, who hath called us unto his eternal glory by Christ Jesus, after ye have suffered awhile, make you perfect, establish, strengthen, settle you. To him be glory and dominion forever and ever. Amen" (1 Peter 5:10, 11). David tells us in one of the Psalms that before he was afflicted he went astray but that after the affliction he kept God's word (Ps. 119: 67). Most certainly, persecution was a significant factor in the spiritual growth of each of these men. Persecution is also a factor in God's dealings with His children today. Because of this truth we may face persecution with all joy, knowing that after we have gone through its furnace we shall be more like Jesus, our Savior.

RADIANT CHRISTIANITY

The third truth that will help a Christian to rejoice in persecution is the truth that persecution allows the Christian an opportunity to show forth the supernatural *radiance* of the Christian life. If everything is going well with you and you rejoice, what makes you different from the non-believers who are in the world? Nothing at all! They too rejoice when circumstances are favorable. If you are able to rejoice when things are not favorable, however, then Jesus Christ may be clearly seen in you, and the supernatural power of the Christian faith is made manifest. Persecution is the dark background for the supernatural radiance of this life.

Again, this truth is best illustrated by a story. Mr. and Mrs. Arthur Mathews and their daughter Lilah were the last missionary family of the China Inland Mission to leave China after the Communist takeover at the end of the Second World War, and the story of their last two years in China is one of great persecution. For the better part of their two-year captivity in China they lived in one small room. Their only furniture was a stool. They could not contact their Christian friends for fear of subjecting them to reprisals for befriending aliens. Their funds were cut off by the government except for the smallest trickle. The only heat they had came from a small stove which they lit only once each day to boil rice for dinner. Even the fuel which they used was made by Mr. Mathews from the refuse that animals deposited around the streets. For a time the couple submitted to the treatment stoically, asking all the while that God would soon deliver them from China. At last a turning point came in their outlook. They realized that Jesus Christ had come from heaven, not merely submitting to the will of his Father, but delighting in it. And they saw that their own experience was comparable. It was an opportunity for the radiance of joyful obedience to be manifested in them and in which their conduct could be a supernaturally effective witness. After this they came to rejoice and even to sing hymns. And they came to accept the privilege of suffering for the sake of Christ with as much joy as they later experienced when they learned of their pending deliverance.

It was a similar knowledge of the opportunities afforded by persecution that taught Hugh Latimer to cry out to Nicholas Ridley as they were both led to the stake in Oxford, England, in 1555, "Be of good comfort, Master Ridley, and play the man; we shall this day light such a candle by God's grace in England as (I trust) shall never be put out." And he was right. For the behavior of Christians in persecutions was then and often still is a great testimony to God's grace.

Rewards in Heaven

There are two more truths that a Christian should also know in order that he may rejoice in persecutions. The first is the *promise of rewards*. Jesus said, "Rejoice, and be exceedingly glad; for great is your reward in heaven" (Matt. 5:12).

There are many Christians who consider even the thought of rewards to be ignoble. But that is because they are thinking only of material or self-exalting things. Actually, the rewards are far more likely to be spiritual — fellowship with Christ and proximity to Him — and they cannot be the least bit self-exalting, for even they flow from God's grace. Do not make your Christianity something so ethereal that you think your conduct should be above the thought of rewards. That is not how the believers of other ages prospered. Abraham looked for a city, with foundations, whose builder and maker is God. Moses chose to suffer affliction with the people of God rather than to enjoy the pleasures of sin for a season because "he had respect unto the recompense of the reward" (Heb. 11:26). Even Jesus "for the joy that was set before him endured the cross . . . and is set down at the right hand of the throne of God" (Heb. 12:2). He said, "Rejoice . . . for great is your reward in heaven."

Finally, the Christian can rejoice in the knowledge that the Lord *Jesus Himself is particularly near* him in the moment of severe persecution. Do you remember the story of the three Hebrew young men who were cast into the midst of the burning fiery furnace? Their names were Hananiah, Mishael, and Azariah, whom the king named Shadrach, Meshach, and Abednego. Three men! But when the king looked into the furnace he said, "Did not we cast three men, bound, into the midst of the fire? . . . Lo, I see four men loose, walking in the midst of the fire, and they have no hurt; and the form of the fourth is like a son of the gods" (Dan. 3:24, 25). In the same way Jesus Christ is particularly near those who are persecuted for His sake, and they can have great joy in this knowledge.

VICTORY IN PERSECUTION

When a Christian can anchor himself in a knowledge of the five great truths that have just been explained, persecution can result in rejoicing. And the rejoicing will — this is the culminating point — lead to greater knowledge.

Job knew suffering and great persecution. But he triumphed through knowledge, and the persecution itself led on to more knowledge. At the beginning Job knew that he was nothing in himself and that he had no rights at all before God. When God allowed the most severe blows of life to fall upon him, Job thrived in the knowledge that there was yet the corresponding grace of God and the inextinguishable love of God for himself. As the trials continued, he came to know that God was testing him and purifying his faith, and he rejoiced in that knowledge. Finally, he learned that God was revealing Himself to him in a new way, and he came to expect an even fuller revelation. For Job, knowledge was the key to spiritual victory and his knowledge actually grew because of it. So should it be for every persecuted Christian.

Chapter 9

Do You Make Men Thirsty?

(Matthew 5:13)

In Matthew 5:13 we come to a new section of the Sermon on the Mount. We pass from a basically abstract definition of the Christian to a functional one. Jesus said, "Ye are the salt of the earth, but if the salt have lost its savor, with what shall it be salted? It is thereafter good for nothing, but to be cast out, and to be trodden under foot of men."

We all know the difference between an abstract definition of a thing and a functional definition, if we think about it. For instance, almost every dictionary definition of a word is abstract. We turn to the word "hunger" in *Webster's New Collegiate Dictionary* and read, "an uneasy sensation, occasioned normally by the want of food." However, we could also define hunger functionally. We could also say, "Hunger is the one and a half billion people in this world who live always on the verge of starvation and who die at the rate of 15,000 daily as the result of malnutrition." The second definition is anything but abstract. And, of course, it is better. In the same way the dictionary tells us that "justice" is "the principle of rectitude and just dealings of men with each other." But we could also say that justice is enacting good laws, caring for the poor, raising children properly, and many other things.

We have the same thing in the sphere of theology. The *Westminster Shorter Catechism* asks the question, "What is God?" And it answers, "God is a spirit, infinite, eternal, and unchangeable, in His being, wisdom, power, holiness, justice, goodness, and truth." But it is also true, even more true, that God is Jesus Christ who died for our sin and who rose again for our justification.

The second definition in each of the cases I have mentioned gives us an understanding of the term in action; it produces the effect that Jesus produced by His further, functional definitions of the true Christian. "Ye are the salt of the earth." "Ye are the light of the world." By these definitions Jesus was saying that while it is true that the Christian is to be poor in spirit, mournful for sin, meek, thirsty for righteousness, merciful, pure in heart, and disposed to make peace, nevertheless he is never to be these things in isolation from a very real and sharply antithetical world. He is to manifest those characteristics in the world. And what is more, he is to practice these things in a way that will affect the world positively, as salt affects the medium to which one applies it.

A Decaying World

This is of great significance for our understanding of the nature of true Christianity, especially in our present day. Jesus was saying, "Those who are My disciples should affect the world positively by the way in which they live." But as I view the world today, there is not nearly enough of this positive action for good in the world by Christians, even though many people are aware that something of this nature is precisely what the world needs.

At the end of the nineteenth century there was a feeling of confident optimism in the western world, based on the belief that an ongoing biological and philosophical evolution would eventually solve all man's troubles and lead to something closely akin to the Greeks' "Golden Age." The idea was that all of human life was advancing and rising upward. Dr. D. Martyn Lloyd-Jones writes perceptively of this age, "It is indeed pathetic to read the prognostications of the thinkers (so-called), the philosophers and poets and leaders, towards the end of the last century. . . . Wars were going to be abolished, diseases were being cured, suffering was going to be not only ameliorated but finally eradicated. It was to be an amazing century. Most of the problems were going to be solved, for man had at last really begun to think. The masses, through education, would cease giving themselves to drink and immorality and vice. And as all the nations were thus educated to think and to hold conferences instead of rushing to war, the whole world was very soon going to be Paradise. That is not caricaturing the situation; it was believed confidently." *

Today, however, there are not many people who think like that.

* D. Martyn Lloyd-Jones, *Studies in the Sermon on the Mount* (Grand Rapids: Wm. B. Eerdmans, 1967), Vol. I, pp. 150, 151.

Where there was once a confident optimism, there is now real pessimism and acute despair. Even the ones who are still confident in some areas express their more limited optimism guardedly. There is an awareness that something more than a theory of progress is necessary, that there must, in fact, be something akin to a new life embodied in a new breed of men. This is what the Gospel of Jesus Christ offers. And yet, what do we find? Instead of the active, permeating, preserving, and transforming power of the Gospel of Jesus Christ always operating in the world through all Christians, too many Christians are sitting on the sidelines without the "savor" provided by the Lord Jesus Christ and fit only — if we are to take Christ's words literally — "to be cast out, and to be trodden under foot of men."

I am well aware that there are good historical reasons why an evangelical church that once gave fuel and impetus to the greatest social movements the world has seen has come to be outdistanced by others and at times even to be hostile to the applications of the Gospel to the contemporary world. Daniel O. Moberg, author of the book, *Inasmuch,* lists ten reasons in his historical study of the neglect of the social aspects of the faith by evangelicals: a preoccupation with valid theological battles, a misinterpretation of the prophecies that in the last days things on this earth will get worse to mean that they will never in any circumstances get better, a belief that social concerns are antithetical to a concern for the salvation aspects of the Church's message, a concern for personal piety, the idea that politics are intrinsically "dirty," a growing conformity to the world's standards in business and political life by Christians, and other things also. But the explanation does not excuse the situation in which we find ourselves today. Nor does the situation itself negate the moral imperatives of Christ's teachings.

According to Jesus, the Christian is clearly to influence his society. And this must be true wherever the principles of the Gospel impinge upon the religious, political, economic, or social issues of the Christian's community.

Uses of Salt

All this falls into a much clearer focus when we consider the actual uses of salt, particularly those that were most valued in ancient times.

First, in Christ's day and for many centuries thereafter (in fact,

until nearly modern times), salt was the most common of all pre-
servatives. There were no refrigerators in ancient times, no deep-
freeze units. The Mediterranean world was largely tropical. In
such a climate and in the face of such conditions, salt was used to
keep things from going bad and becoming rotten, particularly meat.
It was able to resist spoilage and keep putrefaction at bay. When
Jesus said that those who followed Him were the salt of the earth,
therefore, He was teaching that the world apart from God is rotten
because of sin, but that through His power His disciples were able
and actually obliged to have a preserving and purifying effect
upon it.

Do you see this clearly? If you do, the principles involved in
this statement will keep you from the two opposing errors that have
always gone along with programs to express the Christian's social
responsibility. The first error is the thought that the world is basically good and will gradually become better and even perfect
through Christian social action. In opposition to this understanding, Christ says that the world is basically rotten. This means that
even though it may appear healthy for a time, it is dead spiritually.
It means that the life has gone out of the body and that the mi-
crobes of sin will eventually (if left to themselves) reduce it to a
stinking, unapproachable carcass.

The other error is the view that because this is so, because the
world is rotten, the Christian should try to disassociate himself
from the world as much as possible, retreating to a monastery or to
one of our white (or black), middle-class, self-protecting churches.
And he should let the world go to hell. The answer to this error
is that the Christian is to be a preserving force in the world wherever God has placed him. The salt never did any good when it
was sitting on one shelf and the meat on another. To be effective,
the salt had to be rubbed into the meat. In a similar way, Christians must allow God to rub them into the world. And this means
that they must be Christians at work, Christians in politics, Christians at home, Christians everywhere else that a normal life in their
own society would take them.

"Oh," someone says, "that would mean that I would have to be
taken out of the salt shaker and spread around, and I might get
dirty and even seem to dissolve or disappear!" Yes, that is what
it means. But God is the One who provides the flavor, and the
flavor does not disappear when the salt is dispensed or dissolved.

In fact, there is even a sense in which the salt *must* dissolve if the flavor is to be released, and for this reason God sometimes shakes the salt shaker through persecutions so that the salt will fall out and let this happen. Sometimes it will mean that we shall have to dissolve to our own interests, that we shall have to extend ourselves in areas of the world where we do not see many Christians. We shall feel lonely and even depressed, but that is where the salt is active.

I should add a fact that is well known to the medical world. If a body does not give off salt through perspiration, what happens? It retains water, and it becomes bloated. In the same way, the Church will become bloated and desperately unhealthy if the salt is not dispersed in this work of preservation.

SOURCE OF FLAVOR

There is a second thing that salt is good for, and that is to provide flavor. The Christian, through the life of Jesus Christ within and the verities of the Gospel, is to lend flavor to a flavorless, insipid world. The pleasures of the world are unsatisfying without Jesus Christ. They fill for a time. But they are rather like a Chinese dinner, and the person is soon left empty again. Consequently, those who pursue them are doomed to a constant and relentless search for that which will never satisfy the true hunger and desire of their soul. Christians are to be present as those who know something different and whose satisfaction in Christ can be seen and known by their unbelieving contemporaries.

Unfortunately, it often has been the other way around. Non-Christians have looked at Christians and have said, "What an insipid bunch of people; I would never want to be like one of them." The nineteenth century poet and critic A. C. Swinburne wrote of Jesus: "Thou hast conquered, O pale Galilean; the world has grown grey from thy breath." Oliver Wendell Holmes once said, "I might have entered the ministry if certain clergymen I knew had not looked and acted so much like undertakers." And the poet and author Robert Louis Stevenson once wrote in his diary, as if he were expressing an exceptional fact, "I have been to church today, and am not depressed."

Those are honest remarks by people who have seen an insipid Christianity. And if they or their followers are to see something different, they must see it in the only place it can or will be seen — in us. They must see it in you and in me. Do you go around with a long face as if the world and everything you know are depressing? Or do you go about as one who bears within the Spirit of the living God? The second is your true responsibility. It is by doing that, that you show forth the flavor of Christ and Christianity.

Thirst of the Soul

The third thing that salt does is to make one thirsty. And this leads us to ask: Do you make anyone thirsty for Jesus Christ? The non-Christian tends to feel self-satisfied even if he is not, and he naturally goes through life telling himself that circumstances are wonderful. But when a Christian comes into his sphere of vision, there should be that evidence of joy, satisfaction, and peace that makes him look up and say, "That's what I want; that is what I want to be like!" Can that be said of you? Do you make men thirsty for Jesus Christ?

In ancient times during the Feast of Tabernacles in the city of Jerusalem it was the custom for the priests to go to the pool of Siloam each day and to return bearing large containers of water that were then emptied upon the altar in the Temple. This happened for seven days during the feast. On the last day the ceremony was repeated seven times. On that day, during the Feast of Tabernacles in the year that He attended, Jesus Christ stood up and cried in a loud voice, "If any man thirst, let him come unto me, and drink. He that believeth on me, as the scripture hath said, out of his heart shall flow rivers of living water" (John 7: 37, 38). It is true, Jesus Christ can satisfy the great thirst of the human soul. Your responsibility is not to satisfy the thirst yourself, but to point men to Jesus Christ. If you do that, out of you will flow His life and character, and others will see Him and be satisfied.

A Common Substance

I am sure you already have anticipated the last point of this study, for you have doubtless recognized that salt is one of the most common things of life. It is found everywhere. And hence, when Jesus said, "Ye are the salt of the earth," He was saying, "I delight to use little things." He did not say, "Ye are the gold of the earth." He did not say, "Ye are the uranium of the earth." He did not even say, "Ye are the lead," although Christians sometimes resemble lead far more than we like to admit. He said, "Ye are the salt" — a common substance. It is from the common things — from the weak, the foolish, the despised, the things that are not (1 Cor. 1:26-29) — that God brings the greatest glory to His name.

We see that throughout Scripture. When God made man in the garden of Eden, what did He use? Gold? Silver? Iron? No, He used dust. But He breathed into the dust the divine breath of life. When God spoke to Moses in the desert to call him to come forth to be the deliverer of the people of Israel from Egypt, how did He reveal Himself? In a dazzling theophany? In thunder and lightning? In an overpowering vision? No, He revealed Himself in a burning desert bush. When God called David to deliver the Israelites from the Philistine tyranny, did He make use of Saul's armor? No, He used a sling and a few small stones. And when Jesus Christ was born, God did not allow Him to be born in the courts of the Caesars or of a woman of noble ancestry and great culture. He chose a peasant girl, who was probably illiterate, and she gave birth to Jesus Christ in a stable.

God uses the small things and the small people. God uses you and me that He might do His work in the world. As a matter of fact, the smaller you can become, the more effective His work in you will be. Do you know what we are to be? We are to be picture frames within which Jesus Christ is to be seen. God is not interested in its being a gold frame or a beautifully carved frame. He is just interested in its being an empty frame, because He knows that when you come to Him with that, He can put Christ there. And when people look at you, they will see Jesus.

Chapter 10

The Light of the World

(Matthew 5:14-16)

When Jesus Christ described the proper function of His disciples in this world in the Sermon on the Mount He made use of two sublime illustrations. The first was salt. He said, "Ye are the salt of the earth." We already have studied that illustration. The second illustration is light. Jesus said, "Ye are the light of the world. A city that is set on an hill cannot be hidden. Neither do men light a lamp, and put it under a bushel, but on a lampstand, and it giveth light unto all that are in the house. Let your light so shine before men, that they may see your good works, and glorify your Father, who is in heaven" (Matt. 5:14-16).

We need to look at these words carefully, for they are profound. They teach important lessons about the nature of Christ and this world, the imperatives and strengths of the Christian life, and the obligation of a believer to remain in close fellowship with his Lord.

A DARKENED WORLD

The first clear implication of Christ's words is that the world is in darkness where spiritual things are concerned. And the tragedy of the situation is that men actually prefer the darkness to God's light. Several years ago an old woman in the bush country of southern Rhodesia said to a missionary, "You missionaries have brought us the light, but we don't seem to want it. You have brought us the light, but we still walk in darkness." She was speaking only of the life she knew in Africa. But her words aptly describe the reaction of all men to the light of Christ and to the Christian Gospel. Jesus was the light of the world when He was in the world. Today, Christians are the light of the world. The tragedy is that men actually prefer the darkness. That is, they

77

prefer their own imperfect and sinful way of doing things instead of the perfect and holy standards of Jesus Christ.

Part of the problem, of course, is that most men will not admit this. A few years ago a national news magazine made some accurate remarks about the presence of sin and evil in America and the reaction of Americans to it, but they could have been even more accurate if the words had been extended to the world in general. The magazine wrote, "It is the particular heresy of Americans that they see themselves as potential saints more than as real-life sinners." And it added in reference to the young radicals of our society, "Today's young radicals, in particular, are almost painfully sensitive to these and other wrongs of their society, and denounce them violently. But at the same time they are typically American in that they fail to place evil in its historic and human perspective. To them, evil is not an irreducible component of man, an inescapable fact of life, but something committed by the older generation, attributable to a particular class or the 'Establishment,' and eradicable through love and revolution" (*Time,* Dec. 5, 1969, p. 27). Unfortunately, evil *is* an irreducible component of man, and it is no less real because most men are unwilling to acknowledge it.

It was the particular achievement of Jesus Christ that He exposed the nature of the darkness in a way that had never been done previously. And, of course, men hated Him for it. One commentator has written, "The light which reveals the world does not make the darkness, but it makes the darkness felt. If the sun is hidden, all is shadow, though we call that shadow only which is contrasted with the sunlight; for the contrast seems to intensify that which is however left just what it is before. And this is what Christ has done by His coming. He stands before the world in perfect purity, and we feel as men could not feel before He came, the imperfection, the impurity of the world. The line of separation is drawn forever, and the conscience of men acknowledges that it is rightly drawn. Whether we know it or not the light which streams from Christ is ever opening the way to a clearer distinction between good and evil. His coming is a judgment. The light and the darkness are not blended in him, as they are in us, so that opinion can be doubtful." *

* Brooke Foss Westcott, *The Revelation of the Father* (London and Cambridge: Macmillan and Co., 1884), p. 52.

Actually, the coming of Jesus into the world exposed the world's darkness, even where men thought they had most light. When I was very young I spent a number of summers at a Christian camp in Canada. Each summer my friends and I took several camping trips. The trips were fun, as I remember, but the sleeping accommodation was not. The ground was hard. Often it was damp. Generally there were rocks underneath the bedding. I remember lying awake sometimes for most of the night talking or fooling around with the other campers. During a particularly long night we would play with our flashlights. We would shine them in one another's eyes, and the game was to see which light was the brightest. Generally, the flashlight with the brightest reflector or the largest number of batteries won. Now, obviously, the game could be played only in the dark. For eventually the sun came up, and after that the differences between the flashlights faded into insignificance by comparison.

That is what happened when the Lord Jesus Christ came into the world, and that is what men and women still experience today when they come face to face with Him. As long as we live in the darkness and are never exposed to God's light you and I are able to compare the relative merits of human goodness and be totally oblivious to how much in darkness we are. We are able to see the difference between a three-battery character, a two-battery character, and one that has almost gone out. We rate men accordingly. Fortunately, all these distinctions fade away in the presence of the white light of the righteousness of Jesus Christ. For His coming and His presence reveal the depth of the darkness of your character and mine.

What is your reaction to that? It can be one of two things. You can hate Christ for it, as many people have done, and attempt to get rid of His presence in your life. (When Jesus was on earth, those who felt that way crucified Him.) Or you can do what He wants you to do. You can say, "Lord, I see now that my own works are far from perfect. If they seem bright to me, it is only because I am measuring them by my own low standard. I realize that they will never take me to heaven. I ask You to give me that goodness which I do not have, as you have promised to do, and remove my sin forever. I believe in You and Your work of redemption." And Jesus will do that. He is as good as His word. The Bible says, "For he [God] hath made him [Jesus Christ], who

knew no sin, to be sin for us, that we might be made the righteousness of God in him" (2 Cor. 5:21).

"YE ARE THE LIGHT"

At this point you may be saying to yourself something like this:
"Dr. Boice, you began by quoting Christ's statement that Christians are the light of the world, but ever since then, you have
spoken only of Him as the light and of the fact that we are in
darkness. If this is true, how can we say that Christians are the
light of the world? In fact, is it even possible?" The answer to
these questions is that in himself the Christian *cannot* be the light
of the world. However, he *can* show forth light to the extent that
he first receives it from the Lord Jesus Christ and reflects it from
Him to others.

As I have studied this theme throughout the Bible I have been
impressed by the fact that most of the images used to convey it
clearly point this out. For instance, in the verses from the Sermon
on the Mount that we are studying, the Christian is described as a
lamp or a candle. He gives forth light. But he does so only because he first has been kindled by Jesus Christ. In John's gospel,
John the Baptist is described as "a burning and a shining lamp"
by Jesus. Again the point is that John's light is secondary to that
of Christ; John's is a kindled light and exists only because of Christ.

One of the greatest illustrations on this point that I have heard
was often used by Dr. Donald Grey Barnhouse. He used to say
that when Christ was in the world He was a bit like the sun which
is here by day and gone at night. But when the sun goes down
the moon comes up, and the moon is a picture of the Church — of
Christians. It shines, but it does not shine by its own light. It
shines only because it reflects the light of the sun. Jesus said of
Himself in John 8:12, "I am the light of the world." But when He
was thinking of the fact that one day He would be taken out of the
world He said, "Ye are the light of the world." And that is why
the world is in such darkness today. At times the Church is a full
moon, in the midst of revival when a man like Luther or Calvin or
Wesley is here. And at other times the Church is a new moon and
you can barely see it. But whether it is a full moon or a new moon
or only a waxing or a waning quarter it glows because of the sun.
In the same way, you and I can show forth light only if we reflect
the real light of the Lord Jesus.

Do you do that? If you do, you will function a bit like Jesus Himself when He was on earth, only in a smaller version. For one thing your presence will help to expose the evil and the darkness of this world, and you will find that you are not particularly popular for it. You will illuminate dishonest practices in business, gossip in the secretarial pool, loose talk and still looser morals at parties, corruption in local politics, racial prejudice, greed, selfishness, and other things. And they will appear darker, even to non-Christians, because of what you reveal of the holy character of Jesus.

For another thing, you will help faith grow among the weak in faith, just as a plant will grow even in a dark cave if a bright enough light is present. Friends should grow in the Christian life because of what you know and have learned of Jesus. If you are married and have children, the children should grow to full spiritual stature in your home.

Finally, you should also see men and women turn to Jesus Himself through your testimony. In his day, the Apostle Paul taught this by means of an illustration from the Old Testament. When Moses was with God in the mountain his face shone with transferred glory as a result of being with God. The glory was so bright that when Moses came down from the mountain he had to cover his face so that the light on it would not dazzle the people. Using this theme Paul argues in 2 Corinthians 3 and 4 that we also should shine with the same glory as a result of spending time with Jesus Christ, and that others should be able to see Him as He is reflected by us. He concludes by saying, "God, who first ordered light to shine in darkness, has flooded our hearts with his light. We now can enlighten men only because we can give them knowledge of the glory of God, as we see it in the face of Jesus Christ" (2 Cor. 4:6, Phillips).

Do men see Jesus Christ in you? They will not find Him in the world — in the world's literature, culture, or pastimes. They will find Him only as you look to Jesus, as you spend time with Him and thereby allow some of His light to be reflected from your life to those about you.

You may be tempted to think that this applies only to "special" Christians. But the whole point of the illustration is that it applies to every believer in the Lord Jesus Christ. When Jesus Christ said, "Ye are the light of the world," who were the "ye's" who heard

Him? They were not the important people alone, not even His disciples exclusively. They were the whole mass of those who followed Him — rich and poor, small and great, educated and uneducated, Jews and Gentiles, free men and servants, women and children. These were all to reflect Christ's light. And the nobodies (in the opinion of the world) were among them.

The Bible says that "God hath chosen the foolish things of the world to confound the wise; and God hath chosen the weak things of the world to confound the things which are mighty; and base things of the world, and things which are despised, hath God chosen, yea, and things which are not, to bring to nothing things that are, that no flesh should glory in his presence" (1 Cor. 1: 27-29). No matter who you are, if you are a Christian, you are called to reflect Christ's light to those about you.

WALK IN THE LIGHT

Moreover, if you will do this, you also will find that the light of Christ will lead you on in love, grace, and righteousness and will keep you from falling as you move along the dark and treacherous paths of this world. Bishop Westcott, a great biblical scholar of a past generation, has a series of comments on this point that are so relevant to today's world that they deserve repetition. He writes, "We lose the light if we do not follow Christ, and move as He moves. We cannot hold Him back. It is the glory of our faith that it advances with the accumulated progress of all life. And it is our blessing that we are not left to grope sadly and restlessly for our way. That way is a track of light which grows dim only if we loiter or hang back. A Christian cannot rest in anything which has been already gained. New acquisitions of knowledge, new modes of thought, new forms of society, are always calling for interpretation, for recognition, for adjustment. . . . There are the trials of wealth burdened by an inheritance of luxury, which checks the growth of fellow-feeling and enfeebles the energy of Christian love. There are the trials of poverty worn by the struggle for bare existence, which exhausts the forces properly destined to minister to the healthy development of the fulness of life. There is the separation of class from class which seems to become wider with increasing rapidity through the circumstances of modern labor and commerce. . . . There is the impatient questioning of old beliefs which gives an unreal value to the appeal to authority and casts suspicion upon sympathetic efforts to meet doubt.

"But to meet all these dark problems our light — the Light of Life — is unexhausted and inexhaustible. The temple lamps blazed through the early night, but then at last they died out and darkness settled again over the city which lay below. Each borrowed and preparatory light gleamed for a time and afterwards faded away: such lights are consumed in burning. But the Light, which lightens because it lives . . . burns on with changeless splendour. And this only is required of us if we would know its quickening, cheering, warming energies, that we should follow it." *

Do we follow it? Do you? Oh, Christian, let us walk in the light, for then we walk with God. We do not escape the perils, foes, and dangers. But we do see them, and we see our proper path. In His light we see light. We reveal His light. And we do not overlook the goal.

* *Ibid.*, pp. 55-57.

Chapter 11

Christ and the Scriptures

(Matthew 5:17-20)

It is not at all uncommon in our seminaries today for a young man to be taught that if he stands firm on a high view of Scripture as the Church in previous ages has always done, he runs the danger of bibliolatry or Bible-worship. That is, he runs the danger of actually worshiping the Bible instead of the Lord Jesus Christ and of placing it on a pedestal which even Jesus Himself did not assign to it. This argument against the traditional view of the Christian Church on Scripture sounds valid to some persons and even seems pious, but it is misleading. And as used in the hands of some teachers it has greatly harmed the unwary. In opposition to this debilitating and erroneous approach, the careful student of the Bible must maintain that Christ so identified Himself with Scripture and so interpreted His ministry in the light of Scripture that it is impossible to weaken the authority of the one without at the same time weakening the authority of the other. And to accept Christ's teachings is at the same time to accept His high view of God's Word.

What did the Lord Jesus Christ teach about the Bible? He taught many things, and on many occasions, of course, but by far the most comprehensive answer the Lord Jesus ever gave to this question is contained in the verses to which we come now in our study of the Sermon on the Mount. Jesus said, "Think not that I am come to destroy the law, or the prophets; I am not come to destroy, but to fulfill. For verily I say unto you, Till heaven and earth pass, one jot or one tittle shall in no way pass from the law, till all be fulfilled. Whosoever, therefore, shall break one of

84

these least commandments, and shall teach men so, he shall be called the least in the kingdom of heaven; but whosoever shall do and teach them, the same shall be called great in the kingdom of heaven. For I say unto you that except your righteousness shall exceed the righteousness of the scribes and Pharisees, ye shall in no case enter into the kingdom of heaven" (Matt. 5:17-20).

According to these verses Jesus taught that He did not come to supplant the Scriptures or to oppose them. He came to fulfill them and to fulfill them precisely. Before we look at the specific ways in which Jesus Christ fulfilled the Scriptures, we want to look in a general way at the truths He taught about them.

ABSOLUTE AUTHORITY

The first truth that we find in these verses is the truth that the Scriptures — and Christ was of course, referring to the whole of the Old Testament — are absolute. They are eternal and unchangeable. They are the rock upon which the Christian can build. They stand written beyond any alteration or recall. They are the supreme court of all supreme courts. From their verdict there is no further appeal.

Moreover, this is true, not only in a passive, but also in an active sense. For the decision that the Bible gives is an efficacious decision, one that actually brings about the fact stated. We might illustrate this aspect of the Bible's function by a comparison of the Scriptures with the Supreme Court of the United States. Suppose that the Supreme Court is asked for a decision on a matter that is already common practice across the country but which has been challenged by suit. If the Supreme Court finds the practice to be in conformity with the Constitution of the United States, this decision is final. And the practice must stand. If, however, as in the case of segregation in the public schools, the practice is found to be out of conformity with the Constitution of the United States, then the practice must be changed, and the decision reached at the bench of the Supreme Court is one that affects the conduct of millions of citizens and the ordering of their lives.

Clearly, Jesus Christ believed that the Bible was the supreme authority over life in both of these senses. It was the court from which there was no further appeal. And it was the court whose decisions, already recorded, were affecting and would continue to affect the lives of men everywhere. According to Jesus the only possible course of action for anyone, including Himself, was to live in total conformity to it. Even though heaven and earth were to pass away, nothing would pass from this book until everything it speaks of had come to pass.

THE SMALLEST PART

It is also evident from these verses that the Lord Jesus Christ considered each part of the Bible inspired. This is to say that according to His teaching the Bible was not only authoritative; it was authoritative in even the smallest part. Jesus said, "Till heaven and earth pass, one jot or one tittle shall in no way pass from the law, till all be fulfilled."

It is evident, even as we read this unusual phrase today, that the phrase "one jot or one tittle" was a common expression referring to the most minute parts of the law. The thought, also quite common in Judaism, was that not even the smallest part of the law would perish or be forgotten. The "jot" was the smallest letter of the Hebrew alphabet, the letter that we would transliterate by an "i" or a "y." In written Hebrew it resembled a comma, though it was written near the top of the letters rather than near the bottom. The "tittle" was what we would call a serif, the tiny protrusion on letters that distinguishes a Roman type face from a more modern one. In many Bibles Psalm 119 is divided into 22 sections each beginning with a different letter of the Hebrew alphabet. The reader of the English Bible can see what a tittle is by comparing the Hebrew letter before verse 9 in Psalm 119 with the Hebrew letter before verse 81. The first letter is a *beth*. The second one is a *kaph*. The only difference between them is the tittle. The same feature distinguishes *daleth* from *resh* and *vau* from *zayin*. According to Jesus, then, not even an "i" or a "serif" of the law would be lost until the whole law was fulfilled.

Do you believe that? You should because Christ taught it. If you are Christ's disciple, you cannot remain faithful to His teachings and say, "I like the Sermon on the Mount, but I don't like the references to the blood of Jesus Christ; they offend me." You cannot say, "I like prophecy," but then neglect Christ's ethics. You cannot say, "I like the New Testament, but not the Old Testament," "I like certain things that Jesus Christ said, but not other things that Christ said." You must take it all. Jesus taught that "all Scripture is given by inspiration of God, and is profitable for doctrine, for reproof, for correction, for instruction in righteousness" (2 Tim. 3:16).

FULFILLMENT OF SCRIPTURE

Furthermore, Jesus went on to teach that not only is Scripture absolute and not only is every part of it absolute, but also that He had come to fulfill it. This means that Scripture finds its fullest meaning in Him. It is by Him, for Him, and about Him. It is an enigma unless the one who reads it sees the Lord Jesus Christ at its core.

We must remember that Jesus Christ was the author of Scripture during the Old Testament period, that subsequent to that He was the one who came and lived on earth to fulfill it, and then that He inspired the New Testament writers to interpret correctly the things He had already done. If you have ever studied to be a teacher, you will know that one of the first things you are told is that if you want to make your point clear you first have to tell your students what you are going to say, then you have to say it, and finally you have to tell them what you have said. That is what Jesus Christ did. He foretold His coming; He came; and then He told men about it.

CHRIST'S USE OF SCRIPTURE

All these principles are illustrated by Christ's own handling of the Bible and of particular scriptural texts. For instance, just one chapter earlier in the gospel of Matthew, in chapter four, Jesus defeated Satan on the occasion of His temptation by the use of three direct quotations from the Book of Deuteronomy. Jesus had gone into the wilderness to be tempted as a man by the devil. Satan had come to Him and had said, "Look, You don't want to defeat me as a man; why don't You fight temptation by using Your divine powers. Strengthen Yourself supernaturally by commanding that these stones become bread." Jesus replied in effect, "No, I will defeat you as a man by depending on Scripture; for it is written, 'Man shall not live by bread alone, but by every word that proceedeth out of the mouth of God'" (verse 4; cf. Deut. 8:3).

Satan said, "All right then, if You want to use Scripture, we'll do it your way. I am a Bible student myself. And in that capacity I would like to remind you of Psalm 91:11, 12. (And he quotes it incorrectly.) It says, 'He shall give his angels charge concerning thee, and in their hands they shall bear thee up, lest at any time thou dash thy foot against a stone.' Why don't You trust to that promise by throwing Yourself from the temple? When God does bear You up You will have provided a supernatural defense of Your religious claims." Jesus answered that temptation by quoting Deuteronomy 6:16: "Thou shalt not put the Lord, thy God, to the test."

By this time Satan was on the defensive in the battle with Christ, and he became entirely open in his bid for His approval. He said, "All right, I know that You are able to win this struggle and that You will win it. But I can order things so You will not have to die on the cross to rescue this world for Your purpose. The world has been entrusted to me temporarily at least, as You Yourself recognize when You call me the prince of this world; I will give it all to You now if only You will fall down and worship me." Jesus replied with a final devastating sword-thrust from God's word: "It is written, thou shalt worship the Lord, thy God, and him only shalt thou serve" (Deut. 6:13). In the greatest spiritual battle of Christ's life, in a direct encounter with the devil, victory was won by a quotation of three verses from the heart of the Old Testament law.

After His temptation Jesus left the area of the Jordan where it had taken place and went home to Nazareth where He began His formal ministry. He went into the synagogue on the Sabbath day and was asked to read the Scripture. He took the scroll of the prophet Isaiah and opened it to chapter 61, verses 1 and 2, and read: "The Spirit of the Lord is upon me, because he hath anointed me to preach the gospel to the poor; he hath sent me to heal the brokenhearted, to preach deliverance to the captives, and recovering of sight to the blind, to set at liberty them that are bruised, to preach the acceptable year of the Lord" (Luke 4:18, 19). When He had finished reading He put the scroll down and said, "This day is this scripture fulfilled in your ears" (Luke 4:21). This must have been astounding for His hearers, for Jesus was claiming to be the Messiah, the One about whom Isaiah had written. He was identifying His forthcoming ministry with the lines set out for it in Scripture hundreds of years before.

Sometime later, in the early months of the ministry, we find the disciples of John the Baptist coming to Jesus with John's question, "Art thou he that should come, or do we look for another?" (Matt. 11:3). Jesus answered by a second reference to this same section of Isaiah's prophecy, He said, "Do not take My word for who I am. Look at Isaiah and what he foretold about the Messiah. Then see if I am fulfilling it." In other words Jesus also challenged other people to evaluate His ministry in the light of God's Word.

On one occasion the Sadducees came to Him with a trick question about the status of marriage in heaven and the reality of the resurrection. Jesus answered, first, by a rebuke that they did not know either the Scriptures or the power of God and, second, by a direct quotation from Exodus 3:6 in which the point of the quotation consisted in the tense of the Hebrew verb — "I am the God of Abraham, and the God of Isaac, and the God of Jacob" (Matt. 22:32). According to Christ's argument, there must be a resurrection otherwise God would have said, "I *was* the God of Abraham," and not "I *am*." Thus, He proved the doctrine of the resurrection by the difference between two tenses.

On many occasions Jesus appealed to the Scriptures in support of His actions — in defense of His cleansing of the Temple (Mark 11:15-17), in reference to His submission to the cross (Matt. 26: 53, 54). He taught that "scripture cannot be broken" (John 10: 35). He foretold the scattering of the disciples on the night of His arrest in the garden of Gethsemane because, as He said, "It is written, I will smite the shepherd, and the sheep shall be scattered" (Mark 14:27), a quotation from Zechariah 13:7.

We turn to the fifth chapter of John and we find Jesus talking to the Jewish rulers in a long section dealing with His authority and with the witness of His religious claims. He gets to the climax, and it has to do entirely with Scripture. What does He say about it? He says that nobody would ever believe in Him who had not first believed in the writings of Moses, for Moses wrote of Him, "[Ye] search the scriptures; for in them ye think ye have eternal life; and they are they which testify of me. . . . . Do not think that I will accuse you to the Father; there is one that accuseth you, even Moses, in whom ye trust. For had ye believed Moses, ye would have believed me; for he wrote of me. But if ye believe not his writings, how shall ye believe my words?" (John 5:39, 45-47). It is stated as plainly as it can be stated. If you reject the Bible, you will reject Jesus Christ. If you believe the Bible, you will accept Him. He is the subject of it.

We go further in Christ's life, and we find Him hanging on the cross. What is Jesus Christ thinking about there? Scripture! He says, "My God, my God, why hast thou forsaken me?" (Matt. 27: 46), a quotation from Psalm 22:1. He says that He thirsts, and they give Him a sponge filled with vinegar in order that Psalm 69: 21 might be fulfilled. Three days later, after the resurrection, He is on the way to Emmaus with two of His disciples, chiding them because they have not used Scripture to understand the necessity of His suffering. He says, "O foolish ones, and slow of heart to believe all that the prophets have spoken! Ought not Christ to have suffered these things, and to enter into his glory? And beginning at Moses and all the prophets, he expounded unto them, in all the scriptures, the things concerning himself" (Luke 24: 25-27).

ALLEGIANCE TO SCRIPTURE

When we sum it all up, we find that Jesus Christ believed Scripture, that He submitted Himself to Scripture, that He taught that a person would only believe on Him as He believed Scripture. We are left with the question: How can we profess to be followers of Jesus Christ and not hold to the same view of Scripture as He did?

I have done a good bit of work in the general area of New Testament studies. I know that there are difficult areas. All the problems have not been solved, and some may never be solved in this age. I also believe that we need to define our doctrine of Scripture more clearly. We need to say precisely what such words as "inspiration" and "infallibility" mean and what they do not mean. But these are secondary matters compared with the total allegiance of the Christian to the Word of God. Is that your standard? Do you submit yourself to Scripture, as Jesus Christ did? Do you acknowledge Christ as the author, Christ as the subject, Christ as the authoritative interpreter of His own acts? If you do, you will go on from faith to faith and from knowledge to knowledge, understanding more of His ministry and therefore more of what He requires of you as His follower.

Chapter 12

Christ Fulfills the Scriptures

(Matthew 5:17-20)

The first great public utterance of the Lord Jesus Christ on Scripture not only set forth its complete authority, it also contained the categorical statement that the Scriptures were to be fulfilled in their entirety by Him. Jesus said, "Think not that I am come to destroy the law or the prophets; I am not come to destroy, but to fulfill. For verily I say unto you, Till heaven and earth pass, one jot or one tittle shall in no way pass from the law, till all be fulfilled" (Matt. 5:17, 18). We are now to ask: In what sense did Jesus fulfill the law? And in what sense did He fulfill the prophets?

CHRIST AND THE LAW

I believe that without being grossly misleading, there is only one sense in which we can say that Jesus fulfilled the law. He fulfilled the law by dying on the cross and thereby satisfying forever the demands of the law against those who would believe on Him. All other views of Christ's fulfilling the law are misleading in terms of this great purpose, even though they may be quite true in themselves.

You may be asking, "How can it be that something true in itself can be misleading?" Let me give you an illustration. Suppose someone should ask you, "Why was it that George Washington crossed the Delaware on the night of 3 January, 1777?" Well, if you are a humorist, you might answer it as you do the question about the chicken crossing the street — "He crossed it to get to the other side." That would be true, but it would be misleading. You might also say, "The troops were restless and dispirited; and they were in need of some successful action." That, too, would be true, but it also would be misleading. The real reason that Washington crossed the Delaware was to get to the British troops that were in Trenton and defeat them by this unexpected maneuver. And he did it as part of a general strategy for the American War of Independence. To give any other reason, even if it were true, would be to cloud that primary purpose.

It is the same way in terms of Christ's fulfilling the law. Some teachers have said that Jesus Christ fulfilled the law by keeping it perfectly. That is true. There are even Scripture verses to back up the teaching. For instance, Galatians 4:4 says that Jesus Christ was "made under the law." When Jesus was baptized in the Jordan He answered John's objection to baptizing Him by saying, "Permit it to be so now; for thus it becometh us to fulfill all righteousness" (Matt. 3:15). In other words, He was stating His intention of identifying Himself with man in every respect and, as a man, perfectly to fulfill all that the law of God required. Some commentators have pointed out that Jesus also fulfills the law by means of His Spirit in the lives of those who follow Him. Romans 8:4 says that God sent His Son to earth "that the righteousness of the law might be fulfilled in us, who walk not after the flesh, but after the Spirit."

These points are true. And yet, if we look at these interpretations of Christ's coming to fulfill the law, we are likely to miss the main purpose entirely. Jesus came not primarily to live in us by His Spirit, not primarily to obey the law, by keeping it perfectly — although these things are also true — but to die and in dying to cancel the claims of the law against all who would receive Him as their Savior.

This is taught by the law itself. When the law was given, the lamb also was given, and when Moses was chosen to be the law-giver, Aaron also was chosen to be the high priest. In ancient Israel the law and the sacrifices went hand in hand. God had arranged it that way so that when a man sinned before the law (as all men did constantly) he had a means of atonement by which his guilt was cancelled. This innocent sacrifice pointed forward to the full and perfect sacrifice of Christ.

WHY SACRIFICES?

Someone will object, however, "But doesn't the Bible say that God does not desire sacrifices? Doesn't Hebrews 10:4 say that 'it is not possible that the blood of bulls and of goats should take away sins?' And doesn't Psalm 40:6 say, 'Sacrifice and offering thou didst not desire . . . burnt offering and sin offering hast thou not required'?" Yes, it does. "Well, then, how is it possible that these verses exist along with all the other verses that speak of the need for sacrifices in the terms that you have given to it?"

The answer to that problem is to be seen in the purpose for which God established the sacrifices. They were not ends in themselves. If that were so, we would have sacrifices today. Actually, they were signposts to point to the Lord Jesus Christ. God gave them in order to teach over a long period of time that sin meant death, either the death of the individual himself (the sinner) or else the death of an innocent substitute.

It would be possible to say, using modern terminology, that God was establishing a condition reflex in the people much as scientists do with animals today. Take Pavlov as an example. Pavlov was a Russian engaged in pioneer work in the behavioral sciences. He wished to demonstrate that certain physical reflexes could be built into a person or an animal by external conditioning. He took a dog when it was quite young and began to feed it under special conditions. Now, as anyone who has worked closely with animals knows, a dog's mouth begins to produce saliva whenever food is set before him. Pavlov wondered if the physical reflex could be built into the dog to salivate even when there was no food before it. So he did this. Every time the young puppy was to be fed, a bell was first rung and then the food was placed before him. The bell was rung and the food appeared. This went on for a long time. Eventually, when the day came for his test, Pavlov rang the bell as usual but this time had no food available. Still the dog's mouth began to produce saliva; and thus, Pavlov succeeded in showing that a natural physical reflex could be established by an external and artificial stimulus.

That is what God was doing throughout the Old Testament period by means of the sacrifices. He was building a conditioned reflex into the people so that when Jesus Christ should come they would understand His coming, and when they sinned they would know that they needed a substitute. Just as the dog in his dog's brain learned to recognize the sequence "bell means dinner," so the people of Israel would learn to recognize the sequence "sin means death." And they would avoid their own spiritual death by means of a sacrifice. God took centuries to teach this great spiritual lesson, and He did so in order that men would understand Christ's death when He was crucified.

CHRIST AND THE PROPHETS

It is not only true that Jesus Christ fulfilled the law. He also fulfilled the prophets, as the verse states. But He did this in an entirely different way. When we speak of prophecy we are speaking of direct statements in the Old Testament about the One who was to come to deliver Israel and redeem mankind, statements that told who He would be, where He would be born, what He would do, how He would suffer, and what would be the ultimate outcome of His suffering. Thus, when Jesus said that He had come to fulfill the prophets He meant that He had come to fulfill the great statements that had been made about Him in the Old Testament.

It is obvious that this is a subject so large that it could never be covered adequately in any one study, much less part of one. And even if it were covered exhaustively, it would be the case (as John says) that even the world itself could not contain all the books that should be written about it. I propose to set forth briefly the prophecies that are, in my opinion, the major ones. In each case, however, they are passages that already have been picked up by the New Testament writers as pointing to Jesus Christ and for which we therefore have the authority of the Scriptures for our interpretation.

The first is Genesis 3:15. It is the first prophecy in the Bible about the coming of Jesus Christ, and it is interesting that it was spoken not to Adam or Eve, or Moses, or any of the Patriarchs, or any other human being, but to Satan. It was a prophecy that the One who was to be born of the woman would be victorious over him. The verse says, "And I will put enmity between thee and the woman, and between thy seed and her seed; he shall bruise thy head, and thou shalt bruise his heel." This verse was fulfilled at the cross of Christ when Satan succeeded in bringing about the death of the Lord Jesus — though naturally it had been foreordained and brought to pass by God — at which time Jesus decisively defeated Satan and his power. This was one prophecy that Jesus came to earth to fulfill.

Another prophecy is Genesis 22:18, which was spoken to Abraham. The chapter in which it occurs is the chapter that tells of Abraham's obedience in being willing to offer his son Isaac as a sacrifice on Mount Moriah. Today we see that this event portrayed, in a way that the patriarch understood, what God would one day do with His Son for the world's salvation. Abraham was only called upon to *offer* his son. But when the time came for God's offering of His Son, Christ really died, tasting death for all who should call upon Him. He thereby achieved their salvation. It was in this context that God said to Abraham, "And in thy seed [meaning Christ] shall all the nations of the earth be blessed." Years later, the Apostle Paul pointed out clearly that the "seed" was the Lord Jesus Christ, that the promise was one of blessing through Him, and that the blessing promised was to come through Christ's great work of redemption (Gal. 3:13-16).

We turn over the pages of Genesis and come to the words of Abraham's grandson Jacob, spoken to his son Judah on his death-bed. All the words spoken to his twelve sons on this occasion are prophecies, but to Judah there is a special prophecy of a ruler and a lawgiver to come. Jacob says, "The scepter shall not depart from Judah, nor a lawgiver from between his feet, until Shiloh come; and unto him shall the gathering of the people be" (Gen. 49:10). There is no doubt, of course, that this word "Shiloh" is a difficult term. I often have thought and am at least half convinced that originally it was an active participle of the verb *shalach* meaning "the appointed one" or "the one who is sent." This would involve the alteration of a final letter *hay* to a *cheyth,* which certainly is a possibility, but not a certainty. Whatever the case, the word looks forward to a future descendant of Judah who would be both a king and a lawgiver and to whom the Gentile nations would be gathered.

We turn to the Psalms, and there we find great prophecies. For David was a prophet, at least according to Peter who spoke about one of his prophecies on the day of Pentecost. David probably understood more about the significance of Christ's coming than anybody else in the Old Testament period except Isaiah. Thus, we look at Psalm 22 and there we find an awesome description of Christ's death by crucifixion.

Someone will say to me, "Do you mean that when David wrote this Psalm with all its colorful language — I am poured out like water, my bones are out of joint, my strength is dried up like a potsherd, they pierced my hands and my feet, they part my garments among them and cast lots upon my vesture — that he was clearly and literally visualizing a future crucifixion of God's Messiah?" I am not certain. I tend to think that perhaps this was the case, but we read of other Old Testament prophecies which the writers failed to understand. We even have a record that when Daniel prayed to God for understanding he was told that the things he had written were not to be understood in his time but were for a future age. That may have been the case with David. But whatever the case, this Psalm is a magnificent description of death by crucifixion — the best description in all literature, ancient or modern. And the significant thing is that it was written, not in the Roman era when crucifixion was practiced, or even years later by someone reflecting on what it must have been like, but a thousand years before the world had ever seen a crucifixion, and by David who, thus, by the inspiration of the Holy Spirit, looked forward in faith to the One who was to come.

Moreover, it is not only the crucifixion that David pictured. He also foretold the resurrection of Jesus Christ, and the fact that the body of the Messiah would not decompose during the time it lay in the tomb before the resurrection. He wrote, "For thou wilt not leave my soul in sheol, neither will thou permit thine Holy One to see corruption" (Ps. 16:10). Peter quoted these very words on the day of Pentecost to show that they had been fulfilled literally in the death and resurrection of Jesus.

The final passage is probably the greatest single prophecy in the Old Testament — the 53rd chapter of Isaiah. It is great because it explains the significance of Christ's death so clearly. What is that significance? Just this: that when Jesus Christ died on the cross by crucifixion He died not for Himself but for us! Thus, Isaiah says: "He hath borne *our* griefs, and carried *our* sorrows. . . . he was wounded for *our* transgressions, he was bruised for *our* iniquities; the chastisement for *our* peace was upon him, and with his stripes *we* are healed. . . . The Lord hath laid on him the iniquity of *us all*" (vv. 4-6). What is prophesied here is the fact that the coming one, the "seed" of Abraham, who was first mentioned in the earliest chapters of Genesis at the beginning of God's dealings with the human race, was to die vicariously, for others, so that they might be healed. That, Jesus did. And thus this prophecy, among all the others, was one that He came specifically to fulfill.

"FOR THE SAKE OF THE SON"

Have you ever asked yourself in the course of your own study of the Word of God if there is a theme to the Old Testament and, if so, what it is? It is a question with which every Old Testament theologian must grapple and for which a variety of answers has been given. Some say, "The only theme you find there is a historical theme. It is the birth, rise, and development of the Hebrew nation." Others say, "No, what you find in the Old Testament is primarily a record of the evolution of ideas, ideas of God, man, law, justice, and so on." Still others deny that there is a unifying theme at all. What do *you* think? You should be able to say, as every Christian should say, "Oh, it is true that there is a historical side to the Old Testament and that there is a development of ideas in a certain sense; but this is not the theme of the Old Testament any more than it is the theme of the New Testament. The theme of the Old and New Testaments is Christ, Jesus Christ. He is the one who was promised, who came, and whose ministry is now recorded and interpreted for our understanding."

Do you know what Martin Luther said on this point? He wrote, "What purpose other than this proclamation does Scripture have from beginning to end? Messiah, God's Son, was to come and through His sacrifice, as an innocent Lamb of God, bear and remove the sins of the world and thus redeem men from eternal death for eternal salvation. For the sake of Messiah and God's Son Holy Scripture was written, and for His sake everything that happened took place." *

Do you believe that? If you do, you understand what all Scripture and all life is about. If you do not, you are missing the point of it all in God's sight, no matter how perceptive you may be in other areas. According to the Bible, Jesus Christ is the hinge and focal point of history. He has come to be your personal Savior and Lord.

* Martin Luther, *What Luther Says,* compiled by Ewald M. Plass (Saint Louis: Concordia, 1959), Vol. I, p. 69.

Chapter 13

Have You Earned Heaven?

(Matthew 5:20)

The statements of the Sermon on the Mount are the righteous foundation of all God's dealings with men, and when they are accepted they drive a man to the Lord Jesus Christ where alone he finds salvation. On the other hand, if they are not accepted, they will turn a man from Jesus. And they will cause a man to hate Him and despise His teachings.

To a large extent this must have been true as Christ spoke the Sermon. For He was undoubtedly heard by many, including the religious leaders, who stood opposed to every word He uttered. They would have reacted to His teachings as anyone would react to that which condemns him. Jesus had said, "Blessed are the poor in spirit; for theirs is the kingdom of heaven," and the words must have hurt. For the leaders of the people, the scribes and the Pharisees, knew that they were neither poor in spirit nor poor in material things; and yet they had boasted that they knew the way to heaven better than others. Actually, they were rich in pride. Jesus had said, "Blessed are the merciful," and they were not merciful. In fact, there is hardly a phrase in the first section of the Sermon on the Mount that would not have hurt them as they heard it; and they must have acknowledged, at least inwardly, that they were indeed salt that had lost its savor and lamps that gave no light.

At this point Jesus actually named the scribes and the Pharisees directly, and in naming them He brought to an end the false standards of religion and morality that they had so carefully erected. They thought they were scrupulous in interpreting and obeying the law. They thought they were righteous. But Jesus said, "For I say unto you that except your righteousness shall exceed the righteousness of the scribes and Pharisees, ye shall in no case enter

98

into the kingdom of heaven" (Matt. 5:20). He was saying that God will never be satisfied even with such a supposed high standard of righteousness as theirs.

SCRIBES AND PHARISEES

This was a difficult saying to accept, of course, and it was difficult for a number of reasons. First, because the scribes and the Pharisees were so highly regarded. We have a negative image of the Pharisees and the scribes today because of what Jesus Christ said about them and because of the higher standard of righteousness that He revealed. But this was not true before that. For the most part they were highly thought of, so highly, in fact, that even Paul, years later when he stood up before Herod Agrippa to plead his case, boasted that formerly he had lived after the strictest sect of the Jewish religion, "a Pharisee" (Acts 26:5). Hence, even then, to be a Pharisee was a matter of praise. The scribes also were honored as the great masters of the law.

Jesus' words were also difficult to accept because He was not saying that in order for a man to get to heaven he must have a slightly higher degree of the same kind of righteousness that the scribes and Pharisees had been accumulating. The first part of the Sermon should have dispelled any thought of that. He was saying that if a man was to get to heaven he must somehow have a different and better righteousness than these men were showing. And this meant that he must turn his back on human goodness altogether and receive instead the freely offered goodness of God. The Phillips' translation of the New Testament makes this a little clearer by saying, "For I tell you that your goodness must be a far better thing than the goodness of the scribes and Pharisees before you can set foot in the kingdom of heaven at all."

HUMAN RIGHTEOUSNESS

Perhaps you are saying at this point, as people always do, "Well, what is wrong with human righteousness? I think we would be in a bad way without it." I agree with you in part. It certainly is much better to be surrounded by honest, upright, sensitive persons than scoundrels, even if the honest men are not Christians. But the point is that human goodness is not good enough for God. And this means that although it will see a man through this life, often with flying colors, it will not see him to heaven.

There are several reasons for this. First, the righteousness of which men are so proud is an external righteousness and, while men look naturally on the outward appearance, it is God's nature to look on the heart (1 Sam. 16:7). Jesus knew men, and He knew that although the scribes and Pharisees were taking a great deal of trouble to shine up the outside of their lives they were nevertheless unable to do anything about the true state of their hearts. In their hearts they were as sinful and as unacceptable to God as anyone else. On one occasion He said, "Woe unto you, scribes and Pharisees, hypocrites! For ye are like whited sepulchers, which indeed appear beautiful outward, but are within full of dead men's bones, and of all uncleanness" (Matt. 23:27).

Moreover, what Jesus said of the Pharisees is true of every life. To a certain extent you and I can pull ourselves up by our own bootstraps morally. If you are an alcoholic, you can discipline yourself to attend the meetings of Alcoholics Anonymous and get rid of the habit of drink. You can get control of yourself and enter into a useful life. People will even admire you for having overcome this weakness of character. But although you can do all this outwardly, you cannot do anything about your heart. You can be scrupulous in the affairs of your life so that you are not the least bit dishonest in business. But you cannot make your heart loving if your heart is not loving. You cannot become humble if you are proud. You cannot make yourself pure. Hence, the first reason why human righteousness will not get anywhere with God is that the only righteousness of which you are capable is external. God demands a transformation of the heart.

The second reason why Jesus was critical of the righteousness of the scribes and Pharisees is that this external righteousness actually whittled down the standards of the law and therefore nullified it in many important points. These men were great definers. That is, they could tell to the smallest degree exactly what each of the commandments meant. When the law said, "Remember the sabbath day, to keep it holy," they could tell you precisely what one could do on the Sabbath and still keep the law, and what one could not do. Thus, it was possible to move about, but only a Sabbath day's journey; to eat, but not to cook food; to bandage a person who became hurt, but not to apply ointment or anything actively to promote healing, and so on. Jesus said, however, that when you have done that, you still have not kept the law of God; you only have kept your watered-down version of it. And it is quite possible not to go more than a Sabbath's day's journey, not to cook food — or in our day not to go to work, not to take in a movie, not to play golf (or whatever it may be) — and still disobey God's commandment.

Is that not also true with us? God gives a commandment, and, oh! how we rationalize! We can make His commandment say anything we want it to so that we can do what we want to do. God says that human righteousness will always function like that.

Then, too, human righteousness is always self-glorifying instead of God-glorifying. The Westminster Shorter Catechism asks the question: "What is the chief end of man?" And it answers, "Man's chief end is to glorify God, and to enjoy Him forever." If you are going about to establish your goodness, however, you are really seeking your own glorification and not the glorification of God. You are like the Pharisee in Christ's story. The Pharisee went into a public area of the Temple and prayed, "God, I thank thee that I am not as other men are, extortioners, unjust, adulterers, or even as this tax collector. I fast twice in the week; I give tithes of all that I possess" (Luke 18:11, 12). Jesus said, "Do you mean to say that God hears that kind of prayer, the kind of prayer that asks Him to look at how good a man is? Of course not!" And He argued that the prayer God hears is the prayer of the publican that says, "God be merciful to me a sinner."

Jesus knew that when a man will do that, then God will get the glory, even if by God's grace the man does eventually come to live an upright and exemplary life. Paul knew it too. That is why he wrote, "For by grace are ye saved through faith; and that not of yourselves, it is a gift of God — not of works, lest any man should boast" (Eph. 2:8, 9).

There is a fourth reason why human righteousness is unacceptable to God, and it is most important. Human righteousness is a different kind of righteousness from that which God requires; God asks for divine righteousness.

Most people think of goodness much in the way we think of light. That is, they acknowledge that it takes different forms and has varying degrees of intensity, but they believe that basically it is the same thing wherever you find it. At the bottom there is light that you cannot even see. A little higher up the scale there is the dull light that you might find in a cave somewhere that comes from decaying bacteria. There is the kind of light which men produce by incandescence. Then there is the light of the sun on a dark day, followed by the light of the sun of a bright day. And then there is the light produced on the surface of the sun itself. Men say, "Well, that is the way it is with righteousness. The light of decaying bacteria corresponds to the tiny flickers of goodness that are in the worst of men. Most of us resemble incandescent bulbs. Some are the light of the sun on a dark day. And then there is God, and He is like the sun itself."

God says that is all wrong. You can pile human goodness upon human goodness upon human goodness upon human goodness; you can refine and perfect it and polish it, but no matter how hard you try you fall short of God's standard because human righteousness is qualitatively different from the righteousness of God. It belongs to a different realm entirely. For instance, if human goodness can be compared to light, then God's goodness must not be compared to light, but to something like mathematics, or life, or the world of pure thoughts. For that reason, God says, He cannot work with the good deeds that come from men, however much we may think of them, and instead asks us to receive the righteousness of Christ.

THE APOSTLE PAUL

Many years ago there was a Pharisee who found out that these things were indeed true and who experienced a transformation of his life as a result. He is probably the best known rabbi that ever lived. At any rate, he was certainly the one most effective in changing the history of the world. His name was Paul. In his youth he had gloried in his achievements as a Pharisee. He had achieved everything from the pharisaical point of view. Yet near the end of his life he writes that when he looked back to add it all up he recognized that it came to nothing and that the only thing that counted was Christ.

Here is his testimony about it: "If any other man thinketh that he hath reasons for which he might trust in the flesh, I more: circumcised the eighth day, of the stock of Israel, of the tribe of Benjamin, an Hebrew of the Hebrews; as touching the law, a Pharisee; concerning zeal, persecuting the church; touching the righteousness which is in the law, blameless. But what things were gain to me, those I counted loss for Christ. Yea doubtless, and I count all things but loss for the excellency of the knowledge of Christ Jesus, my Lord; for whom I have suffered the loss of all things, and do count them but refuse, that I may win Christ, And be found in him, not having mine own righteousness, which is of the law, but that which is through the faith of Christ, the righteousness which is of God by faith" (Phil. 3:4-9).

Paul lists seven achievements in these verses, including four that were inherited and three that were earned. First, he was a Jew, for he was born of the stock of Israel. This exposed him to all the spiritual blessings — the law, the covenants, the promises — that God had given to the Jewish people. Second, he was a pure-blooded Jew, for he was born of two Jewish parents ("an Hebrew of the Hebrews"). Third, he had been circumcised on the eighth day of life, which meant that he was no proselyte or Ishmaelite, who was circumcised in the thirteenth year. Fourth, he was of the tribe of Benjamin, the one tribe that had remained with Judah in the south at the time of the civil war in Israel. This meant that he belonged to one of the two tribes which had remained faithful to the temple worship and to the law.

Then, too, there were considerable advantages that Paul had won for himself. In the first place, regarding his attitude to the law, he was a Pharisee. This was the strictest sect of Judaism, and to become a Pharisee was a matter of personal choice. Moreover, Paul was a zealous Pharisee, a fact proved by his early persecution of the Church of Jesus Christ. Finally, he worked so hard at his calling that he actually came to consider himself blameless as a Pharisee before the law's standards.

This was a tremendous list of assets from a man's point of view. But the day came when Paul recognized that these things were worthless in the sight of a just and holy God. It was the day on which he met Jesus. Before this happened he thought that he had attained to righteousness by keeping his conception of God's law. Afterward he knew that all this righteousness was as dirty in God's sight as filthy rags. He had once said, "As touching the righteousness which is in the law I am blameless." He now said, "I am the chief of sinners."

Paul had something like a balance sheet in his life. Under assets he had listed all the things he had achieved for himself up to his encounter with Christ on the Damascus road — his birth, his education, his achievements, even the murder of Stephen. But when he met Christ he came to know what true holiness was. He came to see what righteousness was. And, as he looked at all the things he had been accumulating in the white light of God's righteousness, these things seemed filthy. He had no other word for them but "dung." Thus, he moved the whole column of the things which he had considered assets over into the column of liabilities because, he said, "These things have actually kept me from God's righteousness." Under the column of assets he wrote, "Jesus Christ alone."

GOD'S RIGHTEOUSNESS

That is what salvation is all about. Is that what you believe? Or are you still among those who are spending a lifetime accumulating things that you think are going to earn heaven for you? If you are doing the latter, you need to learn that those things will take you to hell. Hell is full of human righteousness. You need to recognize the imperfection of this righteousness and accept the righteousness of God. Christians have always known this and, as a result, have written their recognition of this truth into a number of their hymns. One of the great hymns says:

> *Nothing in my hands I bring,*
> *Simply to thy cross I cling;*
> *Naked, come to thee for dress,*
> *Helpless, look to thee for grace;*
> *Foul, I to the fountain fly;*
> *Wash me, Savior, or I die.*
>
> *Rock of Ages, cleft for me;*
> *Let me hide myself in thee.*

If you will pray that prayer, God will wash you. God will cleanse you. And He will give you the righteousness that is above anything that man can attain and will receive you on the basis of that righteousness into heaven.

Chapter 14

When You Are Angry

(Matthew 5:21-26)

At the end of the Sermon on the Mount we read that the people who heard Jesus "were astonished at his doctrine; for he taught them as one having authority, and not as the scribes" (Matt. 7:28, 29). The statement indicates that the unprecedented authority of the Lord Jesus Christ was startling to His contemporaries. But surprising as this note of authority was, the standard which Jesus set before men was more startling still. The men of Christ's day, like those of our time, were for the most part content with an external righteousness or goodness. By contrast Jesus taught that the only righteousness acceptable to God is a divine righteousness that in time brings about a full transformation of the personality.

Up to the twentieth verse of Matthew 5 the demand for an internal righteousness has been presented positively. Christ has spoken of the character of the Christian man. He is poor in spirit, sorrowful for sin, meek, hungry and thirsty for righteousness, merciful, pure in heart, a peacemaker, persecuted. Because of this he is to be the salt of the world and its light. Now, with verse 21, this changes; the positive side is dropped, and Jesus begins to state the same thing negatively. For centuries the scribes and Pharisees had been teaching that to avoid murder was to keep the sixth commandment; Jesus teaches that men have broken the commandment even if they have only been angry with one another or called one another a fool. The scribes had taught that the seventh commandment was kept if a person avoided sleeping with another man's wife or another woman's husband; Jesus teaches that the commandment is broken even if adultery exists only as a thought in the heart. A man's word must be kept in spirit as well as in letter,

105

according to Jesus. Charity must go beyond the call of mere duty. A man must love his enemies, as well as his neighbors and friends.

In the remainder of this first chapter of the Sermon on the Mount six of these themes are introduced, in each case by the formula, "Ye have heard that it was said by them of old" or "Ye have heard that it hath been said." And in each case the points are similar. True Christian morality must arise from the heart; and, as a result of this, no one but God (who controls the heart) can provide it.

WHAT IS MURDER?

The first of Christ's examples is based on the sixth commandment, the commandment that said, "Thou shalt not kill [meaning murder]." For years, ever since the giving of the law to Israel through Moses on Mount Sinai, this commandment had stood in the decalogue and had been known to Israel. And for the same length of time murder had been defined by most men, including the scribes and the Pharisees, as the external act. They had taken the sixth commandment as found in Exodus 20:13 and had combined it with a verse in Numbers that demanded death for anyone who unlawfully took innocent life (Num. 35:30). The clear implication was that the commandment referred to nothing more or less than this act. We do the same thing, of course, for our dictionaries define murder as "the offense of unlawfully killing a human being with malice aforethought, expressed or implied."

"Well," said Jesus, "is this what murder is? Is murder nothing more than the act? Or if it is, is there no guilt to the man who almost kills another but is prevented from doing so by some unexpected circumstance? Or to the man who would like to kill his enemy but does not do so from cowardice or from fear of getting caught?" This is the way men reason, of course; and they excuse themselves. But the reasoning does not support the intent of God's injunction. "Instead, God is concerned with the heart," says Jesus. "And God is as concerned with anger as with the actual shedding of blood." The Bible reports Christ as saying, "Ye have heard that it was said by them of old, Thou shalt not kill and whosoever shall kill shall be in danger of judgment; but I say unto you that whosoever is angry with his brother without a cause shall be in danger of judgment" (Matt. 5:21, 22).

Nor is this all, for not only is unjustified anger forbidden, but according to Jesus, God will not even excuse a person who is guilty of expressions of contempt. "And whosoever shall say to his brother, Raca, shall be in danger of the council; but whosoever shall say, Thou fool, shall be in danger of hell fire" (verse 22). *Raca* is a term meaning empty; but the insult of it is more in the sound than the meaning. If it means anything, it means "a nothing" or "a nobody." The term *moros,* translated "Thou fool," means one who is a moron morally. It is one who "plays the fool." Hence, it is a slur upon his reputation. Jesus said that these things also make one guilty when measured by God's standards.

Obviously, such a definition of murder searches to the depths of our own beings, and it does not help us much to recall that there is such a thing as righteous anger, or that there is a valid distinction between being angry against sin and angry with the sinner. Of course, there is a righteous anger. Jesus Himself spoke in righteous anger against the hypocritical stand taken by the so-called leaders of his day. Paul spoke in justified anger against the legalizers who were trying to undermine the true faith of the Galatian believers. David gave voice to anger in the imprecatory Psalms. But it is not very often that our anger is like that; and, if we are honest, we must admit that far more often we are angry at some wrong done against ourselves, real or imaginary, some insult, or some undeserved neglect.

Do we commit murder? Yes — by this definition. We lose our temper. We harbor grudges. We gossip. We kill by neglect, spite, and jealousy. And we would learn that we actually do worse things than these if only we could see our hearts as God is able to see them. It is no accident that even in our own speech such things sometimes are termed character assassination, or that we speak of destroying a person by words. This is literally true, and we do it. Jesus says we are not to be that way as Christians.

CURE FOR ANGER

These verses go on to show in a far more positive way what the cure for anger is to be. The first step in that cure, according to Jesus, is to admit that we do get angry.

You would think, of course, that such a point would be obvious and that all men would do this naturally. But it is not obvious, even though modern psychiatry teaches the same thing. The subtlety of the human mind prevents it. A man can do the worst possible things that a person can do in this life — kill, cheat, steal, commit adultery, and so on — and when he is brought face to face with his actions he will find a dozen reasons why they were not faults at all or why it was necessary for him to commit these acts.

Quite a few years ago, in May of 1931, the city of New York witnessed the capture of one of the most dangerous criminals the city up to that time had ever seen. His name was "Two Gun" Crowley. He had shown himself to be the kind of man who would kill at the drop of a hat. Some time before his capture he had been parked at the side of a road when a policeman came up and asked to see his license. Without saying a word Crowley drew his gun and cut the policeman down. Then, as the officer lay dying, Crowley jumped out of his car, took the policeman's revolver and fired another bullet into the body. What did this man, "Two Gun" Crowley, think of himself as a person? We know, because when he was finally captured in his girl friend's apartment at the end of an hour-long gun battle involving hundreds of police, a blood-stained note was discovered that had been written by Crowley during the battle. It said, "Under my coat is a weary heart, but a kind one — one that would do nobody any harm."

Later, Crowley was sentenced to the electric chair. When he arrived on death row at Sing Sing, he did not say, "This is what I get for killing policemen." No! He said, "This is what I get for defending myself." The point is that "Two Gun" Crowley did not blame himself for anything.

Now if that was true of "Two Gun" Crowley and other criminals, how much more true it is of normal men and women like you and me. We sin, but we cover up the sin. We refuse to acknowledge it even to ourselves. No wonder, then, that Jesus taught we are to acknowledge it first of all. We are to admit our anger, acknowledging our guilt, and we are to do this as the first step to its cure.

CORRECT THE INJUSTICE

The second step for those who wish to overcome their anger is to correct the injustice, for there is always injustice on both sides in any normal dispute. Thus, Jesus said, "If thou bring thy gift to the altar, and there rememberest that thy brother hath anything against thee, leave there thy gift before the altar, and go thy way; first be reconciled to thy brother, and then come and offer thy gift" (Matt. 5:23, 24).

Someone will always say at this point, "Oh, but didn't the meaning of the sacrifice lie in the fact that it atoned for sin, that it covered the guilt of the one presenting it?" Yes, but it was never supposed to excuse the necessity for restitution. We must never forget that King David was a saved man who is in heaven today because he looked for the Messiah he knew was coming to save men from their sin, but when he wrote of his daily relationship to God and of his sin he said, "If I regard iniquity in my heart, the Lord will not hear me" (Ps. 66:18). Samuel said to King Saul on the occasion of Saul's first great disobedience to the Lord after he was king, "Hath the LORD as great delight in burnt offerings and sacrifices, as in obeying the voice of the LORD? Behold, to obey is better than sacrifice, and to hearken than the fat of rams" (1 Sam. 15:22).

It is the same today. Men always find it easier to substitute the ceremonial aspects of religion for the demands of a clear conscience before God. And where in ancient times this meant the presentation of sacrifices at the temple in Jerusalem, today it means the attendance of a Christian at church, his participation in a Bible study or prayer meeting, or his giving to the church or missionaries. These things are right in themselves. We should do them. But God says that they are worthless from His point of view so long as there is unconfessed sin in the life of the Christian and failure on the Christian's part to make the sin right. 1 John 3:18, 20 says, "My little children, let us not love in word, neither in tongue, but in deed and in truth. . . . For if our heart condemn us, God is greater than our heart, and knoweth all things." Consequently, we are to confess these things and to make them right insofar as we are able.

The third step in Christ's cure for anger is to do what we must do *immediately*. First, we must admit the wrong in our anger. Second, we must do what we can to correct it. And third, we must do what we can do *immediately*.

This is the point of the next two verses of this chapter, for Jesus speaks of agreeing with your adversary quickly lest terrible consequences follow. These verses do not teach, as some suppose, that God is the adversary and that you and I can lose our salvation if we continue in a course marked out for us by our anger. Jesus did not mean that. Actually, He was merely saying that sin has consequences and that, if you want to avoid the consequences, you must confess and make right the sin as soon as you are able. In this sense the Lord Jesus Christ was only saying in different words what Paul later said to the Ephesians: "Be ye angry, and sin not; let not the sun go down upon your wrath" (Eph. 4:26), and he was recognizing the great principle stated in the twelfth chapter of Hebrews: "Follow peace with all men, and holiness . . . lest any root of bitterness springing up trouble you, and by it many be defiled" (Heb. 12:14, 15).

TRANSFORMATION

The fourth step in the cure of anger must be added to these three obvious steps on the basis of all that Christ is saying. That is: we must ask God to change our heart because only God is able to do it.

One Sunday evening after the seven-thirty service in my church I was talking with my daughter Elizabeth and learned that she was greatly offended because someone had mistreated her, as she thought. He had held her upside down, and she did not like that and was angry about it. She said to me, "I don't like that man; I'm never going to forgive him! I'll forgive Cici and Vicky and Pamela [her friends], but not him." I said, "Oh, you don't want to say that. Jesus tells us that we are supposed to forgive one another; He forgives us, doesn't He?" She said, "Yes, I know. They teach me that in Sunday school and at school, but I don't understand it. What I'd really like to do is kick him." I said, "Yes, that's the way we are. But God wants us to be different."

If you look into your heart honestly when you are offended, you will find that to kick the person is what you would most like to do. It is often what I would most like to do. And yet, we must not do it. In fact, we must even come to the point at which we ask God to change our hearts and minds so that we will not even *want* to do it. For when we do, God will change our minds — we shall be transformed from within by the renewing of our minds (Rom. 12:2) — and we will find it possible to do what beforehand we would have judged impossible.

Moreover, did you know that God says that this will be possible for you even if the other person does not return the favor and maintains a white-hot temperature of anger against you? He writes through Paul in Romans saying, "Dearly beloved, avenge not yourselves but, rather, give place unto wrath; for it is written, Vengeance is mine; I will repay, saith the Lord. Therefore, if thine enemy hunger, feed him; if he thirst, give him drink; for in so doing thou shalt heap coals of fire on his head. Be not overcome by evil, but overcome evil with good" (Rom. 12:19-21). What does this short paragraph mean? It means that we are not to retaliate against wrongs done to ourselves, but that we are to step aside and let the wrath of man work, even to our harm. If you should be saying, "But they *will* do me harm," the answer is "Vengeance is mine; I will repay, saith the Lord." In other words, God says that if we live as He intends us to live, the wrath of man will come, but when it comes He Himself promises to protect our interests. He may protect them here. We may not see how they are protected until we get to heaven. But we shall get to heaven, and there those who have lived as Christ lived shall be vindicated in the presence of the universe.

"Be not overcome by evil, but overcome evil with good." It is a hard statement to accept. In fact, it is an impossible statement if the heart of man is unchanged. But God will change the heart if the life is surrendered to Jesus Christ for transformation.

Chapter 15

Lust and Christian Marriage

(Matthew 5:27-30)

The positive side of the Lord Jesus Christ's second great example of Christian conduct in the Sermon on the Mount is marriage — Christian marriage — and the perversion that is opposed to it is lust. Jesus said, "Ye have heard that it was said by them of old, Thou shalt not commit adultery; but I say unto you that whosoever looketh on a woman to lust after her hath committed adultery with her already in his heart" (Matt. 5:27, 28). According to Jesus, lust is the equivalent of adultery, just as anger is the equivalent of murder. And the standard of His followers is to be, quite simply, chastity before marriage and fidelity afterward. In this Jesus reinforces the whole of the biblical teaching.

A PLAYBOY WORLD

It is evident, of course, that this standard is opposed to the widely accepted standards of our day. For never in the history of the western world since the death of Greek and Roman paganism has fidelity in marriage been so threatened either from within or without, or an unbridled indulgence of free sexual passions been so encouraged or so praised.

In the first place, it is threatened by the mass media which use the lure of sex to push materialism and to glamorize the pursuit of mere pleasure. This is acute simply because the media have a scope and immediacy in this age that they have possessed in no other. Television fills our living rooms with sex-filled advertisements for toothpaste ("gives your mouth sex appeal"), shaving cream ("take it off; take it all off") and detergent ("the stripper").

And the newspapers not only carry reports of sexual crimes that would have been omitted years ago, but also sell movies through advertisements that are both more explicit and more perverted than television. One writer has noted that sex is "the cornerstone of mass persuasion and the symbol par excellence of the life of leisure and consumption." Unfortunately, this view of sex is not sex as God intended it within the bounds of marriage.

The Christian ethic of faithful and monogamous marriage is also threatened in our day, perhaps even more seriously than by the mass media, by a new hedonism symbolized by the so-called "playboy philosophy." Hedonism is the philosophy that makes pleasure the chief goal in life; and it is as evident in the pursuit of the second home, the third car, and the right and proper friends, as it is in adultery and pre-marital sex experimentation. In fact, in the playboy philosophy the two go hand in hand. Thus, the pages of the magazine seem to imply that choosing the right wine or the right stereo is almost as important as finding the right kind of play-mate, the kind of girl whom comedian Mort Sahl identifies as folding in two places and wearing a staple in her navel.

If sex itself were the cause of the problem, then Hugh Hefner's multi-million-dollar empire could be assessed as a prime factor in the moral decline of our time and judged accordingly. As it is, the playboy world has merely capitalized on a "pleasure-first" philosophy rampant in our time and has contributed (albeit greatly) to a weakening of the status of married love and the marriage relationship.

The third major source of the present-day threat to marriage and to the accompanying Christian moral virtues is the so-called "New Morality," popularized by such well-known churchmen as Bishop Robinson of England, Joseph Fletcher, Harvey Cox, the late James Pike, and others. This approach to morality is based for the most part on two fundamental convictions: first, that the proper action in any given set of circumstances is determined by the situation itself and not by any pre-determined norm of ethics (even biblical), and second, that the only absolute demand in the Christian scheme of things is love. Anything is right that does not hurt the other person, and whether it hurts him/her or not is a conclusion to be reached in the context of the situation. Hence, it is not necessarily wrong to commit adultery (according to these spokesmen) so long as the person committing it has the best in-

terests of all the involved parties at heart. It is the same with
stealing, lying, lawlessness, dishonesty, and other things formerly
thought to be vices.

One thing must be said for the new morality: it is opposed to
legalism, and this is biblical. One whole book of the Bible is
written to combat legalism, the book of Galatians. But this does
not mean that anything goes in Christianity; and it does not mean,
for the sake of that reason alone, that the new morality is right.
The Christian is called to freedom by Christ, but it is a freedom
to follow Christ. We are to be like Him as Christians; and it is
He who taught not only that adultery is wrong but that the impure
thoughts that precede it are wrong. In the same way we are called
to love. But the love to which we are called is Christ's love, a love
linked to knowledge, discipline, discernment, and discrimination.

There are several reasons why the new morality is inadequate
even apart from Christ's teachings. For one thing, it is impossible
to define a situation, limited as we are by time and partial knowledge. A couple in the back seat of a car may decide that intercourse outside of marriage will not hurt them and that no one else
need know. But they cannot be sure that it will not hurt them,
and they cannot foresee the consequences. Many such persons are
thereafter haunted by guilt, and thousands of children are without
families today simply because some couple could not foresee the
total situation as they gave vent to their feelings. Moreover, the
new morality presupposes an ability to make a proper decision that
sinful men simply do not have. Who is to determine whether adultery or sex before marriage can be beneficial to the parties concerned? Or free of consequences? Certainly not the couple! They
are the last ones capable of making the decision. And, of course,
the full truth is that no one is capable of such decisions, for the
heart of man is deceitful above all things and desperately wicked.

In spite of these criticisms, however, the new morality contributes to the ethical climate of our day and to a far larger degree reflects it. And the cry, "If it feels good, do it," has almost
become the watchword of our age. Is this standard right? Is it
time for such "freedom"? As Christians, we must say No. But
at the same time we must acknowledge honestly, as C. S. Lewis
has said, that the Christian standard "is so difficult and so contrary to our instincts" that obviously something is wrong both with
us personally and with our society. In other words, we must acknowledge that we are all sinners, even after conversion, and we

are not automatically free from, victorious over, or even innocent of, the world's perversion of sex because of it. *

Is There a Cure?

What are we to do in this situation? We cannot escape. To do so is monasticism, and that is unbiblical. We cannot retreat into celibacy, for God created sex and gave marriage. We certainly cannot give vent to promiscuity or even genteel experimentation. The only answer is that we must fight a debased and perverted morality with a pure one, and we must live and teach what Christ taught as the true way to happiness.

I believe this must start with a clear recognition that the sexual instinct as we see it and know it, has gone wrong. Notice, I did not write that sex or the sex instinct is wrong. Christianity is almost the only great world religion that approves of the body and has thoroughly glorified sex in marriage. I only said that the sexual instinct as we see it and know it, has gone wrong.

For one thing, the appetite for sex, stimulated by our culture, is enormously out of proportion to its function. C. S. Lewis, who makes this point far better than anyone else I know, says wisely, "The biological purpose of sex is children, just as the biological purpose of eating is to repair the body. Now if we eat whenever we feel inclined and just as much as we want, it is quite true that most of us will eat too much: but not terrifically too much. One man may eat enough for two, but he does not eat enough for ten. The appetite goes a little beyond its biological purpose, but not enormously. But if a healthy young man indulged his sexual appetite whenever he felt inclined, and if each act produced a baby, then in ten years he might easily populate a small village. This appetite is in ludicrous and preposterous excess of its function.

"Or take it another way. You can get a large audience together for a strip-tease act — that is, to watch a girl undress on the stage. Now suppose you came to a country where you could fill a theatre by simply bringing a covered plate onto the stage and then slowly lifting the cover so as to let everyone see, just before the lights went out, that it contained a mutton chop or a bit of bacon, would you not think that in that country something had gone wrong with the appetite for food? And would not anyone who had grown up

* C. S. Lewis, *Mere Christianity* (New York: The Macmillan Company, 1958), p. 75.

in a different world think there was something equally queer about the state of the sex instinct among us?" *

The most popular argument against this view today seems to be in the admission that sex is a mess but that it has become so only because it has been hushed up. But in our day it is not hushed up. In fact, it has not been hushed up for the greater part of this century, and still it is terrible. And it is getting worse! We have more divorce, more perversions of sex, more illegitimacy (two to four times as much as in 1940, in spite of the pill), and more downright misery in marriage and outside it than ever before. People are flocking to the marriage counselors and ministers for help to unscramble the ruin they have made of their lives. As Lewis says, it is probably the other way around. The human race hushed up sex originally because it had become such a mess. And if things become bad enough in our day this hushing up of sex may well be reverted to again as the present playboy age gives way to a new Victorianism.

He Who Runs Away

The second thing we must recognize is that if we are to live as God's children in this world, there are times when we shall simply have to run away from the temptation. I do not believe that this is the whole answer, as you will see, for the answer to any evil is never entirely a negation but always a more powerful good. And yet, this is a partial answer and, at times, the only one. Did you know that this was Paul's advice to his converts? He wrote to the Corinthians that they were to "flee fornication" (1 Cor. 6:18). To Timothy, a young preacher, he wrote, "Flee also youthful lusts, but follow righteousness, faith, love, peace, with them that call on the Lord out of a pure heart" (2 Tim. 2:22). In other words, Joseph, who fled from Potiphar's wife, and not David, who invited Bathsheba over to the palace, is to be imitated.

A moment's reflection will show why in some instances this must be so. In most of the temptations of this life, although they may well be severe, the Christian has an ally in reason. He may be tempted to cheat on his income tax; but if he is, his reason will tell him that the computers today are very thorough and that the gain (if there is one) is entirely out of proportion to the loss of money, time, and reputation if he should be caught. Reason

* *Ibid.*

unites with his knowledge of the good and the internal witness of the Holy Spirit to save him. It is the same in many other temptations, but not with love. It is entirely different with love or with the sexual instinct. There is something here that operates apart from reason, or even against it, for it will make lovers of a Montague and a Capulet or of a Duke and Duchess of Windsor. What couple ever sat alone in an apartment reasoning out the relative advantages and disadvantages of pre-marital sex, and then had sexual intercourse on that basis or on that basis avoided it?

It does not work that way. Consequently, if you are in this situation (or if you find yourself in this situation), you must start running like Joseph. Get out of the apartment if you are there. Start the ignition if you are sitting in a car by the roadside. Visit your friends. Even go to see your pastor. But whatever you do, get moving! For neither you nor anybody else is one hundred percent able at all times to avoid these sexual temptations.

CHRISTIAN MARRIAGE

In the final analysis, however, even running is not the solution. Although it will help for the moment, it will not do so permanently. Total victory requires a more powerful and more vigorous philosophy.

Is there such a philosophy? Certainly there is! We should say "theology" rather than philosophy, for it is tied up, as it must be, with the nature and the purposes of God. It is not sex alone, although sex is part of it. It is not abstinence, and it is not indulgence. It is marriage, Christian marriage, marriage on the highest possible plane. It is marriage as God intended marriage to be, marriage as an illustration of the union of the Christian with Christ. I know that much of what passes for Christian marriage is not Christian, and I know that even Christian marriages are often joyless, drab affairs. But the proper antidote is not hedonism or negation, but rather a high and ennobling grasp of what marriage should be and can be when a man and a woman are united by God and enjoy the privileges of sex within that relationship.

We are going to be looking more deeply into marriage in our next study. But before we go on it is necessary to say one thing to each of two different classes of people. The first class comprises those who are not married, and there are always many of them. Sometimes when one speaks about marriage, those who are not married get the feeling that they are incomplete if they remain single. But this is not true. As we shall see, the sexual relationship is only part of being married, and the fullness of sex involves being male and female on a much broader scale, much of which is natural and possible even apart from a sexual relationship. What is more, even as wonderful as it can be, marriage is still only an earthly picture of the greater relationship of Jesus Christ to the Church, and there is always the possibility of wholeness and fulfillment of the whole personality with Him. We all need to remember that.

The second word is to those who are going to be saying as we go on talking about marriage, "Yes, that is all right. That is what marriage should be. One should remain pure before marriage and faithful afterward. But I have not done that, and it is too late for me now." The answer to this type of person is, "No, it is not too late." The glory of the way in which God deals with sinful men and women, which we all are, is that God is able to pick us up where we are and as we are and set us in His way, which is always a way of blessing. God can do that with you no matter how far you have fallen. I would far rather counsel a man or a woman who has become mixed up in a sinful sexual relationship, than attempt to counsel a hypocrite, a gossip, or a person who is overly proud. It is much easier to help one who has yielded to the sins of the flesh than one who has indulged in the sins of the spirit.

All that is true, and yet the best way is to avoid the sins entirely as God gives us grace. He will if we yield to Him and allow Him to bless us in our sexual relationships.

Chapter 16

Christian Marriage

(Matthew 5:27-30)

A firm grasp of what marriage should and can be under God is the only reliable antidote to the pleasure-seeking hedonistic philosophy of our age. This truth is most important, and for that reason we need to develop it further. What is it that makes a marriage Christian? What does it involve? What are God's purposes in marriage? These questions may be answered correctly only by saying that God is the author of marriage and that He established it as the most important illustration in all of life of how God joins true believers to the Lord Jesus Christ in faith and how He does so forever.

A DIVINE INSTITUTION

The basis of everything that is to be said about Christian marriage lies in the fact that God has established marriage and that it is therefore a divine institution.

I suppose that I perform between half a dozen and a dozen weddings each year; and at each of them I begin by calling attention to the truth that God has instituted marriage, for this truth comes first in the marriage service. The groom and the best man and I come out, the bride and her bridesmaids advance down the aisle, and when the wedding march stops and the people are seated, I begin: "Dearly beloved, we are assembled here in the presence of God, to join this Man and this Woman in holy marriage; which is instituted by God, regulated by His commandments, blessed by our Lord Jesus Christ, and to be held in honor

119

among all men. Let us therefore reverently remember that God has established and sanctified marriage for the welfare and happiness of mankind." In the prayer that follows I give thanks to God for the estate of marriage and ask His blessing on the ensuing service.

"God has established marriage." That is the point. And it follows from this that marriage must be governed and directed by His rules, especially if it is to result in the happiness and joy that all men acknowledge should belong to it.

Who is it that originally made the race male and female? The answer is: God (Gen. 1:27)! Who is it that commanded, "Be fruitful and multiply" (Gen. 1:28)? God! Who is it who said, "It is not good that the man should be alone; I will make him an help fit for him" (Gen. 2:18)? God! It was God who brought the first bride to the first husband and thus established the first human family (Gen. 2:22). God's Word declares, "Therefore shall a man leave his father and his mother, and shall cleave unto his wife; and they shall be one flesh" (Gen. 2:24). In the New Testament Jesus Himself reinforced the teaching that marriage is a divine institution (Matt. 19:4-9). It is for this reason that the Church speaks of "holy matrimony." For while we do not believe, as some do, that marriage is a sacrament of the Church, we do believe that God has established it, that His laws should regulate it, and that it is far from being a merely civil or social arrangement.

A very practical consequence follows upon this. For if it is true that God has established the state of marriage, then we must never make fun of it or of anything connected with the marriage relationship. Dr. Donald Grey Barnhouse used to say, "Bite your tongue before you will ever say, 'Well, I want you to meet the old ball and chain' or 'Here's the jailer.'" Dr. Walter A. Maier, who produced the most valuable book on marriage that I have ever read, has written, "To speak disdainfully of married life, to invoke upon it sophisticated sarcasm, is to exalt the puny errors of pigmy minds over the eternal truth of heaven — to blaspheme God." * Both men are right. Consequently, neither you nor I should ever joke about our marriages or the marriage relationship.

* Walter A. Maier, *For Better, Not for Worse* (St. Louis: Concordia, 1935), p. 18.

BODY, SOUL AND SPIRIT

Moreover, the fact that God has established marriage means that you and I are to get our ideas about it, not from the books we may read or from the movies, but from God Himself and from the Bible. I suppose that over the years I have read perhaps ten or twenty books about marriage and sexual problems, and the general impression I have had from the non-Christian books (and sometimes the Christian ones) is that marriage is primarily a matter of sexual compatibility and adjustment. This is part of the truth, of course. But at best it is one-sided, and by itself it is only slightly less misleading than the marriages in movies, where marriage is either a farce or else the institutionalization of romantic love. Neither of these is right, and what the Bible teaches about marriage is quite different.

For instance, as far back as the early pages of Genesis we read that a man shall leave his father and mother and cleave unto his wife, and "they shall be one flesh" (Gen. 2:24). What does this mean? We must not make the mistake of thinking that this refers only to a sexual union, for the Bible uses the word "flesh" in a far broader sense than the meanings we give to it. The word means the person as a whole. Thus, the union in a certain sense makes one person of those who were two persons before. C. S. Lewis has argued that marriage results in something a bit like a two-part mechanism — like a lock and key or a violin and its bow. I would much rather call it a single organism in which the relationship of a wife to a husband or husband to wife is like that of the hand to the head of a person, or the heart to the mind.

Another way of saying the same thing is to point out that man is a trinity as God is a Trinity. Man has a body, soul, and spirit. And thus, the union of one man with one woman in marriage must be a union on each of those three levels if marriage is to be what God intended it to be and the union is to be lasting.

It must be a union of body with body, first of all, which is to say that there must be a valid sexual relationship. This is important. For this reason all of the branches of the Christian Church have acknowledged that a marriage has not actually taken place until the sexual union is consummated. If sexual union does not take place or cannot take place, then the marriage can be annulled as invalid. I always tell couples that this is a vital aspect of the marriage relationship. According to the Bible, neither the man nor the woman is to defraud the other of the sexual experience. The quickest way for the marriage to end up in trouble is for the wife to have a headache every night and go to sleep early to avoid the sex act, or for the husband to lose interest in his wife romantically and to spend his nights elsewhere or with the boys. Sex must be a regular expression of the relationship.

On the other hand, if the relationship is based upon nothing but sex — in other words, if it is a marriage of body with body alone and not of soul with soul and spirit with spirit — then the marriage is weak and inadequate and it is headed for the divorce courts. When the glamour wears off, as it always does if there is nothing more to sustain it, the relationship is finished; and there is either total indifference, a divorce, or adultery. This is the result of a marriage that is based purely on physical attraction.

A better marriage than this is a marriage that is also a union of soul with soul, in addition to being a union of body with body. The word "soul" is a word that had almost passed out of use in the English language until the blacks in our day revived it; but it is a good word, and we would have been poorer for its loss. It refers to the intellectual and emotional side of a person's nature, involving all of the characteristics that we associate with the functioning of the mind. Hence, a marriage that involves a union of souls is a marriage in which a couple shares an interest in the same things — the same books, the same friends — and seeks to establish a meeting of the minds (as it were) both intellectually and emotionally. Such marriages will always last longer.

I believe that at this point a special word must be said to Christians who are married. For whenever a minister speaks like this to Christians, many are already racing ahead of him to point three and are concluding that because their marriages are ones of spirit with spirit, therefore they do not need to worry very much about a union of their minds or souls. This is not right. Not only do we need to worry about it at times, we also need to work toward it. For an emotional and intellectual union does not in itself come naturally.

What does a girl have in her mind when she marries a young man? What is her vision of this new husband? Well, it has something to do with her father and whether she liked him or rebelled against him. It has a little bit of Cary Grant mixed up in it, and perhaps a little of James Bond or Johnny Carson or her minister. What is the vision of the husband? Keith Miller, who wrote the best-selling book *The Taste of New Wine,* said that his vision was probably a combination of St. Theresa, Elizabeth Taylor and . . . Betty Crocker. We each put our own set of names into those categories.

Now, what happens when a girl with a vision of Cary Grant and a man with a vision of Elizabeth Taylor get married and begin to find out that the other person is not much like their vision? One of two things! Either they center their minds on the difference between the ideal and what they are increasingly finding the other person to be like, and then try, either openly or subversively to push the other spouse into that image. Or, by the grace of God, they increasingly come to accept the other person as he or she is, including his or her standards of how they themselves should be, and then under God seek to conform to the best and most uplifting of those standards.

It must be one or the other of those ways. Keith Miller has written, "The soul of a marriage can be a trysting place where two people can come together quietly from the struggles of the world and feel safe, accepted, and loved . . . or it can be a battle ground where two egos are locked in a lifelong struggle for supremacy, a battle which is for the most part invisible to the rest of the world." * If you and I are to have the former in our marriages, then we must work toward it. And we must do it by cultivating the interests and the aspirations of the other party.

A true marriage, then, must be a marriage of body with body and of soul with soul. But it must also be a marriage of spirit with spirit. It is for this reason that the only marriages that can approximate the kind of marriage that God intended to exist in this world are Christian marriages. What does this mean, a marriage of spirit with spirit? Primarily it means that both the husband and the wife must be Christians, for the unsaved person posesses a spirit only in the sense that he supports a vacuum at the center of his life that can be filled only by God. He has a spirit, but the spirit has died — just as Adam's spirit died when he disobeyed God and ran from Him. The only persons who possess a live spirit are those who have been touched by the Holy Spirit and have entered into God's family by faith in the Lord Jesus Christ. Hence, only these can be married in the full sense

* Keith Miller, *The Taste of New Wine* (Waco, Texas: Word Books, 1968), p. 46.

of the word, which means body with body, soul with soul, and spirit with spirit.

If you are a Christian, you must marry another Christian, or else you must not marry at all. If you do marry a non-Christian, then you are willfully choosing much unhappiness, for you will be unable to share that which is most real and most precious to you.

What will happen to you can be illustrated from the case of Solomon. Solomon had been the recipient of many blessings from God, first because of God's promises to his father David and then because of the fact that Solomon had himself determined to walk in the Lord's way. However, after the Temple was finished and Solomon was at ease in Jerusalem, he began to get ideas, one of which was to marry the daughter of the Pharaoh of Egypt. This was not God's will for him, for the princess of Egypt did not worship Jehovah. Nevertheless, he married her even though he knew it was wrong for him to do so. It was one step in his downfall. Someone will say, "How do you know it was wrong?" The answer is that one verse in the story tells us so and indicates that even Solomon knew it. In 2 Chronicles 8:11 we read, "And Solomon brought up the daughter of Pharaoh out of the city of David unto the house that he had built for her; for he said, My wife shall not dwell in the house of David, king of Israel, because the places are holy, to which the ark of the LORD hath come." In other words, Solomon was saying, "I recognize that this woman does not fit in with the things that I know to be true about God; and whenever I bring her around the palace of David or the Temple I feel guilty and my conscience bothers me. The only solution is to build her another house and thereafter to live my life in as nearly separate but equal compartments as is possible."

If you marry a non-Christian, that is what will happen with you. Do not think that you will lift the non-Christian up, and that he or she will become a Christian. That may happen eventually because of God's great grace, but even if it does there will still be years of heartache and sorrow. If the other person is not a Christian or does not become one some time before the engagement, I tell you on the authority of God's Word that he or she is not the husband or the wife for you. The Bible says, "Be ye not unequally yoked together with unbelievers; for what fellowship hath righteousness with unrighteousness? And what communion hath light with darkness?" (2 Cor. 6:14). You will have a marriage of body with body and sometimes even of soul with soul, but you will never have a marriage of spirit with spirit; and that is what God wants your marriage to be.

CHRIST AND THE CHURCH

The final and conclusive proof of all that I have been saying is in the truth that when God created us male and female and established the state of marriage, He did so for a definite purpose. What was it? It was to provide the best illustration in life of how God joins a man or woman to Jesus Christ and how He joins them to Him forever. Someone says, "Didn't God create marriage so there would be children? Isn't marriage for reproduction?" No, it is not. Oh, I know that this is one sideline of marriage, but it is secondary. If it were not, a marriage without children would be incomplete, a failure; and that is not true.

"Well, then, why did He establish it?" He established it as an illustration of the relationship between Christ and the Church. Paul says in Ephesians 5 that a wife is to submit to her husband "as unto the Lord." He says that a husband is to love. his wife "even as Christ also loved the church, and gave himself for it." He concludes by saying of marriage, "This is a great mystery, but I speak concerning Christ and the church" (verse 32). In other words, God established marriage so that a Christian husband and a Christian wife could act out in their own relationship the relationship that Christ has to you and me and thereby point men to Him as the supreme lover, bridegroom, husband, protector, and provider of His Church.

To marry as God intends men and women to marry is to illustrate this most sublime of relationships — the relationship of the Lord Jesus Christ to those who believe on Him, and the relationship of the Church to Jesus, to the one who loved us and who gave Himself for us. If you see this truth, then you are well on the way to a blessed and happy marriage. For you will have the spiritual motivation and overall orientation to make a happy marriage possible.

Chapter 17

Marriage and the Home

(Matthew 5:27-30)

One of the most important things that can be said about a Christian marriage is that within the relationship God has established an organic union between two persons — an organic union, not an organization. But when that is said, it also must be said that marriage does have organizational aspects. And hence, we must give attention to these also. How is a marriage to function after the wedding vows are taken? Is it to be a democracy? Is it to be a dictatorial system? A monarchy? Or is it a republican form of government? What are the duties of the husband, wife, and children to each other and to the Lord?

Many of the answers to these questions are found in the fifth chapter of Ephesians, verses 22 through 30. In this chapter marriage is set forth as an illustration of the relationship of Jesus Christ to the Church, and the duties of the husband and wife to each other are set forth in terms of that relationship. The wife is to submit herself unto the husband "as unto the Lord." The husband is to love his wife "even as Christ also loved the Church, and gave himself for it." Later, in chapter six, children are told to obey their parents "in the Lord, for this is right." And they are to "honor" their father and mother. The parents on their part are to raise their children "in the nurture and admonition of the Lord."

GOD'S WORD TO WIVES

We now want to look at the rules governing each of those relationships. The first word God has is to the wives. It is an unpopular word, especially today, for God says that the wife is to submit herself to her husband. When my wife and I were married in June of 1962, Dr. Robert Lamont of the First Presbyterian Church of Pittsburgh performed the ceremony and spoke for a few minutes from this passage. After the ceremony a woman came up to us and said that she had never heard those things before. We asked, "What things?" She said, "About a wife submitting to her husband," and she added that she was going to go home and tear that page out of her Bible.

What she did not know was that even tearing out the fifth chapter of Ephesians would not have solved her problem, for the same teachings are found throughout the Bible. It is true that Ephesians contains the most extensive passage. It says, "Wives, submit yourselves unto your own husbands, as unto the Lord. For the husband is the head of the wife, even as Christ is the head of the church; and he is the savior of the body. Therefore, as the church is subject unto Christ, so let the wives be to their own husbands in everything" (Eph. 5:22-24). But it is also true that the same thing is said as far back as in the third chapter of Genesis. "Unto the woman he said, I will greatly multiply thy sorrow and thy conception; in sorrow thou shalt bring forth children; and thy desire shall be to thy husband, and he shall rule over thee" (Gen. 3:16). Colossians 3:18 adds, "Wives, submit yourselves unto your own husbands, as it is fit in the Lord." In 1 Peter we read, "In the same manner, ye wives, be in subjection to your own husbands" (1 Peter 3:1). Again the reference is to the standards set for all of us by Christ.

I think that the biggest difficulty with these verses today is that most wives do not realize what they actually mean, and I suspect that most husbands do not understand them either. Not long ago I was counseling a couple who were soon to be married, and I asked if they understood what God meant when He said that the wife was to be in subjection to her husband and that the husband was to love his wife as Christ loved the Church and gave Himself for it. The wife-to-be was wise enough to remain silent. But the man blurted out, "That means that we are to love each other; but whenever we disagree I am to give her a hug and a kiss, and after that we're to do things my way." Well, if the husband thought that, it was no wonder that the wife disliked the teaching. And if husbands in general misunderstand it, who can hold the wives responsible?

What does it mean that the wife is to submit herself to her husband as to the Lord? Well, it certainly does not mean that she is submitting to a form of slavery or tyranny, for we are not called to a form of slavery or tyranny by Christ. It does not mean a type of blind obedience either, for a wife is not a chattel. Neither does it mean that the submission itself is always entirely one-sided, for the verse immediately before this says that we are to submit ourselves *"one to another"* in the fear of the Lord" (verse 21). Actually, the verse means that the wife was created primarily as a helpmeet for the man. And thus, in a very real way she is to subordinate her interests to his.

One of the underlying meanings of the Greek and Latin words translated "be subject" bears this out, for they are constructed of a verb meaning "to set, determine, or place" and a preposition meaning "under." The meaning is "throw oneself under." Thus, the words refer to a type of obedience that is supporting — like a foundation supporting a house or a member of the White House cabinet supporting the President of the United States. The wife is to be this to her husband. If any wife is thinking to herself that this is a demeaning position, she is to remember that the same chapter of 1 Corinthians which says that the "head of the woman is the man" also says that Christ is the head of the man and that God is the head of Christ. No woman should be ashamed to be part of that relationship.

I do not think the position that God sets forth here for the woman necessarily means that the woman cannot have a large measure of independence. For instance, there is no reason why she cannot pursue a career. There are conditions in which a woman can do this and still support her husband within the marriage relationship — for instance, in order to increase the family income at the time when the children are going through college. It does not mean that the woman cannot pursue her own interests. In fact, it is a dull marriage if the wife does not have any outside interests. However, if the two come into conflict — that is, if the wife's career hurts the career of the husband or if her interests lessen her concern for his work and the goals he is pursuing — then the wife is to yield to him in exactly the same way she should yield if her interests came into conflict with the way marked out for her by Jesus Christ.

If someone says, "But isn't that unfair?" the answer is that it is not unfair, for that is the way God made things. Moreover, no wife will be truly happy in her marriage until she is willing to let God trim her interests wherever necessary in order to balance those of the man.

Let me add one more thing for wives before I go on. If you are to be all that God intends you to be as a wife, you must show an interest in what your husband is doing; and for that you must be informed. I know of a marriage in which the wife has never shown any interest in her husband's work and instead has always insisted that he leave the problems of his work at the office. The result has been a sense of unfulfilled need for the husband and an increasingly limited and introverted existence for the wife. How much better it would have been if they could have grown in the man's work and responsibilities together!

Moreover, if you are to be a proper helpmeet to your husband, you must read to be well informed, and you must look attractive. Do not forget that your husband spends the better part of his day with people who are interested in his work and who are therefore at least partially stimulating. The persons he works with are usually making some effort to be attractive, particularly the women. How then is he to be excited about loving you as Christ loves the Church if he comes home to find you with your hair in curlers and so taken up with the household affairs that the most interesting part of your conversation has to do with enzyme detergents or baby food. I know you are busy. Being a housewife is often far from fun. But you must build some time into your schedule in which you can read and inform yourself and keep up your appearance. Read books. Read a good news magazine. Read something about your husband's work and his hobbies. I sometimes think that time spent in this way is as important as time spent reading the Bible. Anyway, it is certainly more important than the time you spend watching television.

GOD'S WORD TO HUSBANDS

All this is only one side of the relationship of course. For if God sets a high standard before the woman, He sets an even higher standard before the man. The wife is to love her husband and submit to him as she loves Christ and submits to Christ. But the husband is to love his wife *as Christ loved us* and gave Himself for us.

Husbands, do you love your wives like that? If you do, you will find that they will have little difficulty in submitting themselves to you in the way that Jesus Christ intended. There is an incident in one of the Greek histories that illustrates this point exactly. The wife of one of the generals of Cyrus, the ruler of Persia, was charged with treachery against the king. After a trial she was condemned to die. At first her husband did not realize what had taken place. When he was told about it he at once burst into the throne room. He threw himself on the floor before the king and cried, "O, Lord, take my life instead of hers. Let me die in her place." Cyrus, who by all historical accounts was a noble and extremely sensitive man, was touched by this offer. He said, "Love like that must not be spoiled by death." Then he gave the husband and wife back to each other and let the wife go free. As they walked away happily the husband said to his wife, "Did you notice how kindly the king looked upon us when he gave you the pardon?" The wife replied, "I had no eyes for the king. I saw only the man who was willing to die in my place."

That is the picture that the Holy Spirit paints for us in the fifth chapter of Ephesians. The husband is to love his wife as Christ loved the Church, and most wives will have little difficulty in obeying a man who is willing to be crucified for them.

Another aspect of this relationship is that the husband is not to criticize his wife publicly. In fact, he is to be her shield and intercessor. The Bible says that Christ gave Himself for the Church, not that He might criticize it, but "that he might *sanctify* and *cleanse* it with the washing of water by the word; that he might present it to himself a glorious church, not having spot, or wrinkle, or any such thing; but that it should be holy and without blemish. *So ought men to love their wives*" (vv. 26-28). To listen to some husbands talk you would think that these verses were never in the Bible. Yet they are, and they mean that if you are a husband, God holds you responsible for the defense of your wife and, to some degree, also for her spiritual growth and understanding.

An equally important verse for husbands is 1 Peter 3:7 which says, "In like manner, ye husbands, dwell with them according to knowledge, giving honor unto the wife, as unto the weaker vessel, and as being heirs together of the grace of life, that your prayers be not hindered." Simply put, this means that God will not even hear the prayers of a man who is too ignorant to know how to treat his wife or too foolish to value her as the greatest gift God has for him on this earth.

What does it mean to dwell with a wife according to knowledge? Well, for one thing, it means to do those little things for her that do not mean much to you but that are everything to a woman. Keith Miller said that for him, dwelling with his wife according to knowledge meant learning to empty the trash basket for her. And it was not easy, for he had always mentally thought of trash baskets as "women's work." Billy Graham writes that dwelling with a wife according to knowledge also means being courteous. He writes, "You remember when you were sweethearts how courteous you were? You used to go around the car and open the door and say, 'Darling, won't you step out?' Now you don't. You remember before you were married how you used to take off your coat and put it down in the mud puddle and tell her to walk over it! Now when she comes to a mud puddle you say, 'Jump, lady, I think you can make it.'"

There might be a most astounding transformation of our homes and our society if only men would learn to treat their wives properly.

Parents and Children

The most important thing that the husband is commanded to be in the Bible is the spiritual head of his home. But since that involves the children as well as the wife, I propose to treat it more broadly in that context. What does the Bible say to children? The Bible says, "Honor thy father and thy mother" (Exod. 20:12). If they are to do that, then you and I must be the kind of fathers and mothers that our children can honor. The Bible says, "My son, keep thy father's commandment, and forsake not the law of thy mother: bind them continually upon thine heart; and tie them about thy neck" (Prov. 6:20, 21). If God tells a son to give such meticulous attention to the instruction received from his parents, it is then implied that the parents must give sound counsel. Clearly, God holds the parents responsible — and particularly the fathers — for the spiritual life of their home.

The Bible teaches that children are to obey their parents. If they do not, the parent is responsible before God to establish discipline and to mete out punishment. Someone says to me, "Do you mean to say that the Bible tells me to spank my children?" Yes, it does. The Bible says, "Chasten thy son while there is hope, and let not thy soul spare for his crying" (Prov. 19:18). The Bible says, "Withhold not correction from the child; for if thou beatest him with the rod, he shall not die" (Prov. 23:13). The Bible says, "He that spareth his rod hateth his son; but he that loveth him chasteneth him early" (Prov. 13:24). The Bible says, "Foolishness is bound in the heart of a child, but the rod of correction shall drive it far from him" (Prov. 22:15). That is the Bible. That is God speaking.

A woman once came to Billy Graham and said, "Mr. Graham, don't you think that all my little boy needs is a pat on the back?" Dr. Graham answered, "Lady, if it is low enough and hard enough, it will be all right."

Let me add that I know quite well that children are all different and that each one requires different handling. Some children do not need to be spanked in order to be disciplined. For some a sharp word is sufficient. The principle, however, is that discipline must be established and maintained, and when the parent is disobeyed there must be chastisement. What is more, there must be chastisement within the general spiritual life and worshipful atmosphere of the home.

Life Out of Death

Now we have touched on many things in this study of the home, but it will be of little benefit unless each of us will put it into effect practically.

Some of what I have said will apply to those who are not married but who are thinking about it. If you are in this category, you must hold these great standards of marriage up before you and evaluate the one you are thinking of marrying in the light of them. Girls, you must look at that fellow and ask, "Can he be as Jesus Christ to me? Can he be for me a man whom I can obey and to whom I can submit, subordinating many of my interests to his?" If you cannot, look elsewhere. You fellows must say, "Am I willing to give of myself for her? Do I love her enough and respect her enough to die for her? Am I willing to be patient with her and even to cover up her faults as God instructs me to do?" If you cannot say those things, then it is not right for you to marry her.

Some of you will be beyond the stage of courtship and the early years of marriage and will be facing problems with the raising of your children. You must not let the difficulties you encounter deter you from the true course of action. Your children may be stubborn, but the Bible does not promise that they will be docile. That is why you may have to spank them. It is possible that they do not even respond to the spanking. Do not give up on that account; keep at it. Isaiah wrote that God's methods with us are "precept upon precept, precept upon precept; line upon line, line upon line; here a little, and there a little" (Isa. 28:10), and His methods must be ours. Moreover, you must pray for your children and ask God to create in you the kind of character that will be winsome and that they can respect.

Finally, there will be some for whom these words seem too late. In your case love has died, and there seems to be nothing that will rescue your marriage from that void. If it were not for what your friends would think of you, you would proceed with a divorce. What should you do? You must yield to the Lord Jesus Christ and let Him rekindle a love that has grown cold and make alive love that has died. A woman once told me that at one point in her marriage her love had died entirely; she had come to hate her husband so much she could have stabbed him with a knife. But as she yielded to Christ and grew in Him, that love was rekindled, and she learned that Jesus is indeed able to bring life out of death, love out of hate, and a true Christian marriage out of sham and hostility.

If you will yield to Christ and His standards, He will begin by making of you a new creation and then end by making all things new.

Chapter 18

Divorce and Remarriage

(Matthew 5:31, 32)

It should be evident from everything that has been said thus far about marriage that according to the teaching of God's Word marriage is for life. In Christian marriage a man and a woman are joined to each other as a Christian is joined to the Lord Jesus Christ, and the relationship in each case is permanent — the one for this life, the other for this life and for eternity.

We know, of course, that not all marriages attain this permanence. As a result we are faced again and again, both within society at large and within the Church, with the problems of estrangement, separation, divorce, and remarriage. What is to be the Christian position in these difficult and tragic situations? Is divorce a permissible option for the Christian? Is it entirely forbidden, or are there conditions under which it is possible? If there are such conditions, is it possible for the Christian then to remarry? Moreover, what is to be the position of the Church toward those who have done whatever of these things are wrong? All these questions are raised for us, not only by the fact that they arise quite naturally out of our previous studies of marriage, but also by the fact that the Sermon on the Mount goes on from the verses we have been studying to raise these problems directly.

In Matthew 5:31, 32 Jesus says, "It hath been said, Whosoever shall put away his wife, let him give her a writing of divorcement; but I say unto you that whosoever shall put away his wife, except for the cause of fornication, causeth her to commit adultery; and whosoever shall marry her that is divorced committeth adultery."

These words should be taken together with a closely related passage in Matthew 19, in which almost the identical words are repeated. The Pharisees had come to Christ testing Him with an

134

interpretation of the major Old Testament passage regarding the grounds for divorce. The passage was Deuteronomy 24:1-4, and they asked on that basis, "Is it lawful for a man to put away his wife for every cause?" Jesus answered, "Have ye not read that he who made them at the beginning, made them male and female; and said, For this cause shall a man leave father and mother, and shall cleave to his wife, and they two shall be one flesh? Wherefore, they are no more two, but one flesh. What, therefore, God hath joined together, let no man put asunder." At this point the Pharisees asked him, "Why did Moses then command to give a writing of divorcement, and to put her away?" Jesus answered, "Moses, because of the hardness of your hearts, permitted you to put away your wives, but from the beginning it was not so. And I say unto you, Whosoever shall put away his wife, except it be for fornication, and shall marry another, committeth adultery; and whosoever marrieth her who is put away doth commit adultery" (vv. 3-9).

Because each of these passages contains the phrase that gives the one permissible ground for divorce — "except it be for fornication" — both of them always have been at the heart of any discussion of these questions.

PERMANENCY OF MARRIAGE

The place to begin in the discussion of these texts is not with the exception itself, however — we shall come back to it later — but with the general direction of the passage. And this, quite clearly, is to assert in the strongest possible language the permanency of marriage. Marriage is of God; hence, men are not to disannul it. In this assertion Jesus was clearly at one with the entire scope of the biblical teaching.

We find this in Genesis. "And the LORD God said, It is not good that the man should be alone; I will make him an help fit for him . . . . And the LORD God caused a deep sleep to fall upon Adam, and he slept: and he took one of his ribs, and closed up the flesh instead thereof; and the rib, which the LORD God had taken from man, made he a woman, and brought her unto the man. And Adam said, This is now bone of my bones, and flesh of my flesh; she shall be called Woman, because she was taken out of Man. Therefore shall a man leave his father and his mother, and shall cleave unto his wife; and they shall be one flesh" (Gen. 2:18,

21-24). These words indicate that marriage was instituted by God for man's welfare, and they imply that the union that makes a man and a woman one flesh is to be permanent throughout both their lives.

We turn from the first book of the Old Testament to the last book of the Old Testament, and we find the same teaching — only in a more direct form. This is important in itself, for some teach that the standards given to Adam and Eve in Eden before the fall have become impossible after it and that God has come to tolerate divorce as a result. Well, has He? "Not at all," says Malachi. In fact, it was because of the multiple divorces in Israel that at that time, according to Malachi, God was no longer hearing their prayers.

Here is the way the prophet says it: "Yet ye say, Why [will the LORD not hear us or receive our offerings]? Because the LORD hath been witness between thee and the wife of thy youth, against whom thou hast dealt treacherously; yet is she thy companion, and the wife of thy covenant. And did not he make one [wife for Adam]? Yet had he the residue of the spirit [i. e., He could have made more]. And why one? That he might seek a godly seed. Therefore, take heed to your spirit [i. e., your breath, that it might not be mingled with the breath of another woman], and let none deal treacherously against the wife of his youth. For the LORD, the God of Israel, saith that he hateth putting away [that is, divorce]" (Mal. 2:14-16). According to this passage, not only does God hate divorce, but He still considers the couple married, regardless of what the parties to the marriage may have done.

When the Lord Jesus Christ argued against the common divorce practices of Judaism in His day, therefore, it was to texts like these that He drew His hearers' attention. And the main line of His teaching was that God does not want divorce; in fact, He hates divorce. The standard, as we noted earlier in these studies, is clearly chastity before marriage and fidelity afterward. And this is to be true regardless of the conduct of the other person.

WHAT IS FORNICATION?

At this point someone will say, "I agree with you in general terms. Certainly that is the ideal. But what of adultery? Doesn't adultery dissolve the marriage contract? And isn't that what Jesus Christ was talking about when He made the exception 'except for fornication' in Matthew?" No, I do not believe that this is what Jesus was talking about either in Matthew 19 or in the Sermon on the Mount. In fact, I believe that Jesus was teaching that the only justifiable ground for divorce was impurity in the woman discovered on the first night of the marriage (in which case there would be deceit involved in the contract) and that even in this case, although the man had the right to an immediate divorce under the standards of the Mosaic law, God's perfect will would always be for a continuation of the marriage.

There are several reasons why I believe this must be so. First, it is the natural implication of the words. For fornication is not the same thing as adultery, and fornication (not adultery) is the word that Jesus uses here. What is adultery? Adultery is unfaithfulness after marriage. That is the only possible meaning of the Greek word *(moicheia),* and it is suggested most vividly by the Latin phrase from which we have derived our word in English. The phrase is *ad alterius torum,* which means "to another's bed." Thus, it is a violation of the marriage contract.

Fornication is a much broader term. In Greek it is a variant of the verb *pernemi* ("to sell"), and it refers to prostitution. This would include the prostitution of a harlot, that involved in any of the basic sexual perversions, and by extension, any sex act performed outside of marriage. The Latin term includes this idea also, for it is based on the Greek noun *fornix,* meaning the arch of a temple where the temple courtesans collected. Thus, it refers in a general way to any sexual impurity.

Unless there are strong reasons for thinking differently, the natural implications of Matthew 5:32 is that although a man may divorce a woman immediately after marriage if he finds her not to be a virgin (in which case he was allowed by the law to remarry and was not to be called an adulterer — Deut. 24: 1-4), he may not divorce her for any other cause. If he does, he forces her into a position in which she may be forced to remarry and thereby forces her to become an adulteress by doing so.

DEUTERONOMY 22 - 24

The second reason why this must be the meaning of the passages in Matthew (5:32 and 19:9) is that each is in essence an explanation of Deuteronomy 24:1-4 which teaches precisely what we already have been saying.

The passage in Deuteronomy is the only statute of divorce to be found in the Old Testament, and it was the one upon which the Pharisees based their far more liberal standards. It says in part, "When a man hath taken a wife, and married her, and it come to pass that she find no favor in his eyes, because he hath found some uncleanness in her; then let him write her a bill of divorcement, and give it in her hand, and send her out of his house. And when she is departed out of his house, she may go and be another man's wife" (vv. 1, 2). In characteristic fashion the people of Christ's day had become most punctilious about the "bill of divorcement" but had become entirely liberal in their interpretation of the crucial word "uncleanness." Thus, there were scribes who taught that the reference could be to so trivial a thing as spoiling the dinner, being troublesome or quarrelsome, or speaking disrespectfully of the man's parents (Hillel). This, Christ rejected.

Actually, this is not the meaning of the passage at all. The meaning is clear from the immediate context. In the first place, the word "uncleanness" is actually the word for nakedness or nudity; and a host of passages show that nakedness was always associated with sex or, in this case, with its impurity. Moreover, it is evident that there is no reference here to adultery, for adultery was punishable by death if it was proved. In that case there would quite obviously be no need for a divorce. What is uncleanness then? Well, if it is a sexual sin in the woman and if it is not adultery (which would be a sexual sin after marriage), clearly it must be a sexual sin before marriage. In other words: fornication. Thus, Jesus was obviously reinforcing this Old Testament teaching.

Someone who knows the Bible well may object. "But isn't it true that fornicators were also punished by death in Israel?" The answer is that although this was the punishment for some types of fornication, it was not the punishment for all, and, consequently, there would be some girls in Israel (perhaps many) who were not virgins at the time of their marriage. If there had been uncleanness during the engagement, the penalty was death just as it would have been for the married woman; for the engagement was considered nearly as binding as the marriage. However, if the girl had been attacked or had been unchaste before there had been an engagement, then she was not executed and, although there were penalties, she was free to marry.

It is worth noting that Joseph took advantage of the legal distinction when he determined to put Mary away privately after he discovered that she was pregnant, rather than have her stoned as an adulteress.

Against this background it is evident that Deuteronomy 24: 1-4 only refers to a case in which a bride or her family have deceived the husband, and it grants divorce in this case and in this case only. In all other cases (and in this one also, according to Jesus, if the man acts as God would want him to act), the standard of marriage is total fidelity and this regardless of the actions of the other partner. In other words, the standard for God's people is to be the love of God for Israel, which is a love in spite of infidelity, or the love of Christ for His Church, which is the love of one who loves us in spite of our unfaithfulness or our running away.

GOD'S STANDARDS

Now that is a high standard and difficult to meet. And it is acutely difficult for many people who are involved in situations of estrangement, divorce, and remarriage. I therefore want to close by saying a few things to these people particularly.

In the first place, we can say that these are standards for Christians, not for the world. This means that believers must not seek to impose them upon all men generally. We believe, of course, that to follow Christian standards would tend on the whole to make men happier than they would be apart from them, and we can point with justifiable alarm to any weakening of the family structure within our society. But the majority of men are not Christians, and it would be both wrong and irrational to expect them to lead Christian lives. Because of this I believe that C. S. Lewis was quite right in suggesting that "there ought to be two distinct kinds of marriage: one governed by the State with rules enforced on all citizens, the other governed by the Church with rules enforced by her own members. The distinction ought to be quite sharp, so that a man knows which couples are married in a Christian sense and which are not." *

Second, because there are many persons who become Christians after they have been married and divorced, sometimes more than once, we must never forget that their previous conduct along with all of their past is wiped clean by their conversion to Jesus Christ and that they therefore have the right to marry for

---

* C. S. Lewis, *Mere Christianity* (New York: The Macmillan Company, 1958), p. 87.

the first time as Christians. The church at Corinth must have been composed largely of persons in this category, for Paul writes that many of them were fornicators, adulterers, idolaters, and so on (1 Cor. 6:9-11). Yet, he terms them "new creatures" in Christ (2 Cor. 5:17). Clearly, when a new creature in Christ meets another new creature in Christ and God leads them together, they have a right to marry and to establish a Christian home regardless of their previous history.

Third, there are cases in which one of the spouses is a Christian and the other is not. What is the Christian to do in these circumstances? Well, this is a situation that Paul also faced not only in Corinth but throughout the Greek cities. His advice was this: first, that the Christian should always stay with the unbelieving spouse if at all possible. For, says Paul, how do you know that you will not be the means by which God will save your husband or your wife (1 Cor. 7:16)? However, it is also possible that the unsaved spouse will not stay with the Christian. In that case, Paul's second point of advice is to let the non-Christian go. But the Christian is thereafter to remain unmarried.

The fourth point is based on the fact that we live in an imperfect world, and this means that there always will be circumstances in which a Christian will have to choose the lesser of two evils. In some circumstances, this could be divorce. For instance, we may imagine a woman married to a brute of a husband, a man who spends his money on drink and then deserts his wife while she must raise and educate the children. Under the laws of the United States, if there is no divorce, it is entirely possible for the man to return at some date just when the children are ready to go to college and claim the money the wife has earned and waste it. In this situation I believe it would be better for the wife to initiate the divorce, even if she is a Christian, for her responsibility is also to the children and to their future.

Finally, it is also true that Christians who marry out of God's will and get divorced, remarry (often to Christians) and that God seems often in His great grace to sanctify and bless the remarriage. Does this mean that in this case God has changed His standards? Not at all. But it does mean that even divorce and remarriage, serious though they are, are not unforgivable and that God is always able to start with His children precisely where they are and bring blessing. The churches should never be closed to such people, and Christians above all men should show mercy.

Perhaps even if such persons marry in rebellion against God's will He may bring repentance, and He may yet greatly bless the new home.

There is hardly a matter in the Christian Church today that is treated with more laxity than divorce and remarriage. As a result, it is always easy to get our standards from what other people do or say or from what we should like the Bible to say. But we must not do that. We must be people of the Book, and we must not lower its standards.

Perhaps you are saying, "But how can I do that? For me the standards are too high." If that is what you are saying, the answer is that God will help you to keep them. The Bible says that God "is able to keep you from falling, and to present you faultless before the presence of his glory with exceeding joy" (Jude 24). And if you still say, "But I have questions about the matter," well, the answer is in John's gospel where Jesus says that if any man really desires to know God's will — whatever it may be — "he shall know of the doctrine, whether it be of God, or whether I speak of myself" (John 7:17). If you will desire that, God will lead you in the way that you should go; and He will bring blessing in your life and marriage.

Chapter 19

For Time and for Eternity

(Matthew 5:31, 32)

At several points in the earlier studies of the nature of Christian marriage it was pointed out that according to the Bible God has established marriage, not primarily to promote happiness among mankind or even for reproduction. He has established it primarily as an illustration of the relationship between the Lord Jesus Christ and His bride, the Church. Marriage is to show that when God joins a man or a woman to Jesus Christ in salvation He does so in love and in a bond that will endure forever. For this reason the possibility of a divorce between Christians — and we must remember that nothing that has been said here applies to a non-Christian marriage — should be unthinkable. Marriage among all true believers should be permanent.

HOSEA AND GOMER

What the Christian attitude should be is illustrated in the greatest and strangest love story in the Bible. It is the story of the prophet Hosea and of his marriage to unfaithful Gomer. It is so poignant and so revealing of God's unfathomable love for us that I propose to conclude our studies of Christian marriage by telling it. I have found in my own study of Hosea and of books about Hosea, however, that no one has told the story with greater insight or more human interest than Dr. Donald Grey Barnhouse, and since I cannot improve upon his study I wish to pass the story on to you in his words. What follows is therefore a composite of the story as it was told in several of his published writings.

"There came a time when the Lord appeared to one of His servants, who became one of His prophets, and told him that he was to enact in his life the relationship of God with Israel. The prophet was told that he was to marry a woman who would become a harlot, and that he was to be faithful to her in spite of her unfaithfulness.

142

"And the Lord said to Hosea, 'Go, take unto thee a wife of whoredoms and children of whoredoms; for the land hath committed great whoredom, departing from the Lord' (Hos. 1:2). In other words, Hosea was to live a dramatic pageant before the nations of Judah and Israel, whom God counted as one nation. Hosea was to play the part of the loving and faithful God. The erring wife would be cast in the role of the perverse nation. She would play the harlot with many lovers even as Israel had left the true God to go after a multitude of strange gods. The heart of the pageant would lie in the fact that Hosea would be faithful to her even in the midst of her greatest unfaithfulness. He would even provide the means for her to continue in her runaway life. And when the lowest point in her folly should be reached she would find her husband there at the nadir of her misery and he would redeem her and bring her back into the joys of truth and righteousness. 'So he went and took Gomer the daughter of Diblaim, and she conceived and bore him a son' (Hos. 1:3).

"Hosea and Gomer had three children, and God dictated the name for each, in order to illustrate the tragedy which their willfulness would bring. Of the first child God said, 'Call his name Jezreel,' (scattered); and God has scattered the Jews all over the world. Gomer next bore a daughter, and God said, 'Call her name Lo-ruhamah,' (not pitied) 'for I will no more have pity on the house of Israel, to forgive them at all.' Hosea was instructed to name the third child, a son, 'Lo-ammi,' (not my people); 'For you are not my people and I am not your God' (Hos. 1:4, 6, 9).

"If we had no more than this, it would indeed be a terrible story. It would appear as though it were possible for God to divorce His people and break the marriage covenant by which He had bound His people to Himself. [And Christians today would be permitted to seek divorce.] But it is at this point that God intervenes to tell us that it will all turn out well and that they will live happily ever afterwards. For we read in the next verse, 'Yet the number of the children of Israel shall be as the sand of the sea, which cannot be measured nor numbered, and it shall come to pass, that in the place where it was said unto them, Ye are not my people, there it shall be said unto them, Ye are the sons of the living God.'

"The names of the three children are now changed by God himself. The first child will still be called Jezreel, but with the meaning 'God sows," instead of God scatters, for the Oriental sowed seed by throwing it to the ground with the same motion that he used for throwing something away. Lo-ruhamah becomes Ruhamah (pitied), 'For I will have pity on them,' and I shall call Lo-ammi, Ammi, 'for they shall be my people' (Hos. 2:22, 23). The new meanings illustrate how God's unchanging love covered the multitude of Israel's sins, even as Hosea's love covered Gomer's sins, and therefore how a Christian's love must cover an erring partner's sins.

GOMER AND HER LOVERS

"Now Gomer left Hosea and lived with other men; and each lover was poorer that the man before him. One day Hosea said to a certain man, 'Are you the man who is currently living with Gomer the daughter of Diblaim?' 'Well, what of it?' replies the man. 'I am Hosea, her husband.' As the man recoiled, Hosea said, 'But I love her, and I know that you don't have enough money to take care of her. Take this money and see that she does not lack for anything.' So the man took Hosea's money and bought clothing, oil and wine for Gomer, who gave her lover credit for providing these things; but Hosea said, 'She doesn't know that I paid the bills.'

"Here is the story as told by God in the words of Scripture: 'Their mother has played the harlot; she that conceived them has acted shamefully. For she said, 'I will go after my lovers, who give me my bread and my water, my wool and my flax, my oil and my drink. . . . And she did not know that it was I who gave her the grain, the wine, and the oil, and who lavished upon her silver and gold, which they used for Baal' (Hos. 1:5, 6, 8).

"No doubt the man who took Hosea's money was thinking, 'There is no fool like this old fool.' But who can explain true love? Love is of God, and it is infinite. Love is sovereign. Love is apart from reason; love exists for its owns reasons. Love does not operate according to logic but according to love. And we can see Hosea lurking in the shadows to catch a glimpse of her who filled his heart; weeping as he sees her embrace her lover and thank him for the gifts which true love has provided, which villainy offers and folly accepts.

" 'Now,' says God, 'that is how I treat you. You run away from Me and I pay your bills. The story of Hosea is a picture of My faithfulness. I am the faithful husband, and you are the adulterous wife. You turn to other gods; you run away, and still I love you.' Man runs away from God and says, 'I've gotten away from Him; I have gotten away from God!' And God touches him on the arm and says, 'My child, I took a shortcut and here I am, to tell you that I love you and am providing for you.' The man pulls away from God and runs; but God says, 'My child, I took another shortcut. I want you for Myself.'

"Someone asks, 'Do you mean God loves us even when we run away from Him?' Of course He does! Have you never run away from God? And does He not give you the strength to run? When we see this love at work through the heart of Hosea we may wonder if God is really like that. But everything in the Word and in experience shows us that He is. He will give man the trees of the forest and the iron in the ground. Then He will give to man the brains to make an axe from the iron to cut down a tree and fashion it into a cross. He will give man the ability to make a hammer and nails, and when man has the cross and the hammer and nails, the Lord will allow man to take hold of Him and bring Him to that cross; He will stretch out His hands upon it and allow man to nail Him to that cross, and in so doing will take the sins of man upon Himself and make it possible for those who have despised and rejected Him to come unto Him and know the joy of sins removed and forgiven, to know the assurance of pardon and eternal life, and to enter into the prospect of the hope of glory with Him forever. That is how much God loves you. He pursues you because He loves you and wants you to commit yourself to Him.

GOMER THE SLAVE

"Thus Hosea kept on loving Gomer, who gradually sank to the depths of degradation. She sank so low that she became a slave; and in accordance with ancient custom in the city of Jerusalem she was put up on the slave block, naked. God told Hosea to buy her.

"We know a great deal about the slave market in ancient times. Almost half the population was in slavery to the other half, and there was scarcely a day and scarcely a city in which human beings were not sold openly in the market. The ancient writers have left us terrible pictures of this sale of human souls. A writer of comedy laughs at the sight of a very fat man being sold in the market place, while the bystanders reflect that he would eat them out of house and home, and one, justifying the bid, says that he has a mill-wheel that is squeaking and that this slave, cut into pieces, would be cheaper than buying grease. Then a female slave is put up for auction, her clothes removed, and the by-standers laugh among themselves as they bid for the body of the slave.

"It was to a scene like that that Hosea was called to go. The Lord told him that he was to go and purchase the wife he had loved so long, but who was now being sold in the market. Suddenly, before the eyes of Hosea, appeared the woman he loved with all his heart. Her veil was taken from her face, her body was exposed to the gaze of the crowd, and the bidding began. Three pieces of silver . . . five . . . eight . . . ten pieces of silver . . . eleven . . . twelve . . . and Hosea then bids fifteen pieces of silver. The market is tense, the low bidders have dropped out. Another voice calls, 'Fifteen pieces of silver and a bushel of barley.' Hosea replies, 'Fifteen pieces of silver and a bushel and a half of barley.' The auctioneer looks around, is unable to get a higher bid, and announces that this woman is sold to Hosea. The curious onlookers gaze at the scene. The husband goes to the wife and helps her with her clothing, puts her veil upon her face and leads her into the anonymity of the crowd.

"Does God love us like that? Listen to the story as it is recorded in the third chapter of Hosea: 'Then said the Lord unto me, Go yet, love this woman, beloved of her friend, this adulteress, according to the love of the Lord toward the children of Israel.' Love *her?* 'Even as the Lord loves the people of Israel.' But Lord, she is a harlot, sold on the auction block as an adulterous slave! 'Go love her,' says God, 'love her, even as the Lord loves you.'

"Now under ancient law a man could do as he pleased with a slave whom he had purchased. If Hosea had taken this woman and had told her that she was to be punished for all her infidelities, and if he had tortured her to death, he would have gone free with but the slightest fine. Men would have thought him indeed vengeful to have wasted fifteen pieces of silver and a bushel and a half of grain in order to wreak his spite upon her. They would have thought that life would have dealt hardly enough with her, and that she would have suffered more as a slave to some other man, or even worse as the slave to some woman, and

that her menial way would bring her a living death when she remembered the life from which she was fallen. But that is all that
would have happened.

GOD'S FAITHFULNESS

"Hosea did not act in this way because he was reflecting the
love of God, and God never acts thus with those whom He has
redeemed by His blood. Hosea took Gomer and led her toward
their home, and as they went he said to her, 'Thou shalt abide for
me many days; thou shalt not play the harlot, and thou shalt not
be for another man: so will I also be for thee.'

"If we examine the words, their poignancy takes hold of the
heart strings. Here is the climax of the expression of love. What
Hosea could not have secured from the free will of a wife he now
has the right to ask of the one who has been redeemed out of
slavery. She was to remain with him in faithfulness. She knew
that this was her place as a purchased slave. She was no more to
play the harlot and be passed from man to man with the loss of
gifts and the daily increasing degradation. But the extraordinary
word is the one that follows, 'So shall I be for thee.' In this moment of home-coming, the love of Hosea shines through at its
brightest. If he is demanding of her a faithfulness that shall be
complete, she must understand that he is not offering her any less
from himself. He will be wholly for her. His faithfulness to her
shall continue. This is the faithfulness of the love of God.

TRUE MARRIAGE

"In the light of this story we see the inner meaning of marriage
as set forth in the Word of God. Marriage is the union of Christ
and the Church.

"In our salvation we were married to Him. He it was who took
the vows first of all: 'I, Jesus, take thee, sinner, to be My bride.
And I do promise and covenant before God and these witnesses,
to be thy loving and faithful Savior and Bridegroom; in sickness
and in health, in plenty and in want, in joy and in sorrow, in faithfulness and in waywardness, for time and for eternity.' And then
we looked up to Him and said, "I, sinner, take Thee, Jesus, to be
my Savior and my Lord. And I do promise and covenant before
God and these witnesses to be Thy loving and faithful Bride; in
sickness and in health, in plenty and in want, in joy and in sorrow,
for time and for eternity.'

"Thus we took His name. We were Miss Worldling; we were married to Him and now bear His name, for Christian means Christ-ian. When we realize the true meaning of this, we understand how important it is to keep His name spotless before the world.

"Christ is the faithful One. We are the ones who slip into flirtation and then into adultery with the world. We are loved by Christ Jesus, but we are drawn aside by our desires and seduced from our love of Christ. Such a seduction is the worst of all transgressions since it is the sin against the love of Christ. He is faithful to the end, loving us when we were unlovely, and taking us through all steps of our wandering to the place of redemption and final attachment to Himself forever.

"Perhaps some believer who reads this may say, 'Lord Jesus, I took You as my Savior, but I have been living a worldly life. Just because I gave You sixty minutes and a few dollars on Sunday morning, I thought I was serving You. But I now confess that I have been faithless to You. From now on, Lord Jesus, I will be faithful to You.' To such God replies, 'I will heal their faithlessness; I will love them freely, for my anger has turned from them. . . . They shall return and dwell beneath my shadow, they shall flourish as a garden, they shall blossom as the vine' (Hos. 14:4, 7).

"Perhaps your life partner has been unfaithful and you are asking yourself, 'Have I the love that Hosea had for Gomer? Has my partner seen that I love him that much? Can I really afford such love?' Your old nature will immediately protest, 'No, you cannot!' But the Holy Spirit will force you to say, 'Yes, I can!'

> *Were the whole realm of nature mine,*
> *That were a present far too small;*
> *Love so amazing, so divine,*
> *Demands my soul, my life, my all.*

"Though you do not possess the 'whole realm of nature' or the world, to give to Christ, you can give yourself to Him in total surrender. Because you love the Lord you can love your erring partner and be faithful." *

* Donald Grey Barnhouse, from *God's Freedom* (Grand Rapids: Wm. B. Eerdmans, 1961), pp. 187-192; *This Man and This Woman*, pp, 21-61; and from parts 37 and 38 of the published radio studies in the *Epistle to the Romans*.

Chapter 20

To Tell the Truth

(Matthew 5:33-37)

There has probably never been a period of history in which the best men of the time have not recognized the need for telling the truth. The great Roman orator Cicero once said, "Nothing is sweeter than the light of truth." Chaucer, the English poet, wrote, "Truth is the highest thing that man may keep." At the same time wise men have also recognized that the truth is not always so attainable. Thus, the English literary critic John C. Collins wrote with some wit, "Truth is the object of philosophy, but not always of philosophers." And Daniel Webster once mused, "There is nothing so powerful as truth — and often nothing so strange."

I believe that the Lord Jesus Christ captured both the need for the truth and the difficulty of attaining it in the fifth chapter of Matthew's gospel when He instructed His disciples: "Ye have heard that it hath been said by them of old, Thou shalt not perjure thyself, but shalt perform unto the Lord thine oaths; but I say unto you, Swear not at all; neither by heaven, for it is God's throne; nor by the earth, for it is his footstool; neither by Jerusalem, for it is the city of the great King. Neither shalt thou swear by thy head, because thou canst not make one hair white or black. But let your communication be, Yea, yea; Nay, nay; for whatever is more than these cometh of evil" (Matt. 5:33-37).

This is the fourth of Christ's six great illustrations of true morality in the Sermon on the Mount (Matt. 5) — victory over anger, purity in sexual matters, faithfulness in marriage, truth, selflessness, and love.

The Taking of Oaths

I believe that if we are to receive the full import of Christ's teaching we must realize that He was not speaking about the taking of oaths primarily. This is the sense in which certain re-

149

ligious bodies in our time have taken Christ's teaching, and hence, they will not swear to the truth of their statements even in a court of law. Actually, Jesus was speaking not against oaths themselves but against the abuses of oaths and the corresponding abuse of the truth that went with them.

We see this most clearly when we look in the broadest way at the positive teaching about oaths throughout Scripture. For instance, as far back as in the book of Deuteronomy we hear Moses commanding the people, "Thou shalt fear the LORD thy God; him shalt thou serve, and to him shalt thou cleave, and swear by his name" (Deut. 10:20). Jeremiah speaks on behalf of the Lord in commanding not only the nation of Israel but also the Gentile nations to swear by Jehovah: "It shall come to pass, if they will diligently learn the ways of my people, to swear by my name, The LORD liveth, as they taught my people to swear by Baal, then shall they be built in the midst of my people. But if they will not obey, I will utterly pluck up and destroy that nation, saith the LORD" (Jer. 12:16, 17). In the New Testament Paul frequently swears by the Lord crying, "As God is my witness" (Rom. 1:9; 2 Cor. 1:23; Phil. 1:8; 1 Thess. 2:5, 10).

It is even more remarkable to notice that at many places in the Bible God takes an oath also. This does not mean that God appeals, as men do, to a higher authority. But it does mean that God takes the most solemn steps to assure men of the truth of His statements.

One of the earliest examples of the taking of an oath by God is in the remarkable story of the execution of His covenant with Abraham. When God had called Abraham out of Ur of the Chaldees into Palestine He promised that the land would be Abraham's and would belong to his seed forever. Abraham had believed God implicitly, for God is the only being in the universe who cannot lie and who has never made a mistake. Abraham had gone to Palestine, and there had grown old. Nevertheless, he had a great problem: he had no children. In response to his concern God took Abraham out of his tent into the clear Near East night and pointed him to the innumerable stars of heaven. "So shall thy seed be," the Lord said.

At this point Abraham asked God for a sign in order that he might learn more about this great and solemn promise. God responded by calling for a heifer, asking Abraham to kill it, and then acting out an oath for Abraham in a ceremony similar to that used by the men of his day. As Abraham waited that evening, waving off the scavenger birds that tried to feed on the sacrifice, God appeared under the symbol of a lamp and of a burning furnace and passed through the pieces of the heifer, thus reaffirming His promise.

What did God say? He said, "Know of a surety," and He went on to outline the next five hundred years of Israel's history. Think of that phrase — "Know of a surety." It means that God does not want a man to know a thing halfway. He does not want us to be doubtful about our salvation or about any of His promises. And so, being able to swear by none higher, He swears by Himself. Thank God, it is so! If any part of salvation depended upon us, we would soon be shaking with fear and doubt. But since all rests upon God, we can be sure and certain.

As we go on throughout the Bible we find God swearing never to destroy the earth again by flood (Gen. 9:9-11), to send a redeemer (Luke 1:68, 73), to raise His Son from the dead (Ps. 16:10; Acts 2:27-31), to preserve and eventually bless Israel, (Isa. 49:15-18), and many other things. Why does God do it? The author of Hebrews tells us why. "So when God desired to show more convincingly to the heirs of the promise the unchangeable character of his purpose, he interposed with an oath, so that through two unchangeable things [that is, the word of God and the oath of God], in which it is impossible that God should prove false, we who have fled for refuge might have strong encouragement to seize the hope set before us. We have this as a sure and steadfast anchor of the soul" (Heb. 6:17-19, RSV).

MAN'S OATHS

Well, if it is true that the taking of oaths is approved throughout the Bible, why is it that the Lord Jesus commands us: "Swear not at all"? The answer is that in Jesus' day the taking of oaths had been greatly abused, and it had come about that the practice was actually weakening the cause of the truth rather than contributing to it.

In Palestine in the time of Jesus there were two unsatisfactory things about the taking of oaths. The first was what William Barclay calls *frivolous* swearing, that is, taking an oath when it was neither necessary nor proper. People who did this swore by their life (or whatever it might be) for almost nothing. The result was that even the most solemn statements appeared to be on this level also. It was exactly as if a servant who lived in the household of an honorable state official should go around talking about the honorable house, the honorable chair, the honorable mop, the honorable dishpan, and so forth. His speech would then have much less meaning when he called the lord of the house "your honor." In opposition to this, Jesus often insisted (as many of the rabbis did also) that the use of an oath to substantiate a simple statement was wrong.

The second perversion of the proper use of oaths by the people of Christ's time was worse. It was *evasive* swearing. People who were afraid to swear by the name of the Lord because they were not telling the full truth began to swear by things, and because mere things were not thought to be as significant as the name of God this second class of oaths was not considered to be binding. Some persons swore by their own life (1 Sam. 1:26) or their health (Ps. 15:4). Others swore by the king (1 Sam. 17:55). Still others swore, as Jesus indicates, by their head, the earth, heaven, the Temple, or Jerusalem (Matt. 5:34-36 cf. 23:16, 22). All such oaths were evasive.

Jesus replied to this perversion, "Woe unto you, ye blind guides, who say, Whosoever shall swear by the temple, it is nothing; but whosoever shall swear by the gold of the temple, he is a debtor! Ye fools and blind; for which is greater, the gold, or the temple that sanctifieth the gold? And, Whosoever shall swear by the altar, it is nothing; but whosoever sweareth by the gift that is upon it, he is bound. Ye fools and blind; for which is greater, the gift, or the altar that sanctifieth the gift? Whosoever, therefore, shall swear by the altar, sweareth by it, and by all things on it. And whosoever shall swear by the temple, sweareth by it, and by him that dwelleth in it. And he that shall swear by heaven, sweareth by the throne of God, and by him who sitteth on it" (Matt. 23:16-22). In other words, life simply cannot be divided into neat little compartments some of which are exempt from God's presence and some of which are not. God is everywhere. He is in every compartment of life. Hence, the truth is as important in one situation and at one time as another.

CONTROL OF THE MIND

I know that you may be saying, "Well, I admit that what Christ was teaching is true. God is truth, and those who are God's should be like Him. It is true, but it is not very easy. In fact, there are situations where shading the truth seems to be demanded by people and where telling the full truth, at least for me, is impossible." Well, I admit that to speak the truth and stand by it will sometimes seem impossible and the more so because we are not naturally constituted to do it. But the answer to the problem is that with God all things *are* possible. Jesus said, "The things which are impossible with men are possible with God" (Luke 18: 27). In His strength many persons who previously could not control their tongues have learned to control them.

In one of the books of Dr. Frank E. Gaebelein, headmaster emeritus of the Stony Brook School for Boys on Long Island and a former associate editor of *Christianity Today,* there is a discussion of the means to control our speech that is quite pertinent to this study. I should like to share it with you. Dr. Gaebelein writes, "Tongue control? It will never be achieved unless there is first of all heart and mind control. The tongue is the servant of the mind and the emotions. In 2 Corinthians 10:5 Paul gives us in a single magnificent phrase the key to victory over the tongue: 'Bringing into captivity every thought to the obedience of Christ.' Whence come our words? They come, of course, from our minds. Antecedent to the word is thought or emotion. Christ only is worthy to have full control of a man's mind. And He who is worthy is also able to do what no man can do for himself. Salvation applies to the whole man. The cleansing of the soul includes also the cleansing of the mind. When any Christian comes to the point of yielding to the Lord — in full sincerity, cost what it may — control of his thought life, the problem of managing his tongue, will be solved, provided that such a surrender goes deeper than the intellect and reaches the emotions and the will. For the Bible makes a distinction between mere intellectual knowledge of God and the trust of the heart.

"It was our Lord Himself who said: 'Out of the abundance of the heart the mouth speaketh' (Matt. 12:34). Words that are truly godly come only from a godly heart. Such a heart is one that is possessed first of all by a deep love for Christ. The heart of the man who really trusts the Lord will express itself in words that are true and edifying.

"It is a humbling thing candidly to consider the totality of what comes from our mouths. We are Christians. Therefore, let us say, we sincerely endeavor and generally succeed in eschewing malicious gossip and impure speech. Nor do we use profanity. But are we therefore perfect in respect to our speech? Well, there is a verse in the last book of the Old Testament that will help us answer that question: 'Then they that feared the Lord spake often one to another: and the Lord hearkened, and heard it, and a book of remembrance was written before him for them that feared the Lord, and that thought upon his name' (Mal. 3:16). In the light of these words, we see that it is not enough to avoid overt sins of speech. The Lord looks to His children to use their tongues to His glory in a positive way. 'They that feared the Lord spake often one to another.' Those words were written of the Jews at one of the lowest ebbs of their national history. Yet there was among them a remnant who really loved the Lord enough to talk frequently about Him. . . .

" 'But,' someone says, 'are we never to engage in pleasantries? Surely all our speech cannot be religious.' That is quite true. Christianity is a religion that hallows the common things of life; our Lord sanctified by His presence happy, normal human relations, as at the marriage feast at Cana. The danger with us is not that of neglect of this aspect of fellowship; it is the opposite danger of leaving the Lord almost completely out of our speech. Honestly now, how often do we speak of Him? How large a place do His blessings, His goodness, and His wonderful grace have in our everyday conversation? Malachi reminds us of the fact that the Lord not only hears us when we speak of Him but that He also treasures our words and writes them in 'a book of remembrance.' It is easy to sing in a meeting, 'O for a thousand tongues to sing my great Redeemer's praise.' Futile wish! We shall never have a thousand tongues. If we had them, we should not know what to do with them — not when the one tongue we have is so strangely silent respecting the Lord who loves us and gave Himself for us." *

* Frank E. Gaebelein, *The Practical Epistle of James* (Great Neck, N.Y.: Channel Press, 1955), pp. 80-83.

Chapter 21

Have We No Rights?

(Matthew 5:38-42)

We live in a day when most people are intensely conscious of their rights. In such a climate it is not unusual for a believer in Jesus Christ to be asking, "What are my rights — as a Christian? Do I have a right to success or wealth? to a home or a family? to a good name? to be respected?" Perhaps you have asked these questions also or others like them. Do you have rights? The verses from the Sermon on the Mount to which we now come answer these questions directly, and they say — striking as it may seem — that there are *no* rights for Christians.

Jesus said, "Ye have heard that it hath been said, An eye for an eye, and a tooth for a tooth; but I say unto you that ye resist not evil, but whosoever shall smite thee on thy right cheek, turn to him the other also. And if any man will sue thee at the law, and take away thy coat, let him have thy cloak also. And whosoever shall compel thee to go a mile, go with him two. Give to him that asketh thee, and from him that would borrow of thee turn not thou away" (Matt. 5:38-42). These verses teach that a follower of the Lord Jesus Christ has no right to retaliation, no right to things, no right to his own time, and no right to his money. In other words, he holds all his possessions in trust from the Lord, and he is obliged to use them as Jesus did, to help others.

"Eating Loss"

Several years ago in the course of my reading I came across a little book by Mabel Williamson, a former missionary under the China Inland Mission, that forcibly develops this theme. It is called, *"Have We No Right—."* And it is full of stories that illustrate how difficult the point we are talking about is for most

Christians. One story is the account of an address by another
CIM missionary, in which he tells of the difficulties he had in
learning this lesson in China.

" 'You know,' he began, 'there's a great deal of difference between *eating bitterness* [Chinese idiom for 'suffering hardship']
and *eating loss* [Chinese idiom for 'suffering the infringement of
one's rights']. 'Eating bitterness' is easy enough. To go out with
the preaching band, walk twenty or thirty miles to the place where
you are to work, help set up the tent, placard the town with pos-
ters, and spend several weeks in a strenuous campaign of meetings
and visitation — why, that's a thrill! Your bed may be made of
a couple of planks laid on saw-horses, and you may have to eat
boiled rice, greens, and bean-curd three times a day. But that's
just the beauty of it! Why, it's good for anyone to go back to
the simple life! A little healthy "bitterness" is good for anybody!

" 'When I came to China,' he continued, 'I was all ready to "eat
bitterness" and like it. . . . It takes a little while to get your
palate and your digestion used to Chinese food, of course, but that
was no harder than I had expected. Another thing, however' —
and he paused significantly — *'another thing* that I had never
thought about came up to make trouble. I had to "eat loss"! I
found that I couldn't stand up for my rights — that I couldn't
even *have* any rights. I found that I had to give them up, every
one, and that was the hardest thing of all.' " *

That comment by a veteran missionary to China rings true.
It is what Christ was teaching. What is more, the lesson involved
is a lesson that must be learned by every Christian. The Apostle
Paul learned it, for he wrote to the Corinthians, "Have we no
right to eat and to drink? Have we no right to lead about a sister,
a wife, as well as other apostles, and as the brethren of the Lord,
and Cephas? Or I only, and Barnabas, have we no right to for-
bear working? . . . Nevertheless, we have not used this right, but
bear all things, lest we should hinder the gospel of Christ. . . .
For though I am free from all men, yet have I made myself servant unto all, that I might gain the more" (1 Cor. 9:4-6, 12, 19).

Paul willingly gave up his natural human rights for the sake of
the Gospel. Although it is difficult, Jesus Christ teaches that we,
His followers, are to do the same.

* Mabel Williamson, *"Have We No Right—"* (Chicago: Moody Press, 1957),
pp. 8, 9.

THE RIGHT TO RETALIATION

The first right that Jesus teaches us to forego is the right of retaliation. It is the first of four rights listed here, and although the list is not comprehensive (and is not intended to be) it is sufficient to indicate the type of character that God requires of us. Jesus said, "Resist not evil, but whosoever shall smite thee on thy right cheek, turn to him the other also."

This is hard teaching, of course. A tendency to insist on our own rights lies deep in the heart of man, and it is nowhere more apparent than in the natural human instinct for retaliation. We believe in fair play. So strong is our sense of it that we naturally tend to justify retaliation as "evening the score' or "giving the other man what he deserves." C. S. Lewis found this idea so universal in the human race that he even used it as the basis of his argument for moral law and for the existence of God in the opening pages of his most popular book, *Mere Christianity*.

Jesus says that this is not the way Christians are to live. Instead of insisting on our rights we are to yield them up, particularly our imagined right to retaliation, in order that the preaching of the Gospel might not be hindered. We shall be abused. We shall be persecuted often, but we are not to fight back. In fact, we are to do as Paul, who also learned this lesson, teaches: "Dearly beloved, avenge not yourselves but, rather, give place unto wrath; for it is written, Vengeance is mine; I will repay, saith the Lord. Therefore, if thine enemy hunger, feed him; if he thirst, give him drink; for in so doing thou shalt heap coals of fire on his head. Be not overcome by evil, but overcome evil with good" (Rom. 12:19-21).

Perhaps someone may object by saying, "That sounds good on paper, but it cannot be done — not in the kind of world we live in. Those words are meant for heaven." Nonsense! It can be done. It is being done. What is more, if you are not doing it, you are not living the kind of special, Christ-like life that God has set before you.

Let me give you an illustration of someone who is doing it. The black evangelist Tom Skinner was converted to Christ while he was leader of the largest, toughest, teenage gang in New York City, the Harlem Lords. His conversion was so real that he left the gang the next day, turning from a life of fighting and violence to preach the Gospel. There was an immediate victory over crime and cruelty. Soon there was victory over hate and bigotry also. Several weeks after his conversion he was playing a football game in which, as his assignment on one play, he blocked the defensive end while his own halfback scored a touchdown. As he got up from the ground to head back to the huddle, the boy whom he had blocked jumped in front of him in a rage and slammed him in the stomach. As he bent over from the blow he was hacked across the back. When Skinner fell the boy kicked him, shouting, "You dirty black nigger! I'll teach you a thing or two."

Skinner said that under normal circumstances the old Tom Skinner would have jumped up from the ground and pulverized the white boy! But, instead, he got up from the ground and found himself looking the boy in the face and saying, "You know, because of Jesus Christ, I love you anyway." Later, Skinner said that he even surprised himself, but he knew that what the Bible had promised was true. He was a new creature in Christ, and it was no longer necessary for him to operate on the old level of tit for tat, hate for hate, or retaliation. Moreover, when the game was over and the opposing end had had some time to think about it, he came to Skinner and said, "Tom, you've done more to knock prejudice out of me by telling me that you loved me than you would have if you'd socked my jaw in."

Do not say that the teachings of the Lord Jesus Christ cannot be followed — if you are a Christian. They can be, if Christ lives in you. What is more, they must be followed. If you are serious about them, why not begin by yielding to Christ's words about retaliation?

OUR GREAT EXAMPLE

Before we go further I want to deal with an objection that someone may be raising. You may be saying, "All of what you say is well and good, but isn't it true that there are situations in which this standard need not be followed? In fact, didn't Jesus even refuse to turn His face Himself when He was struck by the high priest? Didn't He say, 'If I have spoken evil, bear witness of the evil; but if well, why smitest thou me?'"

Well, the first answer to that question is that, although Jesus said what He did, He did not turn around and punch the high priest in the nose. Even to state it that way is ludicrous, and it shows the wide gulf that exists between our reactions and the conduct of Jesus; for we would want to retaliate. That is part of the answer. The full answer, however, is that the situation here involves the law. Christ was being tried by law, and He insisted rightly that the Jewish maxims about not striking an accused person be enforced. The New Testament values law, as does the Bible from beginning to end, and none of these statements suggests that the Christian is to forego the protection that the law affords him. In fact, he is to be thankful for it, and to pray for the authorities.

On the other hand, where the law is not involved, there the Christian is to forego his rights and to refuse retaliation. In other words, his conduct is to be like that of Jesus "who did no sin, neither was guile found in his mouth; who, when he was reviled, reviled not again; when he suffered, he threatened not, but committed himself to him that judgeth righteously; who his own self bore our sins in his own body on the tree, that we, being dead to sins, should live unto righteousness" (1 Peter 2:22-24). To this standard all believers in the Lord Jesus Christ have been called.

THE RIGHT TO THINGS

There are other examples in this section of Matthew's gospel. The next verse talks about things: "If any man will sue thee at the law, and take away thy coat, let him have thy cloak also" (v. 40). There was a Jewish law that limited that for which a man could be sued. A man would have many undergarments, which were light and would correspond to a suit or a dress in our time, but he would have only one cloak, the heavier outer garment that corresponds to a coat. Jewish law recognized that this garment was necessary for a man's well-being, and hence, although he could be sued for his suit, he could not be sued for that which alone would keep him warm in winter or protect him from the chill of the night air if he slept outside on the ground (Exod. 22:26, 27). Naturally, all the poor (and the rich) among Christ's listeners knew this law. So when Jesus said that they were not to be unwilling to spare their coat, He was actually saying that even if the law protected them, they were still not to live by the rights to their possessions.

What does that mean for us? Well, it refers to our property at least — to our homes, automobiles, clothes, food, and other things. And it tells us that these things are not ours to hold and guard jealously. Instead, we must recognize that all that we have comes from the Lord and is to be used in the best possible way to His glory.

THE RIGHT TO OUR TIME AND MONEY

The third example Jesus gave is the right to our time, for He said, "And whosoever shall compel thee to go a mile, go with him two" (v. 41). This is a picture of which we know very little, for it comes from the experience of those who live in an occupied country. In such a situation a member of the conquered nation might at any moment be compelled to serve the conquering power, even if it meant the neglect of things which he considered important and for which time was pressing. To give one example, this was what happened to Simon of Cyrene when he was pressed into service in Jerusalem to bear the cross of Jesus.

Jesus said that if a Roman should come and compel one of His disciples to go a mile with him in order to bear some burden, he was not to do it grudgingly and with obvious resentment. Instead, he was to go two miles with cheerfulness and good grace. To us that means that we are not to be resentful when people call us on the telephone and take up valuable time — just because they do not have anything to do. And we are not to be surly when we are given added work at the office, are saddled with someone else's work, or are sent out for coffee when we are in the middle of something we think important. We are to do it cheerfully and as unto the Lord.

Finally, we are to see that we have no right to our money, for Jesus said, "Give to him that asketh thee, and from him that would borrow of thee turn not thou away" (v. 42). I know we work for our money. We seem to work doubly hard today because the government and the state take so much in taxes, and yet, we are never to say, "Well, what is mine is mine. Let the other fellow work. I did it." We are to respond to his need. And we are to do so cheerfully (2 Cor. 9:7).

This is not speaking of the professional beggar, of course, the kind who will spend all you give him on drink. It is speaking of genuine need. Nevertheless, it does teach that we are to meet that need. Actually, the instruction is exactly the same as that given to us by John, who wrote to those of his day: "But whosoever hath this world's good, and seeth his brother have need, and shutteth up his compassions from him, how dwelleth the love of God in him? My little children, let us not love in word, neither in tongue, but in deed and in truth" (1 John 3:17, 18). Perhaps there are few things that reveal the true depth of our Christianity as clearly as our attitude toward money.

CROSS-BEARING

What is your attitude toward what Christ is saying? Are you still dealing with the question of your rights and your wrongs? Or are you learning to live the kind of life lived for us by the Lord Jesus?

One Bible teacher has written on this subject: "Since the day that Adam took the fruit of the tree of knowledge, man has been engaged in deciding what is good and what is evil. The natural man has worked out his own standards of right and wrong, justice and injustice, and striven to live by them. Of course, as Christians we are different. Yes, but in what way are we different? Since we were converted a new sense of righteousness has been developed in us, with the result that we too are, quite rightly, occupied with the question of good and evil. But have we realized that for us the starting point is a different one? Christ is for us the Tree of Life. We do not begin from the matter of ethical right and wrong. We do not start from that other tree. We begin from *Him;* and the whole question for us is one of Life.

"Nothing has done greater damage to our Christian testimony than our trying to be right and demanding right of others. We become preoccupied with what is and what is not right. We ask ourselves, have we been justly or unjustly treated? and we think thus to vindicate our actions. But that is not our standard. The whole question for us is one of cross-bearing. You ask me, 'Is it right for someone to strike my cheek?' I reply, 'Of course not!' But the question is, Do you only want to be right? As Christians our standard of living can never be 'right or wrong,' but the Cross. The principle of the Cross is our principle of conduct. . . . 'Right or wrong' is the principle of the Gentiles and tax gatherers. My life is to be governed by the principle of the Cross and of the perfection of the Father." *

If you are a Christian, learn soon this great spiritual lesson. Do not stand on your rights. The second mile is only typical of the third and the fourth. The cloak is only typical of all our possessions. Our time is not our own. When Jesus died for us on the cross, He did not do it to defend our right or His. It was grace that took Him there. Now, as His children, we are called to the same life of self-sacrifice and Christ-like service.

* Watchman Nee, *Sit, Walk, Stand* (Fort Washington, Pa.: Christian Literature Crusade, 1966), pp. 25, 26.

Chapter 22

Love Your Enemies

(Matthew 5:43-47)

For most people the verses that we are now to study are the heart of the Sermon on the Mount, and there is a sense in which this is both true and proper. They deal with love — Christian love. As such they contain a highly "concentrated expression of the Christian ethic," as William Barclay notes in his commentary, and they deal with it profoundly.

Jesus said, "Ye have heard that it hath been said, Thou shalt love thy neighbor, and hate thine enemy; but I say unto you, Love your enemies, bless them that curse you, do good to them that hate you, and pray for them who despitefully use you, and persecute you, that ye may be the sons of your Father, who is in heaven; for he maketh his sun to rise on the evil and on the good, and sendeth rain on the just and on the unjust. For if ye love them who love you, what reward have ye? Do not even the tax collectors the same? And if ye greet your brethren only, what do ye more than others? Do not even the heathen so?" (Matt. 5:43-47).

These verses carry the core of Christian ethics up to anchor it in the character of God, for they teach that the Christian is to love others, not as a man loves his friends, but as God loves.

DIVINE LOVE

I believe that we must put the heart of the teaching in this way, for we miss the point of the verses unless we see that the standard is a love of which only God is capable.

This is evident in several ways. For one thing, verse 45 says that we are to do this in order to be sons of our Father who is in heaven, and this means that we are to do it in order that we might be Godlike in our conduct. Because God's love is without discrimination, because it extends to the just and to the unjust alike, our love is also to be without discrimination. Because it results in action, our love is to express itself in action. We are to love those who are, by all human standards, our enemies.

The fact that this is a divine standard and not a human one is also clear in the word for love that occurs in this passage. The Greek language has four distinct words for love, and whenever one of them occurs (as opposed to another) the choice is almost always significant. The first word for love is one that the Bible never uses. It is the word *eros,* and it refers to sexual love. From it we get our words "erotic" and "erogenous." The Bible is aware of this kind of love, of course; but in biblical times the sexual love of the Greeks had become so perverted and debased that the word *eros,* that suggested it, was rejected in biblical language as something contaminated. It is interesting, moreover, that the same thing happened years later when Jerome came to make the Latin translation of the Bible, for he chose the Latin word *caritas* while rejecting the equally common but erotic word *amor.* Thus in 1 Corinthians 13, the older, Authorized Version of the Bible speaks of faith, hope and *charity,* not love. And it does not use the word amorous at all.

The second Greek word for love is *storge.* It refers to family love. This is the love that a father and mother have for their children and that children have for their parents. This word is not in the New Testament either, although it could be.

The third word for love is *philia.* It refers to strong affection, and from it we get our words philanthropy (meaning a love for men), philharmonic (a love for music), Anglophile (a lover of England), and the name Philadelphia (city of brotherly love). This was the word which Peter used when Christ asked him if he loved with the highest of love. Peter, conscious of his recent denial, replied, "Yea, Lord, thou knowest that I *love* thee" (John 21:15-17). It is the highest love of which man in himself is capable.

There is a fourth word for love, however, and it is divine love — *agape.* It is the word that Christ used the first two times that He put His question to Peter, "Simon, son of Jonah, *lovest* thou me?" — and, of course, it is the word which Jesus uses here in the Sermon on the Mount. This love is one that loves without variableness. It loves even when the object of the love is hateful or unlovely. You might say that it is love for no reason at all, or love even when there are ample reasons to discourage it. It is Godlike love. The point is that such love, not erotic or family or even affectionate love, is to characterize our lives as God's children.

LOVE ON THE CROSS

We have not really seen the true extent of this divine love until we go one step further. It is true that the love to which we are called is God-love *(agape)* and that this is an inscrutable love that exists entirely apart from the possibility of being loved back. But where do we see this love if, indeed, it is God-love? Where is it demonstrated? The answer is that we see it only in Jesus Christ and in Him preeminently at the cross.

Years ago, when I first began to study the subject of God's love, I made an interesting discovery that is pertinent here. I noticed that there is hardly a verse in the New Testament that speaks of God's love without also speaking in the same context of the cross. This suggests that to the biblical writers God's love was acknowledged to be seen there, not elsewhere. Think of the verses. There is John 3:16 "For *God so loved the world, that he gave* his only begotten Son, that whosoever believeth in him should not perish, but have everlasting life." Galatians 2:20: "I am crucified with Christ: nevertheless I live; yet not I, but Christ liveth in me; and the life which I now live in the flesh I live by the faith of the Son of God, who *loved me and gave himself for me.*" 1 John 4:10: "Herein is love, not that we loved God, but that *he loved us, and sent his Son to be the propitiation* for our sins." Romans 5:8: "But God commendeth his love toward us in that, while we were yet sinners, *Christ died for us.*" In each case the cross is made the measure of God's love.

Moreover, it is not merely the fact of Christ's suffering that makes God's love so wonderful. It is also the fact that He suffered for sinners, and this means for those who were in themselves naturally repugnant to Him.

Every so often during the summer we hear of a lifeguard who has rescued some person from drowning, and once in a while of one who has lost his life while trying to save a person. Stop a moment and image yourself in his position. You are the handsome lifeguard, and a beautiful girl is drowning. Would you risk your life for hers? You are probably saying, "I am not sure, of course; but yes, I think I might." I agree with you. Many persons would do it, or attempt to do it. But now picture in your mind the most contemptible person you know — one who has wronged you or cheated you, a pervert, a murderer — imagine him drowning. Would you give your life for his? It is not so easy to answer the question this time, for it now begins to show us something of the love of the Lord Jesus Christ for us. That is why the Bible says, "For scarcely for a righteous man will one die; yet perhaps for a good man some would even dare to die. But God commendeth his love toward us in that, while we were yet sinners, Christ died for us" (Rom. 5:7, 8). It was while we were hideous to God that He loved us and died for us.

There is one point here that should also be mentioned. The same verses that tell us that Christ died for us while we were yet sinners also tell us that He died for us while we were helpless, without strength. There was no possibility of our ever helping ourselves out of our lost condition.

Many persons think that there is a good bit that they can achieve for themselves spiritually, but the Bible teaches differently. For one thing, it says that apart from God's saving work through Christ natural man cannot understand Christ's teachings. Thus, Jesus spoke even to the religious leaders of His day, saying, "Why do ye not understand my speech?" and answered, "Because ye *cannot* hear my word" (John 8:43). In other words, the natural man has ears to hear, but he hears not.

Second, the natural man cannot receive the Holy Spirit. For Jesus said to His disciples, "I will pray the Father, and he shall give you another Comforter, that he may abide with you forever; even the Spirit of truth, whom the world *cannot* receive" (John 14: 16, 17). This verse teaches that no one can be saved by receiving the Spirit as an act of his own will.

Third, the Bible teaches that the unsaved man cannot use his will to submit himself to God's law. In fact, he is impelled to rebel against it. "The carnal mind is enmity against God; for it is not subject to the law of God, *neither,* indeed, *can be,*" we are told in Romans 8:7, 8.

Fourth, "the natural man receiveth not the things of the Spirit of God; for they are foolishness unto him, *neither can he* know them, because they are spiritually discerned" (1 Cor. 2:14). The unsaved person cannot understand God's truth. Finally, 2 Peter 2: 14 says of the person apart from Christ that having eyes full of adultery he *"cannot* cease from sin."

If we put all these teachings together we see that God's love is to be measured by the fact that while we were sinners and were unable to hear His word, receive the Holy Spirit, submit to His law, understand His teaching, or cease from sin Christ died for us. That is God's love. That is the full measure of God's love. It is that love to which we are called as God's children.

LOVING, NOT LIKING

At this point a person may be saying, "Well, if that is the standard, I may as well admit right now that I cannot attain it." That is true. In yourself you cannot attain it. That love is possible only to those in whom the Lord Jesus Christ is working and in whom His love dwells. If you are not a Christian, you must begin by becoming one and asking Him to create that love in you, or, if you are a Christian but are far from the Lord, you must draw near to Him and ask Him to work out that love in you.

It is possible, however, that you are a Christian and that you are attempting to walk with the Lord, and yet you find this love remote and unattainable. If that is your case, you may be helped by a very important distinction. That distinction is that loving is not necessarily the same thing as liking. To like someone is to have a certain emotional feeling toward them, and because we cannot entirely control our feelings it is not always possible to like everybody. I am not even sure that we should. I believe, for instance, that there is a sense in which we can say that God does not really like the way we are. But He does love us, and that is an entirely different thing. Love is not a matter of the feelings; it is a matter of the will. And because it is of the will and not of the feelings, it is something that is always possible and that may always express itself in good actions. This we can do — whether or not we feel like it.

Moreover, this is implied in the commands to love that God gives us. If love depended on our feelings, it would be foolish for Jesus to say, "Love one another" or "Love your enemies." It could not be done. But if love is a matter of the will and if our wills are surrendered to Him, it can be done; and we can love our enemies just as we can also bless them that curse us, do good to them that hate us, and pray for them that despitefully use us and persecute us. Certainly Jesus implied this as He linked these four positive commands together in this saying.

I have found the late C. S. Lewis of Cambridge, England, most helpful at this point. Lewis writes, "The rule for all of us is perfectly simple. Do not waste your time bothering whether you 'love' your neighbour; act as if you did. As soon as we do this we find one of the great secrets. When you are behaving as if you loved someone, you will presently come to love him. If you injure someone you dislike, you will find yourself disliking him more. If you do him a good turn, you will find yourself disliking him less. . . . The difference between a Christian and a worldly man is not that the worldly man has only affections or 'likings' and the Christian has only 'charity.' The worldly man treats certain people kindly because he 'likes' them; the Christian, trying to treat every one kindly, finds himself liking more and more people as he goes on — including people he could not even have imagined himself liking at the beginning." *

If you are having difficulty with the need to love others, try this suggestion and see if God will not use it to lead you into a fuller experience of His great love and power.

CHRIST IN YOU

It is important that we do come to this fuller experience of God's love because it is from such loving conduct that the Gospel of Christ is communicated to the unsaved world. Someone has said that God has really given men five gospels. There is the gospel according to Matthew, the gospel according to Mark, the gospel according to Luke, the gospel according to John, and the "gospel according to you." How, then, do men come to know God? They come to know Him through Jesus Christ. And how do they come to know Jesus Christ? They come to know Him as they see Him in the Scriptures and in your conduct. You are the closest some men and women will ever get to Jesus Christ. If they do not see Christ's love in you, they will never see it.

Some time ago I read a story in one of the books of Dr. H. A. Ironside that illustrates this graphically. Once when Ironside was in Ganado, Arizona, at a Presbyterian Mission Hospital there, he met a poor Navajo woman who had been nursed back to health through the consecrated work of a Christian doctor and the Navajo nurses. She had been cast out by her own people when they thought she was going to die, and was found after three or four days of exposure. After nine weeks in the hospital she recovered enough to begin to wonder about the unexpected care she had received. She said to one of the nurses, "I can't understand it. Why did the doctor

* C. S. Lewis, *Mere Christianity* (New York: The Macmillan Company, 1958), pp. 101, 102.

do all that for me? He is a white man, and I am in Indian. I never heard of anything like this before."

The Navajo nurse, a Christian, said to her, "You know, it is the love of Christ that made him do that." She said, "Who is this Christ? Tell me more about Him." The nurse called a missionary to explain the Gospel. The staff began to pray. Several weeks passed. Then a day came when she was asked, "Can't you trust this Savior, turn from the idols you have worshiped, and trust Him as the Son of the living God?" As the Navajo woman pondered her answer, the door opened and the doctor stepped in. The face of the old woman lit up. She said, "If Jesus is anything like the doctor, I can trust Him forever." She came to the Lord Jesus Christ and accepted Him as her Savior.

Do you see what it was that reached her? It was love. But it was not man's love. It was God's love manifest in a man. God's love! That is what you and I are to show forth to an ungodly and rebellious world, and we are to do it as sons of our Father so that many may come to faith in His unique Son.

Chapter 23

Perfecting the Saints

(Matthew 5:48)

At an early point in the Sermon on the Mount the Lord Jesus Christ taught that if a man is to enter heaven he must possess a greater measure of righteousness than the righteousness possessed by the scribes and the Pharisees, the most religious and respected men of His day. As He taught this doctrine a person might easily have said, "You teach that a man can enter heaven only if his righteousness exceeds the righteousness of the scribes and the Pharisees. All right, then, how much in excess of their righteousness must the saved man's righteousness be? If the Pharisees can be credited with having attained seventy or seventy-five percent of the standard, what must our goodness be? Is seventy-six percent sufficient? Or is eighty percent necessary? How good must a saved person be?"

To these questions Jesus now answers with a statement that is devastating to all human attempts to earn heaven, a statement that is meant to turn men to God's grace and away from all man-made attempts at salvation. Jesus said, in summary of all His previous teaching, "Be ye, therefore, perfect, even as your Father, who is in heaven, is perfect" (Matt. 5:48).

I believe that this verse is the most important verse in the Sermon on the Mount. It is the climax of the first of the Sermon's three chapters, and it is the midpoint, the pinnacle, from which much of the later teaching follows. I believe that if you understand this verse, you understand the essence of all that Jesus Christ is teaching. And, what is more, you understand the heart of the Christian Gospel and of the Bible generally.

169

PERFECTION

What does it mean, "Be ye, therefore, perfect, even as your Father, who is in heaven, is perfect"? What is perfection? The first and the best way to answer this question is by studying the words that are translated "perfection" in the Old and New Testaments.

The first word is *tam* or *tamim*. It means to be entirely "without defect" or "without blemish." Thus, it is used of the sacrificial animals that were to be without blemish and without spot (Exod. 12:5; 29:1; cf. 1 Peter 1:19; Eph. 5:27). It has a negative connotation. The second word is *shalem,* which means "whole" or "complete." This word speaks of perfection in a positive sense. *Shalem* is related to the common Hebrew greeting *shalom* ("peace"); it suggests the ideas of security, soundness, and well-being. In the New Testament the major word for perfection is *teleios.* This word means "complete" as when a ship is fitted out perfectly for sea or a legion of soldiers is equipped in all respects for battle. In the moral realm the word means "blameless."

When these various definitions of the word are put together they show us that God's standard for a man is complete and utter moral rectitude. He is to have nothing lacking of all that he should be, and he is to have no blemishes. In short, he is to be as blameless as the Lord Jesus Christ.

When we have said this, however, we have also made it clear that no one lives up to this standard. For all men fall short of such perfection, and in doing so they show themselves to be sinners. That is what sin is. Romans 3:23 says, "For all have sinned, and come short of the glory of God." The verb in that verse is a word taken from the practice of archery, and it refers to the arrows of those who fall short of and therefore miss the target. In other words, if the target were to be set up at one end of a football field and all the archers were to line up at the other end of the field and shoot their arrows, the verb would refer to the shots of all those who did not reach the target. That is what all men have done. God's standard is a bull's-eye, and no one has ever hit it or ever will. All men fall short. Consequently, no one will ever enter heaven by his own efforts.

"Well, then," you say, "what is a person to do? What am I to do? The answer is that you must turn away from your own efforts completely and receive instead the perfection which God has already taken steps to provide for you. Nothing that you will ever do will be perfect. Only what God does is perfect. Hence, if you are to reach the perfection which God requires, it must be as the result of His working for you and in you.

GOD'S WORKING

In the course of my preparation for this study as I looked up all the verses in the Bible that speak about perfection, I came across a paragraph that I had never noticed before but which was striking to me, chiefly because it makes this point so succinctly. In the eighteenth Psalm David speaks of perfection twice, once of God's perfection and once of man's. The point of the verses is that God is responsible for both kinds. In verse thirty David writes, "As for God, *his way is perfect.*" Then two verses farther on he adds, "It is God who girdeth me with strength, *and maketh my way perfect*" (v. 32). Who is God? God is the One who is perfect. What does He do? God works to perfect sinful men.

Now, how does He do it? The answer to that question is a tremendous answer because it involves the whole counsel of God. It has several parts. First, God begins by perfecting the record. Second, He works at perfecting us in this life. Third, He perfects us completely in all ways at the moment of our death.

How does God work to perfect the record? And what does that mean anyhow? Well, the background to what that means is to be found in the fact that sin consists in far more than what it does merely to the individual sinner. Sin involves others, and sin is an offense to God's justice. It cannot be ignored or even simply forgiven. It must be dealt with. Consequently, God the Father sent God the Son to die for the sin of others, bearing sin's penalty and cancelling all claims of justice against the sinner forever. This is the meaning of the cross of Jesus Christ. It is not simply an example, still less a meaningless tragedy. It is the place at which God punished sin and cancelled its claims against all those who should believe in Jesus. The author of Hebrews speaks of this aspect of God's work of perfecting His children when he writes, "For by one offering he [Christ] hath perfected forever them that are sanctified" (Heb. 10:14).

The second way in which God works to perfect the believer is to begin to perfect him more and more in this life. This too is necessary. It is true that the believer has been perfected forever by his faith in Christ in one sense, but it is equally true that he is far from perfect in another sense. Paul knew this. Thus, when he wrote to the Philippians he wrote of two distinct types of perfection. He said, "Not as though I had already attained, either were already *perfect*; but I follow after, if that I may apprehend that for which also I am apprehended of Christ Jesus" (Phil. 3: 12). And then, practically in the next breath he added, "Let us, therefore, as many as be *perfect,* be thus minded" (Phil. 3: 15). Clearly, although he knew that his record had already been cleared before God on the basis of his faith in Christ, he was aware of the practical work of his being perfected that still lay before him.

Each Christian should also find this to be true in his own experience. When a person first believes in Jesus Christ as Savior, he normally has a great sense of joy and gratitude to God for removing the penalty of his sin, the sin that had previously condemned him. He is thankful. He is liberated. At the same time, however — and quite apart from these things — he is still not much different in terms of his natural inclinations and conduct than he was previously. Before he believed the Gospel he was filled with many wrong ideas about who God was and what He was like. He was wrong about himself and about what God required of him. He had bad habits. Now he is saved, but many of these wrong ideas and wrong actions remain. What is to happen? Well, he is to begin to learn that many of these things must change. He is to develop a distaste for sin and a hunger for righteousness. In other words, he is to experience the second aspect of God's work of perfecting.

This does not mean that the man is getting better and better so that the day will come when he will be able to say that he no longer sins. Some Christians must have said this in John's day, for he wrote to them, saying, "If we say that we have no sin, we deceive ourselves, and the truth is not in us" (1 John 1: 8). It means that the man is becoming more and more ready to turn to God for daily and sometimes hourly forgiveness and cleansing.

It is the old principle of the seesaw in theology. It is the principle that if God is up in theology, man is down; and if man is up, God is down. Both can never be up or down at the same time. Some persons have man up and are always talking about how well man is doing, but then they have a very small God because there is not much need of Him if a man can manage so well on his own. Others, the ones who know their Bibles, have man down. Then God is everything, and He becomes increasingly wonderful to them. That is what God wants because He knows that as we get lower He will get higher and we will look to Him for the help, strength, and encouragement which we so desperately need.

The final stage of God's work in perfecting the saints is to perfect them completely in the moment of death. It is this fact that transforms death for Christians. Death is an enemy — even the Bible calls it that. But it is also the portal to that total perfection which we will never know in this life. Paul called death "a gain" (Phil. 1:21), and when he compared the life of eternity to the continuation of this life he said that the first was "far better" (Phil. 1:23). He knew that death brings the believer into the presence of the Lord Jesus Christ, and he knew that it results in the believer's becoming Christlike. He becomes like Jesus in holiness, knowledge, love, wisdom, humility, obedience, and all His other perfections.

That is salvation. It is past, present, and future; it touches every aspect of our living.

An Inflexible Purpose

I want to present one more verse on this subject. It is a great verse, for it teaches that God's purposes in this process which I have been describing are absolutely unshakable and that, therefore, what God has begun in the moment of your salvation He will work to continue without interruption throughout life. The verse is Philippians 1:6: "Being confident of this very thing, that he who hath begun a good work in you will perform it until the day of Jesus Christ." In other words, if you are a believer in Jesus Christ, God already has begun the work of perfecting you; and because God does not change, His purposes will not change. God never begins a thing that He does not intend to finish.

Do you see what that means? For one thing, it means that no one who has believed in Jesus Christ will ever be lost. Were you the one who was responsible for your becoming a Christian? Not at all! It was God. He called you. He straightened out the record. If there was ever a moment in your life in which you seemed to be seeking God, it was only because He was there beforehand moving you to do it. That is why we sing:

I sought the Lord, and afterward I knew
He moved my soul to seek Him, seeking me;
It was not I that found, O Saviour true;
No, I was found of Thee.

God finds us. God calls us. God perfects us. And God never begins a thing that He does not intend to finish.

Second, it means that you will inevitably become like Jesus. What does the verse say? It says, "He who hath begun a good work in you will perform it until the day of Jesus Christ." What is the "good work"? Well, the answer is not given very clearly here in Philippians, but it is given clearly in Romans 8:28, 29. Here Paul speaks of God's great purpose in calling the Christian, which is "to be conformed to the image of his Son, that he might be the firstborn among many brethren." God is so delighted with Jesus Christ that He has set the whole course of creation and human history in motion just so He could call out a race of sinful human beings, put His life within them, and transform them to be like His Son. The result is that there will then be millions of "Christs" where there was only one before. This does not mean that we shall become divine, of course. The Bible does not teach that. But we shall be like Him. We shall be like the Lord Jesus; and we shall be so inevitably, because it is God Himself who does the transforming.

The third thing this verse means is that God will not give up in His purpose of making you become like Jesus Christ, even though you may want Him to give up. There are times when you will. The day will come in your Christian experience when you will sin and find that you like it. You will say to yourself, "I think I would just like to keep on sinning this way." What will happen then? The answer is that God will begin to work on you. He will begin to poke you and to prod you and to whittle you, even to knock you around a bit if necessary, until you get out of your sin and back into the way He has marked out for you.

Moreover, the prodding will get rougher and rougher so long as you persist in your own way. Why? Because God must be true to His nature, and His nature is set against sin. He loves you, but He must lead you aright. He must be true to His own purposes, and His great purpose is to make you become like the Lord Jesus.

As far back as in the book of Hosea there is a picture of how God did this with the Jewish people in Hosea's day. The people had been disobedient, and God had been forced to judge them for their sin. Yet He continued to love them. So He says that He is going to come to them like a moth, gently, in order to get them back to Himself. He says, "Therefore will I be unto Ephraim like a moth, and to the house of Judah like rottenness" (Hos. 5:12). However, if Israel will not repent, says God, then, "I will be unto Ephraim like a lion, and like a young lion to the house of Judah: I, even I, will tear and go away; I will take away, and none shall rescue him" (v. 14). It is a great principle. God is determined to lead you in righteousness. So when you sin, He will deal gently if He can. But He will also deal roughly when He must. In fact, He will even break your life into little pieces if He is forced to do it.

Oh, Christian, learn this lesson, and do not force God to come to you as a roaring and ravaging lion! Learn to recognize the flutterings of the moth — those slight inconveniences, those little failures, that restlessness, that miscarriage of your plans — that warn you of God's displeasure at your present course of action and of His desire to turn you back to Himself. If you learn that, you will go on from strength to strength, and you will rejoice that He who hath begun a good work in you will keep on perfecting it until the day of Jesus Christ.

Chapter 24

How To Invest in God's Program

(Matthew 6:1-4)

In today's world charity is practiced on a wide scale and is thought to be the natural product of the innate benevolence of the human spirit. Actually, that is not so. True charity came into the world through Christianity, and the charity we see today — in the United Fund, in the Red Cross, in hospitals, in benevolent foundations, in government — is purely a by-product of the Gospel of the Lord Jesus Christ.

THE SOURCE OF CHARITY

I do not mean to suggest by this that there was never such a thing as a gift to the poor in pagan lands in the pre-Christian era. We read in ancient sources of those who would toss a few coins to a beggar and thereby gain a reputation for magnanimity from their contemporaries. But such a display was infrequent at best, and it was motivated by a desire for men's praise rather than a genuine concern for the recipient. Before Christ's time there were no homes for the sick or poor, no orphanages. There was a world of toil and poverty, of the exposure of unwanted children, of slavery, of great hunger side by side with great affluence, and appalling indifference. After Christ came there was an instant and sacrificial love of the believers for each other. This was followed by care for the poor, hospitals, reform laws in the status of women, the establishing of change in labor laws, the abolition of slavery, and other things.

The proof that this is true is seen in the awe by which the ancient world first viewed the life of the early church. For instance, as early as A.D. 125 the Athenian philosopher Aristides

176

delivered a defense of the faith to the Emperor Hadrian, in which he said of normal Christians:

> They do not commit adultery nor fornication, they do not bear false witness, they do not deny a deposit, nor covet what is not theirs: they honor father and mother; they do good to those who are their neighbors. . . . They love one another: and from the widows they do not turn away their countenance: and they rescue the orphan from him who does him violence: and he who has gives to him who had not, without grudging. . . . When one of their poor passes away from the world, and any of them sees him, then he provides for his burial according to his ability; and if they hear that any of their number is imprisoned or oppressed for the name of their Messiah, all of them provide for his needs, and if it is possible that he may be delivered, they deliver him. If there is among them a man that is poor or needy, and they have not an abundance of necessaries, they fast two or three days that they may supply the needy with their necessary food. *

It is evident from this spirited apology that the charity of the early church was a new and amazing thing to its contemporaries. Their awe of it is the best evidence that true charity entered the world with Christianity.

There is one apparent exception to this truth. In Judaism, nurtured as it was on the Old Testament Scriptures, there was a strong concern for charity, particularly the giving of alms. The Old Testament taught this duty. Proverbs 19:17 says, "He that hath pity upon the poor lendeth unto the Lord, and that which he hath given will he pay him again." Proverbs 29:7 says, "The righteous considereth the cause of the poor." Psalm 41:1 pronounces a blessing upon the one who does so, saying, "Blessed is he that considereth the poor." The rabbis even amplified this teaching, adding that "alms-giving delivers from death and will purge away all sins" (Tobit 12:9).

The problem, however, was that charity in Judaism, like other aspects of morality, was largely external. And although it was far more common than in the cultures of Greece or Rome, it was performed, nevertheless, with similar motives. Only with the coming of Jesus Christ did motives change, and only in the

---

* *The Apology of Aristides,* edited with an introduction and translation by J. Rendel Harris, Vol. 1 of "Texts and Studies," edited by J. Armitage Robinson (Cambridge: the University Press, 1891), pp. 48, 49.

power of His Spirit did charity flow from a divine love welling up internally.

We now come to a series of verses in which this new spirit of charity is revealed for the first time. Because of its historic significance we will proceed from these verses to consider the subject in the light of the New Testament generally. In the opening verses of chapter six of Matthew's gospel Jesus said, "Take heed that ye do not your alms [i.e., your good deeds] before men, to be seen by them; otherwise ye have no reward of your Father, who is in heaven. Therefore, when thou doest thine alms, do not sound a trumpet before thee, as the hypocrites do in the synagogues and in the streets, that they may have glory from men. Verily I say unto you, They have their reward. But when thou doest alms, let not thy left hand know what thy right hand doeth, that thine alms may be in secret; and thy Father, who seeth in secret, shall reward thee openly" (Matt. 6:1-4).

The phrase "let not thy left hand know what thy right hand doeth" points to an absence of ostentation, not only before men, but also before the giver himself. It is indicative of a charity inspired by the presence of Christ in the heart. In that spirit men and women have since given, even to their own hurt and without any prospect of thanks or appreciation.

FIRST GIVEN TO THE LORD

The first obvious principle of these verses is that true charity must come forth from a life that has first been surrendered to God. We are to give for His approval and before Him.

Have you ever noticed that this is what made the Philippian Christians such outstanding examples of giving? The Philippians had learned to give first because of their love for Paul, who was their father in the faith. When he left them after his first visit to Philippi to go on to Thessalonica, they soon sent messengers to find out how he was doing. When word came back that he was in financial need they took up a collection and sent it to him. Later, when they heard that the need continued, they did the same thing again. Paul refers to this in his letter to them saying, "For even in Thessalonica ye sent once and again unto my necessity" (Phil. 4:16). They continued to do this throughout his life, sending to him even at the last when he was a prisoner in Rome.

Sometime during the course of his long association with this church — presumably during his second missionary journey —

Paul presented the need of the poor at Jerusalem. We do not know much about the state of the Christian Church there, but since it was an outlying and underdeveloped area of the Roman Empire it was probably true that it was much like the Appalachian region of the United States today or like Scotland in the last century. That is, there was probably just not enough work for normal men to earn sufficient wages. The case of the poor was so bad that the church there practiced a form of voluntary communism in which the believers shared their possessions. When the first council of the church met in Jerusalem, a request was made through Paul for help from the Gentile congregations.

This request Paul honored. He wrote to the Galatians in his report about the council, "Only they would that we should remember the poor; the same which I also was diligent to do" (Gal. 2:10). At Philippi he presented the case of these believers, none of whom any of the Philippian Christians had ever seen, and the response was so overwhelming that the believers at Philippi actually competed for the privilege of giving. Having learned to give to Paul in his need, they were ready to give even more liberally to others.

How do we know this? We know because some time later Paul wrote to the Corinthians of the outstanding charity of the Macedonian church. He wrote, "Moreover, brethren, we make known to you the grace of God bestowed on the churches of Macedonia, how that in a great trial of affliction the abundance of their joy and their deep poverty abounded unto the riches of their liberality [that is the Lord's formula: joy, plus great poverty, equals abounding liberality]. For to their power, I bear witness, yea, and beyond their power they were willing of themselves, beseeching us with much entreaty that we would receive the gift, and take upon us the fellowship of the ministering to the saints. And this they did, not as we hoped, but first gave themselves to the Lord, and unto us by the will of God" (2 Cor. 8:1-5).

Here was a church composed entirely of those who a few years previously had known nothing more than the values of the Greek and Roman world, and yet they were competing beyond their actual resources to give to poor Jews in a distant area of the empire. What made the difference? The answer is in the last phrase — "And this they did, not as we hoped, but first gave themselves to the Lord and unto us by the will of God." They gave because they had first given themselves to the Lord Jesus.

SPIRITUAL GIVING

The second great principle of Christ's teaching is that through his stewardship a Christian is to look for spiritual rewards. If he gives spiritually as God leads him to give, he will receive spiritual rewards from God. If he gives to please men, he will have rewards from men — but not from God. Jesus said, "But when thou doest alms, let not thy left hand know what thy right hand doeth, that thine alms may be in secret; and thy Father, who seeth in secret, shall reward thee openly" (Matt. 6:3, 4).

Once again this is amplified most profitably in one of Paul's statements to the Gentile churches. It occurs in the letter to the Galatians, and it includes the much quoted phrase: "Whatever a man soweth, that shall he also reap" (which, incidentally, has nothing to do with sowing wild oats but with the giving of money; in fact, the whole last chapter of Galatians is primarily concerned with this subject).

Paul writes, "Let him that is taught in the word share with him that teacheth in all good things [that is, the members of a church should give money to support their pastors]. Be not deceived, God is not mocked, for whatever a man soweth, that shall he also reap. For he that soweth to his flesh shall of the flesh reap corruption [that is, if he spends his money on his body or on his lower nature, the money will be gone and the body will dissipate also]; but he that soweth to the Spirit shall of the Spirit reap life everlasting [that is, if he spends his money on spiritual things, the Spirit of God will see that he gets a great reward in heaven]. And let us not be weary in well doing; for in due season we shall reap, if we faint not. As we have, therefore, opportunity [that is, depending upon the amount of our income and the ups and downs of the stock market], let us do good unto all men, especially unto them who are of the household of faith" (Gal. 6:6-10).

Paul's great principle here is that money spent on the body — to clothe, feed, house, or entertain it — while it has value for this life, has no lasting fruit for eternity. Money spent in obedience to the Lord, to spread the Gospel and to meet the needs of those who are poor and suffering, will have results not only in this life but in eternity also.

I wonder if you have noticed that these verses also contain another principle that we need especially to remember. It is the principle that we are not to be weary in well-doing. I sometimes think, as I see the numerous requests that come to a church for money — many from very worthwhile causes — and as I pass along scores of these to the members of my congregation as objects for their giving, that there is no end to the task and that responding to the needs themselves seems burdensome. Perhaps you feel this at times, and you become weary. Well, Paul knew this too, for he refers to it. And yet, he says we are not to complain. There will always be one more cause for an offering, but let us give to it as we are best able. Let us not become weary. Let us take confidence in the promise that we shall reap eventually (in this life and in heaven) if we do not lose heart.

SACRIFICIAL GIVING

There is one more point about how we are to give away our money that is not stated explicitly in Christ's teaching in the Sermon on the Mount and yet is involved precisely because it is Christ's teaching and flows from His character. It is the principle of sacrificial giving. The Bible points to it in Christ's case when it says, "For ye know the grace of our Lord Jesus Christ, that, though he was rich, yet for your sakes he became poor, that ye through his poverty might be rich. . . . Therefore [and again Paul is referring to the offering for the Jerusalem saints], perform the doing of it, that as there was a readiness to will, so there may be a performance also out of that which ye have" (2 Cor. 8: 9, 11).

Have you ever been led of the Lord to give sacrificially, perhaps even of that which you do not yet have? Let me tell you how Dr. Oswald J. Smith, pastor of the well-known People's Church in Toronto, Canada, first learned to give sacrificially. He was sitting on the platform of the People's Church for the first time since commencing his ministry there. It was at the time of their annual missionary convention. He was unaware of their normal procedure, and he was somewhat surprised to see the ushers going up and down the aisles handing out envelopes. Surprise turned to amazement and amazement to horror, however, when one of the ushers had the "audacity," as he said, to walk up the aisle and hand him an envelope. He read on it, "In dependence upon God I will endeavor to give toward the missionary work of the church $ _____ during the coming year."

He had never seen such a thing before. As he had a wife and child to keep and was at that time earning only twenty-five dollars a week, he had never given more than five dollars to missions at any one time previously, and that only once. He started to pray, "Lord God, I can't do anything. You know I have nothing. I haven't a cent in the bank. I haven't anything in my pocket. Everything is sky-high in price." It was true. World War I was on.

But the Lord seemed to say, "I know all that. I know you are getting only twenty-five dollars a week. I know you have nothing in your pocket and nothing in the bank."

"Well, then," he said, "that settles it."

"Oh, no, it doesn't," the Lord answered. "I am not asking you for what you have. I am asking you for a faith offering. How much can you trust Me for?"

"Oh, Lord," said Dr. Smith, "that's different. How much can I trust you for?"

"Fifty dollars."

"Fifty dollars!" he exclaimed. "Why, that's two weeks salary. How can I ever get fifty dollars?" But again the Lord spoke, and with a trembling hand Oswald Smith signed his name and put the amount of fifty dollars on the envelope. Well, he has written since that he still doesn't know how he paid it. He had to pray each month for four dollars, but each month God sent it. And at the end of the year, not only had he paid the whole amount, he had himself received such a blessing that he raised the amount to one hundred dollars during that year's missionary conference. He went on to give much more later and to lead People's Church into an ever-expanding and ever more effective program of home and world missions.

That is real sacrificial giving, and it is born solely of the Christian Gospel. If you are concerned about your giving (as you should be if you are a Christian), then begin by yielding yourself to the Lord, seek out spiritual causes, and ask the Lord to lead you in His own pattern of giving.

Chapter 25

How To Pray

(Matthew 6:5-8)

The second great example of godly living discussed by Jesus Christ in the second chapter of the Sermon on the Mount is prayer. It is an important subject, for prayer is at least partially confusing to us all.

There are some Christians, hyper-Calvinists — you probably know some — who believe that it is hardly necessary to pray. These say that everything is in God's hands and that He does what He wants to do whether or not you ask for it. There are some Arminians — those who make a great deal of man's supposed part in salvation — who believe that almost everything is contingent upon prayer and that God will do very little unless we ask for it. In between are more of us — some Calvinists and some Arminians — who believe that God is indeed in charge of things and is accomplishing His own purposes but who, nevertheless, also believe that God responds to our prayers and, in fact, even urges us to pray to Him. Unfortunately, we are often uncertain about prayer anyway. We wonder how we should pray, what we should pray for, and sometimes whether we should even pray at all.

Some time ago I heard a story that illustrates how some of these questions trouble even very mature Christians. At one point in the course of their very influential ministries George Whitefield, the Calvinistic evangelist, and John Wesley, the Arminian evangelist, were preaching together in the daytime and rooming together in the same boarding house each night. One evening after a particularly strenuous day the two of them returned to the boarding house exhausted and prepared for bed. When they were ready

183

each knelt beside the bed to pray. Whitefield, the Calvinist, prayed like this: "Lord, we thank Thee for all those with whom we spoke today, and we rejoice that their lives and destinies are entirely in Thy hand. Honor our efforts according to Thy perfect will. Amen." He rose from his knees and got into bed. Wesley, who had hardly gotten past the invocation of his prayer in this length of time, looked up from his side of the bed and said, "Mr. Whitefield, is this where your Calvinism leads you?" Then he put his head down and went on praying. Whitefield stayed in bed and went to sleep. About two hours later Whitefield woke up, and there was Wesley still on his knees beside the bed. So Whitefield got up and went around the bed to where Wesley was kneeling. When he got there he found Wesley asleep. He shook him by the shoulder and said to him, "Mr. Wesley, is this where your Arminianism leads you?"

The story shows that we all have some things to learn about prayer, and it teaches that because no one understands the ways of God as perfectly as we ought to understand them, prayer is, therefore, at least partially confusing to us all.

PRAYING TO GOD

These problems were also present in Christ's day, so when Jesus began to speak about prayer in the Sermon on the Mount, He began to deal with them directly. He did so, first by instruction and then by a sample prayer that we call the Lord's Prayer. The instructions say, "And when thou prayest, thou shalt not be as the hypocrites are; for they love to pray standing in the synagogues and at the corners of the streets, that they may be seen by men. Verily I say unto you, They have their reward. But thou, when thou prayest, enter into thy room, and when thou hast shut thy door, pray to thy Father, who is in secret; and thy Father, who seeth in secret shall reward thee openly. But when ye pray, use not vain repetitions, as the pagans do; for they think that they shall be heard for their much speaking. Be not ye, therefore, like unto them; for your Father knoweth what things ye have need of, before ye ask him" (Matt. 6:5-8).

Many foolish things have been written about these verses. Some persons have understood the verses to mean that there is to be no such thing as public prayer, but this is foolish because both the disciples and Jesus Himself prayed publicly. Some have said that there is to be no such thing as prayer with others, no prayer meetings. But this is nonsense, too, and the practice of Jesus and of the early Christians refutes it.

Actually, these verses are concerned with the tendency of men to pray to themselves and to other persons rather than to God. They teach that prayer must always be made to God and that as a consequence it must be made in the knowledge that God is more ready to answer us than we are to pray to Him. Let me make this the first great principle of true prayer. True prayer is *prayer that is offered to God, our heavenly Father.*

Someone is going to say, "But isn't that obvious? Aren't all prayers offered to God?" The answer is No. All prayers are *not* offered to God. In fact, I would be willing to argue that not one prayer in a hundred is really offered to God, our heavenly Father. You say, "Oh, I think I know what you mean. You are referring to the prayers of the heathen, those that are offered to idols." Well, partially. But there are other prayers also that are not offered to God. You say, "Oh, you must mean prayers to the saints." Yes, those too. But not only those. I believe that not one prayer in a hundred of those who fill our churches on a Sunday morning is actually made to Almighty God, the Father of our Lord Jesus Christ. They are made to men or to the praying one himself, and that includes the prayers of the preachers as well as those of the members of the congregation. Years ago a minister from New England described an ornate and elaborate prayer offered in a fashionable Boston church as "the most eloquent prayer ever offered to a Boston audience." This was perceptive, for he meant that the prayer was much more concerned with impressing the preacher himself and his listeners than with approaching God.

Do your prayers bring you into the presence of God, or do they make you like the Boston preacher? Isn't it true that often, perhaps most of the time when you pray, you are really thinking far more of your friends, your busy schedule, or what you are asking for than you are of the great God whom you are approaching and of whom you are asking it? Dr. Reuben A. Torrey, the great Bible teacher and evangelist, used to say correctly that "we should never utter one syllable of prayer, either in public or in private, until we are definitely conscious that we have come into the presence of God and are actually praying to Him." *

* Reuben A. Torrey, *The Power of Prayer* (Grand Rapids: Zondervan, 1955), p. 75.

This is supported by Dr. Torrey's own description of how he learned this principle. He writes, "I can remember when that thought transformed my prayer life. I was brought up to pray. I was taught to pray so early in life that I have not the slightest recollection of who taught me to pray. . . . Nevertheless, prayer was largely a mere matter of form. There was little real thought of God, and no real approach to God. And even after I was converted, yes, even after I had entered the ministry, prayer was largely a matter of form.

"But the day came," Torrey writes, "when I realized what real prayer meant, realized that prayer was having an audience with God, actually coming into the presence of God and asking and getting things from Him. And the realization of that fact transformed my prayer life. Before that prayer had been a mere duty, and sometimes a very irksome duty, but from that time on prayer has been not merely a duty but a privilege, one of the most highly esteemed privileges of life. Before that the thought that I had was, 'How much time must I spend in prayer?' The thought that now possesses me is, 'How much time may I spend in prayer without neglecting the other privileges and duties of life?'" *

Have you learned this lesson? Or are you still like so many Christians who do not really know what it is to pray to God? I believe that the psychiatrists are entirely right when they say that much of our prayer is mere wish-fulfillment, for we often pray merely by reciting things that we would like to see happen. Instead of this, Jesus taught that we are to pray only when we are conscious of being in God's presence and are truly communing with Him.

THROUGH THE LORD JESUS CHRIST

A question arises at this point. For if it is true, as we have said, that prayer is communing with God, the question naturally comes up about the means of access to Him. How can a sinful, human being approach a God who is holy? Is it even possible? If it is, what does it mean in terms of the way that you and I can approach Him? The answer to this question brings us to the second great principle of true prayer. True prayer is *prayer offered to God the Father on the basis of the death of Jesus Christ, His Son.* The author of the book of Hebrews puts it like this: "Having

* *Ibid.,* pp. 76, 77.

therefore, brethren, boldness to enter into the holiest by the blood of Jesus . . . let us draw near with a true heart in full assurance of faith" (Heb. 10:19, 22). Jesus taught the same principle when He said, "I am the way, the truth, and the life; no man cometh unto the Father, but by me" (John 14:6).

What does that mean? Well, it means that if we were to approach God as we are, apart from Jesus Christ, God would have to turn from us. God is holy — the verse from Hebrews says "holiness" — and He must turn from all that is unholy and imperfect if He is to be true to His Word and true to His nature. If it were not for Jesus Christ, God would have had to turn a deaf ear to every prayer ever offered by any human being. However, He also tells us that anyone can be purified in His sight through faith in the death of Jesus Christ and that in this state he may come. In fact, he is even urged to come.

This means, of course, that prayer is for believers only. It is not for the heathen. It is not for the atheist. It is not for the good man who, though good morally, nevertheless regards Jesus as nothing more than a man. Prayer is for Christians, and it is for Christians exclusively. The best man or woman in this world is unable to come into the presence of God on the basis of any self-merit. Nor can that person receive anything from God on the grounds of his or her own goodness. And yet, on the ground of the shed blood of Jesus Christ, the worst sinner who ever walked on the face of this earth but who has turned from his sin and accepted Jesus Christ as his Savior can come any day of the year, at any hour of the day or night, and with boldness can speak out of the longing of his heart and receive from God what he asks for.

Isn't that wonderful? In fact, it is doubly wonderful because it is possible only on the basis of the death of the Lord Jesus Christ. True prayer is prayer to God the Father through the Lord Jesus Christ.

In the Holy Spirit

But prayer is one thing more. It is prayer to God the Father. Yes. It is through Jesus Christ. But it is also *in the Holy Spirit*. This is the third great principle of prayer. That is why Ephesians 2:18 says of the Jews and Gentiles, "For through him [that is, through Jesus Christ] we both have access by one Spirit unto the Father."

We see at once, of course, that this verse reinforces the truth we have just been considering, for it says that prayer is to be made through the Lord Jesus Christ. This is not the only idea in the verse, however, for it also says that prayer is to be made in the Holy Spirit. It is the work of the Holy Spirit to lead us into God's presence, to point out God to us, and thus to make God real when we pray. Perhaps I can point this up by the underlying meaning of the word "access." The Greek word that lies behind our English translation is *prosagoge*, which means literally "an introduction." The Holy Spirit introduces us to God. Thus, the Holy Spirit makes God real to us while, at the same time, instructing us how we should pray (Rom. 8:26, 27).

Have you ever begun to pray and had the experience that God seems to be far away and unreal to you? If you have, one of two things may be wrong. First, it may be that sin or disobedience to God is hindering you. The Bible quotes David as saying, "If I regard iniquity in my heart, the LORD will not hear me" (Ps. 66:18). If that is the case, you need to confess the sin openly.

It may also be the case, however, that things are filling your mind or that worries are obscuring the sense you should have of God's presence. What are you to do in this case? Should you stop and pray again another time? Certainly not, for it is then that you probably most need to pray. Instead of stopping, you should be still and, looking to God, ask Him to work through His Holy Spirit to make Himself real to you and to lead you into His presence. Many Christians find that their most wonderful times of prayer are those in which they start without a clear sense of God's presence but come to it fully by praying.

CONFIDENCE

All this is really an exposition only of the first part of Jesus' introduction to prayer in the Sermon on the Mount. There is a second part also. It is the part in which Jesus teaches that God is more willing to answer our prayers than we are to pray and that, as a result, the Christian who prays in God's will can pray with great confidence. Jesus said, "But when ye pray, use not vain repetitions, as the pagans do; for they think that they shall be heard for their much speaking. Be not ye, therefore, like unto them; for your Father knoweth what things ye have need of, before ye ask him" (vv. 7, 8). Perhaps it was these words of which John Newton was thinking when he wrote:

> *Come, my soul, thy suit prepare:*
> *Jesus loves to answer prayer;*
> *He, Himself has bid thee pray,*
> *Therefore will not say thee nay.*

There is a great deal involved in this, of course, for it certainly does not mean that God will grant any stupid thing we ask for. God is willing. But if we are to receive the things we ask for, we must have a knowledge of God's will and God's ways. These are given to us only through Scripture.

One of the greatest verses on prayer in the Bible is 1 John 3:22, which says, "And whatever we ask, we receive of him, because we keep his commandments, and do those things that are pleasing in his sight." It is a remarkable statement and totally in keeping with Jesus' teaching in the Sermon on the Mount. John says that his prayers always are answered and that he has full confidence that they always will continue to be answered. It is so remarkable that we cannot help but ask, "John, how can you make such a statement? Our prayers are not always answered, or they do not seem to be answered. Yet you say that you always receive the things you ask." "Well," John says, "just read the verse more carefully. I say that I receive the things I request, but I also say why. It is because I keep His commandments and do those things that are pleasing in His sight."

I have already referred to Dr. Reuben A. Torrey in this study, but I would like to do so once more by citing a story from his writings. During his first pastorate there was a woman who attended his church often but who was not a member. When Dr. Torrey asked her about this fact she replied that she was not a member simply because she did not believe the Bible. Torrey said, "Why do you not believe the Bible?" She answered, "Because I have tried its promises and found them untrue." Torrey asked her to give one promise which she had found to be untrue. She said, "The promise that says that whatever things you desire when you pray, believe that you shall receive them and you shall have them. Once I prayed for something very earnestly, but I did not receive it. Isn't it true that this promise failed?"

Torrey said, "No, not at all."

"But doesn't it say that you shall receive whatever you ask for

if you believe it?" Torrey agreed that it said something like that.
But he said, "You first have to ask yourself if you are one of the
'ye's.'" She did not know what he was talking about, so he asked
again, "Are you one of the people to whom the promise is made?"

"Why," she said, "isn't it made to every professing Christian?"
Torrey said, "Certainly not! God defines very clearly in His Word
just to whom His promises to answer prayer are made." She
said, "It does?" When she asked to see the verse, he took her to
this last verse which we have been studying: "Whatever we ask,
we receive of him, because we keep his commandments, and do
those things that are pleasing in his sight." The prayers that God
answers are made by those believers in Jesus Christ who keep His
commandments and do those things that please Him. Torrey said,
"Those are the 'ye's.' Do you keep His commandments?" The
woman then admitted that she did not. And she came back to
God and eventually became one of the most active and useful
members of his congregation.

I believe that there are thousands of Christian men and women
just like this woman. But it is unfortunate, and it need not be
true of anyone. Are you one of the "ye's"? Are you one who
knows God's Word, who seeks to keep His commandments and
who tries to please Him? If you are, then you may pray with great
confidence — to God the Father, through the Lord Jesus Christ,
and in the Holy Spirit.

Chapter 26

Our Father, Our Daddy

(Matthew 6:9)

One of the most important lessons that a Christian must learn in life is how to pray. We already have spoken about the meaning of prayer, and we have seen that prayer is talking with God. It is prayer to God the Father, on the basis of the death of the Lord Jesus Christ, and in the Holy Spirit. Now we want to see *how* we should talk with God, bearing in mind that God is for us both our heavenly Father and the holy, righteous God of the universe. The text for our study is the prayer that Christ taught His disciples in answer to their request, "Lord, teach us how to pray." It is recorded in Luke 11:2-4 and in Matthew 6:9-13.

THE LORD'S PRAYER

As we study this prayer it is important for us to realize that it was given to the disciples and to us as a pattern for prayer and not primarily as a prayer to be recited. Joachim Jeremias, who has written one of the major studies on this prayer, calls it a "primer" upon which our prayers should be patterned. Oh, it is used as a prayer by Christians in most churches every Sunday, and this is not wrong. If a congregation is to pray together, it must have an established text; and it is at least as wise to use the text provided by the Lord Himself as to use prayers provided by men. But that is not the primary reason for His giving it. Luke tells us that the disciples had been watching Jesus pray and wanted to learn to pray as He did. He was not reciting prayers or they could have learned to pray as He did merely by memorizing them. He was communing with God. And thus, when they said, "Lord, teach us to pray," Jesus answered by giving them the so-called Lord's Prayer as a pattern.

191

The same thing is evident from the way the longer version of the prayer appears in the Sermon on the Mount, for Jesus said, "After this manner . . . pray" or "Pray like this." He did not say, "Pray these exact words," but "Pray *like* this." Hence, the so-called Lord's Prayer is a pattern.

Christians have always called this the Lord's Prayer, and it is His in the sense that He gave it. But it is far more accurate to call it the disciples' prayer, or even our prayer. Jesus gave the prayer. But Jesus Himself could not pray it, for it contains a prayer for the forgiveness of sins; and He was sinless. He gave it for us. Thus, it contains, as Samuel Zwemer once wrote, "every possible desire of the praying heart; it contains a whole world of spiritual requirements, and combines in simple language every divine promise, every human sorrow and want and every Christian aspiration for the good of others." *

The greatest minds of the Christian Church have always known this, and as a result the Lord's Prayer has been used throughout the centuries as an outline for countless expositions of the nature of prayer and Christian doctrine. In the early church, Origen, Gregory of Nyssa, Tertullian, Cyril of Jerusalem, and Cyprian all wrote substantial expositions of the prayer. Augustine did the same. Dante expounded its significance in the eleventh canto of his *Purgatorio*. Meister Eckhart summed up the principles of scholastic theology by the categories that the prayer suggests. Luther gave countless expositions of the true meaning of the Lord's Prayer to the heirs of the Protestant Reformation. And in the Presbyterian churches an exposition of the Lord's Prayer forms the last nine questions of the Westminster Shorter Catechism.

Andrew Murray said that it is "a form of prayer that becomes the model and inspiration for all other prayer, and yet always draws us back to itself as the deepest utterance of our souls before God." **

OUR FATHER

The first words of the Lord's Prayer are an address to God as our heavenly Father. Jesus said, "After this manner, therefore, pray ye: Our Father, who art in heaven." These words tell us who can pray and what the privileges of access are for them.

* Samuel M. Zwemer, *Prayer* (New York: American Tract Society, 1959), p. 23
** Andrew Murray, *With Christ in the School of Prayer* (Westwood, N.J.: Fleming H. Revell, 1967), p. 27.

If we are to understand the full importance of these words, we must realize clearly that no Old Testament Jew ever addressed God directly as "my Father" and that, as a result, the invocation of the Lord's Prayer would have been something new and startlingly original to Christ's contemporaries. This fact has been documented beyond any doubt by a late German scholar, Ernst Lohmeyer, in a book called *Our Father* (a study of the Lord's Prayer), and by the contemporary biblical scholar Joachim Jeremias in an essay entitled "Abba" and in a booklet called *The Lord's Prayer*. According to these scholars three things are indisputable: (1) the title was new with Jesus, (2) Jesus always used this form of address in praying, and (3) Jesus authorized His disciples to use the same word after Him.

It is true, of course, that in one sense the title "father" for God is itself as old as religion. Homer wrote of "Father Zeus, who rules over the gods and mortal men," and Aristotle explained that Homer was right because "paternal rule over children is like that of a king over his subjects" and "Zeus is king of us all." In this case the word "father" most simply means "Lord." The point to notice, however, is that the address was always impersonal. In Greek thought God was called "father" in the same sense that a king is called a father of his country. Zeus was imagined to rule over men.

In contrast to such sweeping statements, the Old Testament uses the word "father" as a designation of God's relationship to Israel, but even this is not very personal. And it is not frequent either. In fact, it occurs only fourteen times in the Old Testament. Israel is called the "firstborn" son of God (Exod. 4:22). David says, "As a father pitieth his children, so the LORD pitieth them that fear him" (Ps. 103:13). Isaiah writes, "But now, O LORD, thou art our father" (Isa. 64:8). But in none of these passages does any individual Israelite address God directly as "my Father," and in most of them the main point is that Israel has not lived up to the family relationship. Thus, Jeremiah reports the Lord as saying, "I thought how I would set you among my sons, and give you a pleasant land, a heritage most beauteous of all nations. And I thought you would call me, My Father, and would not turn from following me. Surely, as a faithless wife leaves her husband, so have you been faithless to me, O house of Israel, says the LORD" (Jer. 3:19, 20, RSV).

Actually, in the time of Jesus the distance between men and God seemed to be widening, and the names of God were increasingly withheld from public speech and prayers.

This trend was completely overturned by Jesus. Jesus always called God "Father," and this fact must have impressed itself in an extraordinary way upon the disciples. Not only do all four gospels record that Jesus used this address, but they report that He did so in all His prayers (Matt. 11:25; 26:39, 42; Mark 14:36; Luke 23:34; John 11:41; 12:27; 17:1, 5, 11, 21, 24, 25). In fact, the only exception is one that enforces the significance of the phrase, for it is the cry from the cross: "My God, my God, why hast thou forsaken me?" That prayer was wrung from Christ's lips at the moment in which He was made sin for mankind and in which the relationship He had had with His Father was temporarily broken. At all other times Jesus boldly assumed a relationship to God that was never assumed by His contemporaries and which would have been thought highly irreverent or blasphemous by most.

This is of great significance for our prayers. Jesus was the Son of God in a unique sense, and God was uniquely His Father. He came to God in prayer as God's unique Son. But now He reveals that this same relationship can be true for those who have believed in Him and whose sins were soon to be removed by His suffering. They were to come to God as God's children. God was to be their own individual Father. Thus, Jesus could announce to Mary in triumph after His death and resurrection, "But go to my brethren, and say unto them, I ascend unto *my* Father and *your* Father, and to *my* God and *your* God" (John 20:17). Today it is as God's children that believers in the Lord Jesus Christ come to Him.

GOD'S CHILDREN

This first phrase of the Lord's Prayer, properly understood, cuts to pieces that false doctrine of the universal fatherhood of God that has been so popular in this century. According to the Bible, God is most certainly not the father of all men. He is uniquely the Father of the Lord Jesus Christ, and He becomes the Father only of those who believe on Christ and who are united to Him in faith through the Holy Spirit.

Jesus did not teach this only by implication. On one occasion He said it directly to those who thought they were God's children but who were, according to Jesus, actually children of the devil. In the eighth chapter of John we are told that Jesus had been teaching in Jerusalem and had made the statement, "And ye shall know the truth, and the truth shall make you free" (v. 32). The Jews answered Him, "We are Abraham's seed, and were never in bondage to any man. How sayest thou, Ye shall be made free?" (v. 33). "I know that ye are Abraham's seed," Jesus responded, "but ye seek to kill me . . . If ye were Abraham's children, ye would do the works of Abraham" (vv. 37, 39). At this point the people grew angry and accused Him of being illegitimate. In righteous anger the Lord replied, "If God were your Father, ye would love me; for I proceeded forth and came from God; neither came I of myself, but he sent me. Why do ye not understand my speech? Even because ye cannot hear my word. Ye are of your father the devil, and the lusts of your father ye will do" (vv. 42-44). Thus, He put to an end forever the misleading and totally devilish doctrine that God is the Father of all men and that all men are His children.

Let us submit to the Word of God, and let the truth of the Word sweep the mind clean of all such false ideas. There are two families and two fatherhoods in this world. There is the family of Adam, into which all men are born, and there is the family of God, into which some men are reborn by faith in the Lord Jesus Christ. These latter were once children of darkness; they are now children of light (Eph. 5:8). They were dead in trespasses and sins; they are now alive in Christ (Eph. 2:1). They were once children of wrath and disobedience; they are now children of love, faith, and obedience (Eph. 2:2, 3). These are God's children. These and only these can approach God as their Father.

ABBA, FATHER

We still have not seen everything there is to see about this word "Father," however, for when Jesus addressed God as Father He did not use the normal word for father. He used the Aramaic word *abba,* and *abba* means "daddy." Mark states this explicitly in his account of Christ's prayer in Gethsemane, *"Abba,* Father, all things are possible unto thee" (Mark 14:36). And Paul tells us clearly that the early Christians adopted the Lord's own mode of praying: "For ye have not received the spirit of bondage again to fear; but ye have received the Spirit of adoption, whereby we cry, *Abba,* Father" (Rom. 8:15). "Because ye are sons, God hath sent forth the Spirit of his Son into your hearts, crying, *Abba,* Father" (Gal. 4:6).

What does *abba* mean? Well, the early church fathers, Chrysostom, Theodor of Mopsuestia, and Theodoret of Cyrus, who came from Antioch (where Aramaic was spoken and who probably had Aramaic-speaking nurses) unanimously testify that *abba* was the address of a small child to his father. * And the Talmud confirms this when it says that when a child is weaned "it learns to say *abba* and *imma* (that is, 'daddy' and 'mother')" (*Berakoth* 40a; *Sanhedrin* 70b). To a Jewish mind a prayer addressing God as "daddy" would not only have been improper, it would have been irreverant to the highest degree. It was something quite new and unique when Jesus taught His disciples to call God "Daddy."

Do you know the God of the universe as your "daddy"? It is your privilege if you are a believer in the Lord Jesus Christ. I know there are times when you must come to Him sadly, like a child who has just broken the living-room window. But there are other times when you can come to Him snugly, as a child curls up on his father's lap at the end of the day. However you come, you can never change the relationship. He is yours. He is your daddy.

My Daddy

Is He my daddy? If He is, then He will help me in the days of my infancy. He will teach me to walk spiritually, picking me up when I fall down and directing my steps securely. That is why Hosea can report God as saying, "Yet it was I who taught Ephraim to walk, I took them up in my arms; . . . I led them with cords of compassion, with the bands of love. . . . I bent down to them and fed them. . . . How can I give you up, O Ephraim! How can I hand you over, O Israel! (Hos. 11:3, 4, 8, RSV). Surely such a God will keep me from falling and will present me faultless before the presence of His glory with exceeding joy (Jude 24).

Is He my daddy? If He is, then He will care for me throughout all the days of this life and bless my days abundantly. The laws of the United States recognize that a parent must care for his children. So does God. He has set down the rule that "the children ought not to lay up for the parents, but the parents for the

* Joachim Jeremias, *The Lord's Prayer,* trans. by John Reumann (Philadelphia: Fortress Press, 1964), p. 19.

children" (2 Cor. 12:14). And if this is true on the human level, it is also true of the relationship of a man or a woman to God. The Lord Jesus Christ said, "Be not anxious for your life, what ye shall eat, or what ye shall drink; nor yet for your body, what ye shall put on. Is not the life more than food and the body than raiment? . . . Consider the lilies of the field, how they grow; they toil not, neither do they spin, and yet I say unto ycu that even Solomon, in all his glory, was not arrayed like one of these. Wherefore, if God so clothe the grass of the field, which today is, and tomorrrow is cast into the oven, shall he not much more clothe you, O ye of little faith? Therefore, be not anxious saying, What shall we eat? or, What shall we drink? or, With what shall we be clothed? For after all these things do the Gentiles seek. For your heavenly Father knoweth that ye have need of all these things. But seek ye first the kingdom of God, and his righteousness, and all these things shall be added unto you" (Matt. 6:25, 28-33).

Is He my daddy? If He is, then He will go before me to show me the way through this life. That is why Paul can write, "Be ye, therefore, followers of God, as dear children" (Eph. 5:1).

Is He my daddy? If He is, then I shall know that I belong to Him forever; and I shall know that while I am being led, taught, and educated for life's tasks, nothing shall interfere with His purpose in Christ concerning me.

Chapter 27

The Names of God

(Matthew 6:9)

The opening words of the Lord's Prayer teach us who those are who can pray and what the privileges of access are for them. We say, "Our Father, who art in heaven," implying that God may be approached as a father by those (and only those) who have been reborn into His spiritual family. It is entirely possible, however, that a person may be a member of God's family and know this and yet know very little about praying. Consequently, six petitions follow, the purpose of each being to instruct us in general terms what we are to pray for and how we are to do it.

The petitions say, "Hallowed be thy name. Thy kingdom come. Thy will be done in earth, as it is in heaven. Give us this day our daily bread. And forgive us our debts, as we forgive our debtors. And lead us not into temptation, but deliver us from evil" (Matt. 6:9-13).

GOD'S DESIRES

The most important thing that can be said about these sentences is that the first three clearly are concerned with God's honor while the second three are concerned with man's interests and, moreover, that this is not coincidental. Andrew Murray says, "There is something here that strikes us at once. While we ordinarily first bring our own needs to God in prayer, and then think of what belongs to God and His interests, the Master reverses the order. First, *Thy* name, *Thy* kingdom, *Thy* will; then, give *us,* lead *us,* deliver *us.* The lesson is of more importance than we think. In true worship the Father must be first, must be all. The sooner I learn to forget myself in the desire that He may be glori-

198

fied, the richer will the blessing be that prayer will bring to myself. No one ever loses by what he sacrifices for the Father." *

Many people think of prayer as something that brings God into line with their own desires instead of something that brings them into line with His will. They learn that sometimes from the prayers of others, and they do it naturally themselves. As children, many persons were once taught to pray:

> *Now I lay me down to sleep;*
> *I pray the Lord my soul to keep;*
> *If I should die before I wake,*
> *I pray the Lord my soul to take.*

Thus, the idea that prayer consists of presenting a list of personal requests becomes entrenched early in their thinking.

As the person grows older the pattern repeats itself on a more sophisticated level. The person finds himself offering some small thing to God in return for the things that he wants from Him. It is the idea of a deal. Jacob did this the morning after he had run away from home to save his life and had seen the vision of a ladder extending up to heaven and of angels ascending and descending upon it. He was worried about his future at that point. So he prayed, "If God will be with me, and will keep me in this way that I go, and will give me bread to eat, and raiment to put on, so that I come again to my father's house in peace; then shall the LORD be my God: and this stone, which I have set for a pillar, shall be God's house: and of all that thou shalt give me I will surely give the tenth unto thee" (Gen. 28:20-22). How noble of Jacob!

Unfortunately, we often pray first for things (that might take us from God), for friends (that might compete for His friendship), or for an ordering of events (that might accomplish our plans, but not His). Instead, we must learn to begin our prayers with thoughts of God's honor and the advancement of His purposes in history.

HALLOWED BE THY NAME

The first of the six petitions in this prayer establishes the proper order, for it is a prayer for God's honor. It is "Hallowed be thy name." The word "hallowed" is a word that has lost much of its

* Andrew Murray, *With Christ in the School of Prayer* (Westwood, N.J.: Fleming H. Revell, 1967), p. 28.

meaning today simply because it has dropped out of common speech, but it is related etymologically to other words we do know. The Greek word translated here as "hallowed" is the word from which we also get our English word "holy." It is translated in other places as "saint" or "sanctify." Usually it refers to setting something apart for God's use. Objects that were used in the temple were holy or sanctified because they were set apart for God's use in the temple worship. Christians are called holy for the same reason.

I know of only one major text in the Bible in which the word is used of God. But this one text gives us the slightly different meaning of "hallowed" in the Lord's Prayer. 1 Peter 3:15 says, "But *sanctify* [that is the word] the Lord God in your hearts, and be ready always to give an answer to every man that asketh you a reason of the hope that is in you, with meekness and fear." Here Peter means, "Give God the place in your heart that He deserves."

It is the same in the Lord's Prayer, only here the scope of God's rule is much broader. In fact, it is as broad as the first of the Ten Commandments upon which it may be patterned. In Exodus 20:2 and 3, we read, "I am the LORD thy God, who have brought thee out of the land of Egypt, out of the house of bondage. Thou shalt have no other gods before me." In the same way, we are to pray, "Our Father, who art in heaven" (that corresponds to the words "I am the LORD thy God . . ."), "hallowed be thy name" (that corresponds to the command that there might be no other God before Him). If I were to rephrase this first part of the Lord's Prayer, I believe I would say, "My Father in heaven, my first desire is that in everything you might have pre-eminence."

GOD'S NAMES

All these thoughts naturally become more pointed when we move from the word "hallowed" to the word "name." For we can ask ourselves, "What is the name of God?" and "What does it mean to hallow it?" Actually, when we do this we soon find that there are many names of God — hundreds, in fact — and we learn that each describes some aspect of God's nature. When we "hallow the name" we are therefore honoring God in relation to some aspect of His character.

Let me put this in terms of a question. Do you hallow the name of God? For instance, do you honor Him in His name of

Elohim, the name that acknowledges God as Creator? It is the third word in the Bible, the name that heads the account of creation. We are told in that passage that "God [*Elohim*] created the heaven and the earth." He was responsible for the sun, moon, stars, and planets. He created the trees and the mountains, the flowers of the field and the plains. He formed all living things. He formed man of the dust of the earth and breathed into him the divine breath of life. Do you honor Him as the one and only Creator? The eighteenth century poet Isaac Watts was one who who did this. He wrote:

> *I sing the mighty power of God,*
> *That made the mountains rise,*
> *That spread the flowing seas abroad,*
> *And built the lofty skies.*
>
> *I sing the goodness of the Lord*
> *That filled the earth with food;*
> *He formed the creatures with His word,*
> *And then pronounced them good.*
>
> *Lord! how thy wonders are displayed*
> *Where're I turn mine eye!*
> *If I survey the ground I tread,*
> *Or gaze upon the sky.*
>
> *Creatures as numerous as we*
> *Are subject to Thy care;*
> *There's not a place where we can flee,*
> *But God is present there.*

When we pray "Hallowed be thy name," we ask that God might be honored as the Creator by ourselves and by others.

What about the related name *El Elyon?* This name means "God the Most High" and refers to Him in relation to His rule over the heavens and the earth. Do you honor God in that?

The name *El Elyon* occurs first in the Bible in the account of Abraham's meeting with Melchizedek, the king and high priest of Salem. Abraham was returning home after his battle with the kings of the plains and the deliverance of Lot. We read in the account, "And Melchizedek, king of Salem, brought forth bread and wine; and he was the priest of the most high God [*El Elyon*]. And he blessed him, and said, Blessed be Abram of the most high

God, possessor of heaven and earth" (Gen. 14:18, 19). This verse defines the title, for it refers to God's sovereign rule over His creation. Exactly the same meaning occurs in a great hymn of praise to God by Moses, in which Moses says, "Remember the days of old, consider the years of many generations. Ask thy father, and he will show thee; thy elders, and they will tell thee. When the Most High divided to the nations their inheritance, when he separated the sons of Adam, he set the bounds of the people according to the number of the children of Israel" (Deut. 32:7, 8).

We need to ask whether we honor God as ruler of heaven and earth. We do not honor Him as ruler of earth when we doubt His sovereignty in our lives and in the lives of others. We do not honor Him when we complain about the state of the world or ask how we are ever going to get through this week, this month, this year. We honor Him when we acknowledge Him as the one who does all things well, who cares for us, and who continually works (as the Westminster Shorter Catechism says) to preserve and govern all His creatures and all their actions.

Perhaps you have come to hallow God as *Elohim* and *El Elyon*. Well, then, what about His great name *Jehovah*, the name by which God reveals Himself as Redeemer? Do you know Him as the One who has redeemed you and who has saved you from sin?

A verse from the early chapters of Genesis makes this saving relationship clear. We read that God had determined to destroy the earth with a flood because of the great wickedness of men, but we also read that with equal determination He had planned to save Noah and his family within the great ark. God gave Noah the plans for the ark. As God the Creator, He told him to take into the ark two of every variety of animal. Then, as Jehovah the Redeemer, He also told him to take in seven of every clean animal, many of which would later be used as blood sacrifices for sin. The story continues, "And they that went in, went in male and female of all flesh, as God had commanded him: and the LORD [*Jehovah*] shut him in" (Gen. 7:16). Who saves? Jehovah saves. This is the meaning of the name "Jesus." It is Jehovah who promised redemption to the fallen Adam and Eve in the garden. It is Jehovah who spoke to Noah. Jehovah appeared to Abraham promising a redeemer through his seed. Jehovah even taught Abraham the new name *Jehovah Jireh,* which means "the

Lord will provide." All this we experience personally when we enter into Christ and are sealed into Him by God.

Do you know God as your Redeemer? Do you know Him as the One who came in Jesus Christ to die for you, to lift you out of slavery to your sins, to draw you back to Himself in love? You can never honor God properly until you honor Him in this great aspect of His character. In Jesus Christ, the Redeemer, we see the fullness of God's love.

How about the name *Adonai?* This name means "Lord." Is He your Lord? Is He the One to whom you give your highest allegiance? Is He the One who directs your life? You cannot hallow Him as Lord unless you do so practically.

What about that greatest name of all, the Lord Jesus Christ? In Him all other names are combined. In Him the characteristics of God are made manifest. One hymn writer has written:

> *O could I speak the matchless worth,*
> *O could I sound the glories forth*
>   *Which in my Savior shine,*
> *I'd soar and touch the heav'nly strings,*
> *And vie with Gabriel while he sings*
>   *In notes almost divine.*
>
> *I'd sing the characters He bears,*
> *And all the forms of love He wears,*
>   *Exalted on His throne:*
> *In loftiest songs of sweetest praise,*
> *I would to everlasting days*
>   *Make all His glories known.*

If we do that, then we shall be truly hallowing God, and we will be giving Him that place in our lives which He deserves.

None Like Him

Do these names and their content describe your own feelings toward God? They do not exhaust Him, but they remind us that there is none in the universe like Him. We have called Him *Elohim, El Elyon, Jehovah, Jehovah Jireh, Adonai,* the Lord Jesus Christ. But He is also the Father, the Son, and the Holy Spirit. He is Alpha and Omega, the beginning and the end. He is the Ancient of Days, seated upon the throne of heaven. He is the child of Bethlehem, lying in a manger. He is Jesus of Nazareth. His titles are Wonderful Counselor, the Mighty God, the Everlasting Father, the Prince of Peace. He is the righteous judge of the universe. He is our rock and our high tower.

What more can we say of our God? Can we say that He is the Way? Certainly, for He is the Way, the Truth, and the Life. He is the source of our life, the sustainer of life; He is life itself. He is the light of the world, the bread of life. He is the good shepherd, the great shepherd, the chief shepherd. He is the Lord of hosts. He is the King of kings. He is the faithful One. He is love. He is the God of Abraham, Isaac, and Jacob, of Moses, David, Isaiah, Elizabeth, Anna, Simeon, and John the Baptist. He is the God of Peter, James, John, Timothy, Apollos, and Paul. And He not only is their God, He is my God.

Is He your God? If so, you can raise your voice with those of all generations of the Christian Church and sing to His honor:

> *O for a thousand tongues to sing*
> *My great Redeemer's praise,*
> *The glories of my God and King,*
> *The triumphs of His grace!*
>
> *My gracious Master and my God,*
> *Assist me to proclaim,*
> *To spread through all the earth abroad*
> *The honors of Thy name.*
>
> *Hear Him, ye deaf; His praise, ye dumb,*
> *Your loosened tongues employ;*
> *Ye blind, behold your Savior come;*
> *And leap, ye lame, for joy.*

Chapter 28

Thy Kingdom Come

(Matthew 6:10)

The second petition of the Lord's Prayer is related to the first one, for it is a request that the kingdom of God might come. What is God's kingdom? This question is not so easily answered, for the views of Bible teachers and commentators often have differed greatly, and the Bible presents so many aspects of God's kingdom and presents them in so many lights that any short answer is incomplete and often misleading.

Some time ago in one of the question-and-answer periods connected with a series of talks I was giving, I was asked whether the kingdom of God as mentioned in the Bible was past, present, or future. The questioner had in mind the debate on that subject that had been going on in scholarly circles for some years, involving such names as T. W. Manson and C. H. Dodd of England, Rudolf Bultmann and Martin Dibelius of Germany, and Albert Schweitzer. I replied with a summary of that debate and then with the statement that the biblical viewpoint could not be expressed adequately even in those three terms. In one sense the kingdom certainly is past, for God always has ruled over men and history. But at the same time it also is present and future. God rules today and will continue to rule. The Lord Jesus Christ declared to the men of His day that "the kingdom of God is in the midst of you [meaning himself]" (Luke 17:21), but He also instructed His disciples to pray, "Thy kingdom come." In other words, the more one studies the statements in the Bible about the kingdom the more one feels that it transcends any of these temporal concepts.

205

The Kingdoms of Men

Perhaps the most important thing to be said about the kingdom of God is that it is *God's* kingdom. This means that it is exalted far above the kingdoms of men and is infinitely superior to them.

We look into the pages of history and see the kingdoms of this world rising and falling across the centuries. Historians tell us that the world has known twenty-one great civilizations, but all of them have endured only for a time and then have passed away. Egypt was once a mighty world power; today it is weak. It is unable to contend even with the tiny state of Israel. Babylon was mighty, but today it has passed into history and its former territory is divided. Syria, once strong, has become an archeological curiosity. Greece and Rome have fallen. Moreover, we know that even the United States of America and the Soviet Union, although now at the pinnacle of world power, will not be able to escape the inexorable law of God for history: "Righteousness exalteth a nation, but sin is a reproach to any people" (Prov. 14:34). Pride can bring each of them down also.

The normal course of the kingdoms of this world is described in a remarkable way by God in the Book of Daniel. Belshazzar, king of Babylon, had given a party, in the course of which he had defiled the vessels taken from the Temple of God at Jerusalem. In the midst of the party, handwriting had appeared on the wall of the palace, and Belshazzar became frightened. The writing said, "Mene, mene, tekel, upharsin," meaning "God hath numbered thy kingdom, and finished it; thou art weighed in the balances, and art found wanting; thy kingdom is divided, and given to the Medes and Persians" (Dan. 5:25-28). Daniel then said to the king, "The Most High God gave Nebuchadnezzar, thy father, a kingdom, and majesty, and glory, and honor. . . . But when his heart was lifted up, and his mind hardened in pride, he was deposed from his kingly throne, and they took his glory from him. And he was driven from the sons of men, and his heart was made like the beasts, and his dwelling was with the wild asses; they fed him with grass like oxen, and his body was wet with the dew of heaven, till he knew that the Most High God ruled in the kingdom of men, and that he appointeth over it whomsoever he will. And thou, his son, O Belshazzar, hast not humbled thine heart, though thou knewest all this" (Dan. 5:18, 20-22). That night, in accord with the writing, Belshazzar was killed, and Darius reigned in his place.

This is the course of all kingdoms of men. God allows a man or a group of men to rise above others in power. The triumph of the group brings pride, and God removes them, bringing them into the jaws of death. Men rise and fall, but over all the seething course of human history God reigns. God is sovereign over human history, even over those realms that are now in rebellion against Him. His kingdom prevails. This aspect of the expression "the kingdom of God" brings comfort to those who would otherwise be in turmoil or anxious about chaotic world events. Hence, Jesus told his disciples to be anxious for nothing (Matt. 6:25-34), and He added that although there would always be "wars and rumors of wars," nevertheless, His followers were not to be troubled by them (Matt. 24:6).

GOD'S KINGDOM ON EARTH

There is also an aspect of God's kingdom on earth by which He is seeking to bring into being a race of men obedient to Himself and in tune with His purposes in history. In one sense this had begun even in the Old Testament period, for the Word of God came through Nathan to David the king, saying, "The LORD telleth thee that he will make thee an house. And when thy days be fulfilled, and thou shalt sleep with thy fathers, I will set up thy seed after thee, which shall proceed out of thine own body, and I will establish his kingdom. . . . And thine house and thy kingdom shall be established forever before thee; thy throne shall be established forever" (2 Sam. 7:11, 12, 16). David immediately recognized that this could never come about by man's doing, and so gave God all the glory for it. Later, the promise to establish David's house was expanded and repeated, and the prophets looked forward to the time when the Lord Jesus Christ, Jehovah, would reign over the whole earth from Jerusalem (Isa. 24:23; Zech. 14:9, 16).

When the Lord Jesus Christ came to this earth and began His formal ministry, the kingdom of God came in another sense and was closer. In Christ it was among mankind. Thus, Jesus said, "The kingdom of God is in the midst of you." Now as His Spirit works in the lives of those who have been given Him by the Father, there is a sense in which the kingdom also comes in men. Thus Paul, who went about "preaching the kingdom of God," defines it in its internal aspects as "righteousness, and peace, and joy in the

Holy Spirit" (Rom. 14:17). This kingdom comes today whenever and wherever God's righteousness, peace, and joy transform a life and bring the fullness of spiritual blessing.

THE WHEAT AND THE TARES

Unfortunately, many teachers and churchmen have gone from the statements that I have just been making to the totally erroneous assumption that because the kingdom of God comes wherever men believe in Christ and respond to the Gospel, the kingdom in this sense will therefore inevitably go on expanding until all or nearly all the world believes.

This view was a very popular one in the nineteenth century, but it is totally false. It is false biblically, and history itself has destroyed it. Let me give you an example. Toward the end of the nineteenth century a man named Sidney L. Gulick wrote a book called *The Growth of the Kingdom of God* that was subsequently translated into Japanese in an attempt to persuade Japanese students to become Christians. The book was more restrained than some, but its argument was based on what the author believed to be the demonstrable success of the preaching of the kingdom of God in the growth of Christian influence in the world and the increase of church adherents.

He wrote, "The Christian powers have increased the territory under their rule from about seven percent of the surface of the world in 1600 to eighty-two percent in 1893, while the non-Christian powers have receded from about ninety-three percent to about eighteen percent during the same period. At present the Protestant nations alone rule about twice as much territory as all the non-Christian nations combined." He added, "During the [first] ninety years of the religious history of the United States more persons have come under the direct influence of the Christian Church than during the first thousand years of Christianity in all lands combined." * Needless to say, the Japanese were hardly convinced by this line of argument. And since the equation between the truth of religion and world dominion had been made so eloquently, the Japanese attack on Pearl Harbor and the resulting war in the Pacific was the natural result, rather than the conversion of their oriental country.

* Sidney L. Gulick, *The Growth of the Kingdom of God* (Chicago: Student Missionary Campaign Library, and New York: Fleming H. Revell, n.d.), pp. 28, 162, 164.

Today the harsh reality of two world wars, a cold war, and the acknowledged decline of the influence of the Christian religion in this country and elsewhere have taken the enthusiasm for this sort of reasoning out of everyone.

The surprising thing about this line of reasoning, however, is that it was followed in spite of the fact that the Lord Himself spoke in such warning tones against it. You say, "What do you mean? Didn't Jesus teach that His kingdom would go on expanding until it conquered the whole earth?" No, He did not! In fact, He taught almost the opposite. He taught that large portions of the world would never be converted, that the devil's children would be present in the Church until the end, that His rule would come in totality only at the close of time, and that even then it would be established only by His power and in spite of the continuing and bitter animosity of men.

You say, "Where did He teach that?" He taught it in a whole series of parables called the parables of the kingdom recorded for us in Matthew 13. There are seven parables in that chapter, beginning with the sower who went forth to sow and ending with the story of the dragnet. They are intended to preview the course of Church history.

The first parable is the parable of the sower. Jesus said that a man went out to sow seed. It happened that some of it fell on a hard surface where it was devoured by birds; some of it fell in shallow ground and sprang up quickly only to be scorched by the sun; some fell among thorns and was choked by them; some fell on good ground where it produced in some cases a hundred handfuls of grain for one handful, in others sixty for one, and in still others thirty for one. He then explained the parable, showing that the seed was the Word of His kingdom and that the Word was to have different effects in the lives of those who heard it. Some hearts would be so hard that they would not receive it at all, and the devil's cohorts would soon snatch it away. Others would receive it as a novelty, as did the men of Athens in Paul's day, but they would soon lose interest, particularly in the face of persecution. The third class would consist of those who allow the Word to be choked out by their delight in riches. Only the fourth class was to be made up of those who would hear the Gospel and in whom it would take root.

If this parable means anything at all, then, it means that the

Church age is to be a seed-sowing age in which only one part of the preaching of the kingdom of God will bear fruit. It is obvious that the parable does away with the idea that the preaching of the Gospel will be more and more effective and will inevitably bring a total triumph for the Church as time goes on.

The second parable that Jesus told makes this same point, but even more clearly. It is the story of the wheat and the tares. Jesus said that a man went out to sow grain in his field but that after he had done it an enemy came and sowed tares. The two plants grew up together, the one true wheat, the other a plant that looked like wheat but which was useless as food. In the story the servants wanted to pull up the tares, but the owner of the land told them that they were not to do this lest they uproot some of the wheat also. Instead, they were to let both grow together until the harvest, at which time the grain would be gathered into the barns and the tares would be burned.

When Jesus was alone with His disciples He explained that the field was the world, the wheat represented those who belonged to Him, and the tares represented the children of the devil. In other words, according to the Lord Jesus Christ, the Church would always contain within it those who were God's true children and those who were the imitation children of the devil. Moreover, since some of His children would look so much like those whom the devil counterfeited, no one was to try to separate the two on this earth lest some Christians should perish with the non-believers. The point of the parable is that these unsatisfactory conditions will remain until the end of this age.

All the other parables make similar points; that is, that the extension of the kingdom of God in this age always will be accompanied by the devil's influence and always will be imperfect. The parable of the mustard seed points to the abnormal growth of church structure. The parable of the leaven teaches that in this age the kingdom of heaven in one sense always will encompass evil. The stories of the field with treasure in it and the pearl of great price tell of the sacrifice that Christ made to win us for Himself. The final parable, the parable of the dragnet, points to the day in which the Son of God will judge all men. In that day the net will be pulled to shore, and those who have been made righteous through the death of the Lord Jesus Christ will be gathered to the Lord, while the bad will be put away from Him forever.

THE COMING KINGDOM

It should be evident from the imperfect nature of the kingdom of God, as we see it today, that there is yet to be a kingdom in which the rule of the Lord Jesus Christ will be totally recognized.

Christ Himself taught this. He not only told His disciples that there was to be a spiritual kingdom throughout the Church age; He also taught that there was to be a literal, future kingdom as well. In one parable He compared Himself to a nobleman who went into a far country to receive a kingdom and was then to come back. In the meantime, however, the nobleman left gifts in the hands of his servants, charging them to be faithful and to be ready to give a good accounting at his return (Luke 19:11-27). On another occasion, after the resurrection, the disciples asked Jesus, "Lord, wilt thou at this time restore again the kingdom to Israel?" (Acts 1:6). He answered, "It is not for you to know the times or the seasons, which the Father hath put in his own power [in other words, you are right about the fact of the kingdom; but it is none of your business to know when]. But ye shall receive power, after the Holy Spirit is come upon you; and ye shall be witnesses unto me both in Jerusalem, and in all Judaea, and in Samaria, and unto the uttermost part of the earth" (vv. 7, 8).

For us the work of the kingdom of God falls in the last of those great statements. We are His witnesses, and we are to bear the message of God's rule through Christ throughout our cities, states, nation, and world.

What is God doing in this age? God is calling out a people to Himself. He is taking persons of every imaginable condition and from every part of this globe — ethical leaders, politicians, clerks, judges, workmen, housewives, savages and sophisticates, persons like yourself — and He is turning them into men and women in whom Jesus Christ is present and in whom His winsome and righteous character can be seen. In this spiritual aspect the kingdom of God is the rule of Jesus Christ in the lives of those who have been spiritually reborn and who are being daily and increasingly transformed. Therefore, when we pray, "Thy kingdom come," we ask first that God's gracious rule may come in us, and second that it might come through us to others. Moreover, we take confidence in the fact that it will one day come fully in power in the personal rule of the Lord Jesus Christ at the end of history.

Chapter 29

Your Will or God's?

(Matthew 6:10)

The third petition of the Lord's prayer asks that the will of God might be done in earth as it is in heaven. This request is an important one, for the only things we can properly pray for as Christians are things which are in God's will. No Christian can pray, "Lord, I am about to commit adultery, and I want You to keep me from getting caught so I can get away with it." No Christian can pray, "Lord, make me smart enough to cheat my partner on this deal." No Christian can ask the Lord to help him lie convincingly. A Christian simply cannot pray this way. A Christian must always pray, "Thy will be done in my life as it is in heaven."

MANY WILLS

If we are to understand the fullness of what this statement means, we must begin by realizing that all the troubles that exist in this world exist because someone, or some group of people, wants man's will instead of the will of God. The Bible says, "As for God, his way is perfect" (2 Sam. 22:31; Ps. 18:30). Only God is perfect. Consequently, any way that is not God's way is imperfect; it is sinful, and thus it is contributory to the problems of this world.

I believe that this truth can be most clearly illustrated from the fall of Satan, from that act of the will by which Lucifer, the son of the morning, became the devil, the one who disrupts or destroys. The story is told in Isaiah 14:12-14: "How art thou fallen from heaven, O Lucifer, son of the morning! How art thou cut down to the ground, who didst weaken the nations! For thou hast said in thine heart, I will ascend into heaven, I will exalt my throne above the stars of God; I will sit also upon the mount of the congregation, in the sides of the north, I will ascend above the heights of the clouds, I will be like the Most High." In that short passage Satan says, "I will" five times. And the point of the passage is that this event marked the entrance into the universe of a second will, one in opposition to God's will, and that this beginning was the origin of sin.

Lucifer said, first, "I will ascend into heaven." This phrase teaches us that sin began on earth where Satan had been placed to do God's bidding and that Satan's first rebellious thought was to move into heaven and to take charge of its government. His second cry was, "I will exalt my throne above the stars of God." Since the word "stars" often is used in the Bible as a symbol for God's servants or messengers (Job 38:6, 7; Rev. 1:16, 20), this statement may well mean that Satan was determined to take a place above that of God's other creatures.

Third, Satan boasted that he would "sit also upon the mount of the congregation, in the sides of the north." This is not a reference to any earthly congregation of men, for men had not yet been created. This is the congregation of those angelic beings near to God of whom the Psalmist was writing when he said, "And the heavens shall praise thy wonders, O Lord; thy faithfulness also in the congregation of the saints. For who in the heavens can be compared unto the Lord? Who among the sons of the mighty can be likened unto the Lord? God is greatly to be feared in the assembly of the saints, and to be had in reverence of all those who are about him" (Ps. 89:5-7). In other terms, Satan also desired to rise above the angelic hosts that were closest to and surrounding God.

Satan's fourth cry was to "ascend above the clouds." These are the clouds of God's glory, the clouds that surround His person. From this point the fifth and final step was to displace God Himself. Hence, Satan declared in final arrogance, "I will be like the most High." Satan said, "I will ascend into heaven . . . I will exalt my throne . . . I will sit upon the mount of the congregation . . . I will ascend above the clouds . . . I will be like the Most High . . . I will . . . I will . . . I will . . . I will . . . I will." God answers, "Yet thou shalt be brought down to sheol, to the sides of the pit" (Isa. 14:15).

At this point it is proper to ask, "What did God do when He was faced with the emergence of this second, rebellious will in His universe?" Two courses were open to Him. He could have struck Satan down immediately, blotting him out, and then have created another even more beautiful creature to replace him. But if He had done that, He always would have been faced with the possibility of the emergence of an infinite series of similar rebellions, followed by similarly harsh judgments and new creations. He could have done this, but instead He chose a second way. Instead of condemning Satan instantly, God withheld His judgment and stepped aside a bit in order to allow the rebel to try every ounce of his own wisdom and every possible course of action open to him so that it might be demonstrated through the course of what we call history that nothing good will ever come of any will that is in opposition to God's.

This is precisely what we find in history. When Satan rebelled, the cohesion of the universe was broken. First there were two wills, one perfect and one corrupt. Then there were four wills, one perfect and three corrupt. This was followed by eight wills, one perfect and seven corrupt. And the multiplication went on until today there are billions of wills — including yours and mine — and every one but God's is corrupt and the source of unending sins and rebellions. Rebellion against God's will leads not to joy and happiness but to misery. It proves that there is no life, joy, peace, happiness, or any other good thing apart from a complete dependence upon God and a willing submission to Him.

RENEWED FROM WITHIN

Someone will say, "That is all very well and good; but what does that have to do with me?" Well, it has everything to do with you, for happiness and joy will come to your life only as you allow God to bend your will to His.

In our last study I asked the question, "What is God doing in this age?" The answer was that God is taking persons of every imaginable condition and from every part of this globe and turning them into men and women like Jesus Christ, into men and women in whom God's kingdom comes. In the light of our present discussion we can see that it also would be possible to say that God is taking persons with sinful and rebellious wills from every imaginable condition of life and from every part of this globe and then — by means of the new life which He gives them freely through the Holy Spirit — bringing their wills into perfect conformity to His own. Such persons are learning to will as God wills, and the day will come when they will be able to say, as Jesus did, "I do always those things that please him" (John 8:29). Now they pray, "Thy will be done in earth, as it is in heaven."

GOD'S WORD

What is God's will? That is the next valid question. For someone will say, "I agree that I should want God's will, and to some degree — thanks to His new life within — I do want it. However, what is God's will? How can I, a sinful person, know what a holy and righteous God requires?" There is only one answer: We may know the will of God by coming to know the Word of God, and we know the Word of God only as we study it and the Holy Spirit throws His divine light upon its pages.

In his excellent study on prayer Andrew Murray writes: "The great mistake here is that God's children do not really believe that it is possible to know God's will. Or if they believe this, they do not take the time and trouble to find it out. What we need is to see clearly in what way it is that the Father leads His waiting, teachable child to know that his petition is according to His will. It is through God's holy word, taken up and kept in the heart. . . . " *

In the Bible God's will is expressed in great principles. Take John 6:40 as an example. I believe that this verse can be called the will of God for all unbelievers. It says, "And this is the will of him that sent me [that is, God the Father], that everyone who seeth the Son, and believeth on him, may have everlasting life; and I will raise him up at the last day." If you are not a Christian, God's will for you begins here. In one sense God's entire will for you is wrapped up in the life and ministry of the Lord Jesus Christ, and God will not take you on to other things until you believe in Him. He will not teach you spiritual calculus until you have mastered rudimentary math.

Another great verse that also speaks explicitly of the will of God is Romans 12:1, 2. It is an expression of God's will for a Christian. "I beseech you therefore, brethren, by the mercies of God, that ye present your bodies a living sacrifice, holy, acceptable unto God, which is your reasonable service. And be not conformed to this world, but be ye transformed by the renewing of your mind, that ye may prove what is that good, and acceptable, and perfect, will of God." Any Christian can accept as an unchangeable prin-

* Andrew Murray, *With Christ in the School of Prayer* (Westwood, N.J.: Fleming H. Revell, 1967), p. 163.

ciple the truth that anything that contributes to his growth in holiness and the surrender or renewal of his mind is an aspect of God's will for him and that anything that hinders his growth in holiness is not.

A Christian also may claim any of God's promises, for they are certainly God's will for his life and the lives of all others. James 1:5 says, "If any of you lack wisdom, let him ask of God, who giveth to all men liberally, and upbraideth not, and it shall be given him." So if you go to God as a believer in the Lord Jesus Christ and ask for wisdom, you can be absolutely certain that you are praying in God's will and that your prayer will be answered. Here is another, "Be anxious for nothing, but in everything, by prayer and supplication with thanksgiving, let your requests be made known unto God. And the peace of God, which passeth all understanding, shall keep your hearts and minds through Christ Jesus" (Phil. 4:6, 7). In other words, God wills that you have peace even in the midst of life's calamities, and He promises to impart it to you if you will lay your request before Him.

Are you saying, "But, none of these verses covers the little things in life, the things with which I am wrestling"? Well, let me give you a verse for those. In Philippians 4:8 we read, "Finally, brethren, whatever things are true, . . . whatever things are lovely, whatever things are of good report; if there be any virtue, and if there be any praise, think on these things." The verse means quite simply that you are to pursue the best things that life has to offer. If they are the best things for you, then do them. If not, do something else. Just be sure that you get your understanding of the will of God from Scripture.

If you will do that, then you will be able to pray to God with absolute confidence, and you can know and rejoice in the fact that your will is being increasingly conformed to His. John the evangelist wrote to the believers of his day: "And this is the confidence that we have in him, that, if we ask any thing according to his will, he heareth us; and if we know that he hear us, whatever we ask, we know that we have the petitions that we desired of him" (1 John 5:14, 15).

"IF IT BE THY WILL"

To be faithful to this text, however, I must also say that there are Christians who use the idea of God's will in a way that is entirely antithetical to everything that I have been saying. There are

Christians who make a great show about praying according to God's will but who, in spite of their words, are actually using the idea to save face. By this I mean that they pray with so little assurance that God will ever answer their prayers that they constantly add "if it be Thy will" to each of them, as if to say to each other and to themselves that they already know in advance that the thing they are asking for will not happen. Many of these Christians are astonished when God actually does answer some prayer.

Let me give you an example of this type of praying from the early days of the Christian Church, when Herod Antipas was the reigning king in Palestine. Under his rule Peter was imprisoned in Jerusalem, and the Christians were worried. Peter had been imprisoned before and released. But Herod had just killed James, the brother of John, and there was every reason to think that he would execute Peter also. The Christians began to pray. They were praying in one part of Jerusalem — at the house of Mary, the mother of John Mark — but as they were praying God was already at work in another part of the city releasing Peter from prison (cf. Acts 12:5-10).

We do not know what the Christians were saying. They may have been praying that God would comfort Peter, that God would stay the hand of Herod, or (which is more likely) that God would deliver the aged apostle from the prison. But I am sure they were praying, "if it be Thy will," for they were not expecting God's answer. As they prayed Peter came to the door of the house and knocked. A maid named Rhoda went to see who was there. She was so astonished that she returned to the praying group without even letting Peter in. When the ones who were praying were told that it was Peter, they simply would not believe it. They said, "You are mad." The story continues, "But she constantly affirmed that it was even so. Then said they, It is his angel. But Peter continued knocking; and when they had opened the door, and saw him, they were astonished. But he, beckoning unto them with the hand to hold their peace, declared unto them how the Lord had brought him out of the prison" (Acts 12:15-17).

How many of our prayers are like that! In many of our churches prayer has become a form or a duty, and Christians pray without any sure expectancy of God's answer. The prayer meeting has been removed from the week's events or is ill attended, and the leaders think they can arrange God's blessing without asking for it. Jesus phrased this prayer as He did to teach us that we are to live and pray so much in the sphere of God's name, God's kingdom, and God's glory that we may be bold in saying, "Thy will be done." And we may ask in confidence that God's will may be done in our lives and in our churches.

It was a sense of being in the center of God's will that gave Luther his great boldness in prayer. In 1540, Luther's great friend and assistant, Frederick Myconius, became sick and was expected to die within a short time. On his bed he wrote a loving farewell note to Luther with a trembling hand. Luther received the letter and instantly sent back a reply: "I command thee in the name of God to live because I still have need of thee in the work of reforming the church . . . The Lord will never let me hear that thou art dead, but will permit thee to survive me. For this I am praying, this is my will, and may my will be done, because I seek only to glorify the name of God." The words are almost shocking to us, as we live in a more sensitive and cautious day, but they were certainly from God. For although Myconius had already lost the ability to speak when Luther's letter came, in a short time he revived. He recovered completely, and he lived six more years to survive Luther himself by two months.

We are never so bold in prayer as when we can look into the face of God and say, "My Father, I do not pray for myself in this thing and I do not want my will done. I want Thy name to be glorified. Glorify it now in my situation, in my life, and do it in such a way that all men will know it is of Thee."

Chapter 30

What To Pray For

(Matthew 6:11)

One of the first great lessons that a Christian must learn about prayer is to put God's interests first. But after that there comes the area of our own interests — our work, families, homes, friends, finances, and other things. These are also important, and not only to us. What about these interests? Are we also to pray about them? The Bible says, "Yes." Moreover, it teaches us that we are to pray again and again for each one.

In the prayer which we have been studying Jesus taught His disciples to begin to pray for *God's* name, *God's* kingdom, and *God's* will — "Hallowed be thy name, thy kingdom come, thy will be done" — but having prayed for these things and thus having established a correct set of priorities they were then to pray for human interests also. The last petitions say, "Give us this day our daily bread. And forgive us our debts, as we forgive our debtors. And lead us not into temptation, but deliver us from evil." These are requests for physical needs, forgiveness of sins, and spiritual victories. The prayer ends with a new acknowledgment of God's glory.

These three petitions cover all our physical and spiritual needs. On this point Dr. D. Martyn Lloyd-Jones has accurately written, "Our whole life is found there in those three petitions, and that is what makes this prayer so utterly amazing. In such a small compass our Lord has covered the whole life of the believer in every respect. Our physical needs, our mental needs and, of course, our spiritual needs are included. The body is remembered, the soul is remembered, the spirit is remembered. And that is the whole of man." *

* D. Martyn Lloyd-Jones, *Studies in the Sermon on the Mount* (Grand Rapids: Wm. B. Eerdmans, 1967), Vol. II, pp. 67, 68.

Our Willing God

The first request deals with our physical needs, for the phrase "our daily bread" includes by implication all the needs of life. It is a prayer for food and clothing, a home, a good job, and many other physical necessities. At the same time it should be evident that it does not encourage us to pray for superfluities. Philippians 4:19 says that God "shall supply all your *need* according to his riches in glory by Christ Jesus," but it does not say that God shall supply all your *wants*. God gives many of us the obvious luxuries of life, sometimes, so it seems, to our spiritual hurt. But we are nowhere told to ask for these things. We are told to ask only for necessities.

The basis of our asking for life's necessities is found in God's avowed purpose to give us what we ask for. A master cares for the needs of his servants. A general meets the needs of his soldiers. A father provides for the needs of his sons. Each is willing. In the same way, our Father cares for those who have become His children through faith in the Lord Jesus Christ.

If you are saying, as some people do, "But how can I know that God is willing to answer my requests for life's necessities?" the answer is that Jesus taught that God was willing. In fact, He taught it in the next chapter of the Sermon on the Mount in a passage that is actually the best possible commentary on this petition in the Lord's Prayer. Jesus said, "Ask, and it shall be given you; seek, and ye shall find; knock, and it shall be opened unto you; for every one that asketh receiveth; and he that seeketh findeth; and to him that knocketh it shall be opened. Or what man is there of you whom, if his son ask bread, will he give him a stone? Or if he ask a fish, will he give him a serpent? If ye then, being evil, know how to give good gifts unto your children, how much more shall your Father, who is in heaven, give good things to them that ask him?" (Matt. 7:7-11).

This passage says three things about prayer. First, we must be God's children before we can come to God. Second, as God's children we are invited and even urged to come. And third, God delights to answer those who do come. When we come to God in prayer through the Lord Jesus Christ and in His Holy Spirit, we do not come as God's enemies. We come as God's children and therefore as close members of His family. There are many things that an earthly father would not do for a stranger. There are many more things that he would not do for an enemy. But there is almost nothing that he would not do for one of his beloved sons or daughters. In the same way, we come to a God who is not distant, harsh, stingy, or begrudging in His gifts. We come to a God who is loving, willing, and merciful, and who is anxious to be known and loved by His children. This God urges us to come.

Moreover, He urges us to come regularly and repeatedly, for the prayer says, "Give us *this day* our *daily* bread." The idea of regular and repeated prayer is suggested twice (once by the words "this day" and once by the adjective "daily"), and anything repeated twice in an abbreviated prayer of only sixty-five words (seventy-two in Greek) is important.

For many years commentators and linguists did not know the exact meaning of the Greek word translated "daily" *(epiousios)*, and even today, there is still some doubt. This was because the word did not occur in either literary or popular Greek, and, therefore, because there was no means to check it, several interpretations seemed possible. Now, however, the word has been found again in a papyrus from upper Egypt which seems to reveal its meaning. The manuscript is part of an account book, and the relevant inscription reads: "½ obol for *epious* —." At this point the writing is broken off, but there is little doubt that the last word is the one that occurs in the Lord's Prayer and that it refers to what we would call a daily ration. Probably the phrase belonged to a shopping list and is therefore a reminder to someone to buy supplies for the coming day.

This meaning is supported by a seemingly parallel inscription in Latin found at Pompeii which contains as part of a list of expenditures the words "five asses for *diaria* [a term based on the Latin word for day]." Since both of these expressions would seem to be pointing to items that were part of a day's ration for a person or a group of persons it would be natural to take the word *epiousios* in this sense. In this case, the fourth petition in the Lord's Prayer would be a request that God grant us daily our daily ration of life's necessities.

Our Daily Bread

When we see that this prayer is a simple prayer for the things which we have need of every day and that God invites this type of praying, certain great truths emerge from it.

First, it shows that God cares for our bodies. There always have been some in the Christian Church who have tried to minimize the body in the belief that only the soul or the spirit is important. Sometimes this type of religion has taken the form of asceticism or celibacy. At other times there has been outright abuse of the body. None of this is biblical, and it is contradicted by the whole tenor of the Bible as well as by explicit teaching. Jesus showed us that. William Barclay notes that Jesus spent "much time healing men's diseases and satisfying their physical hunger. He was anxious when He thought that the crowd who had followed Him out into the lonely places had a long road home, and no food to eat before they set out upon it. . . . We can see what God thinks of our human bodies, when we remember that He Himself in Jesus Christ took that body upon Him. It is not simply a *soul* salvation, it is *whole* salvation, the salvation of body, mind and spirit, at which Christianity aims." *

Second, this part of the prayer also teaches that if we live as God intends us to live we are to live one day at a time. That is, we are not to be anxious about the unknown future or to fret about it. We are to live in a moment-by-moment dependence upon God.

I am convinced that the meaning of this request must vary slightly from one culture and society to another. Basically, it means that we are not to take thought for tomorrow, but to ask God only for what we need for today. But this has a different meaning in a society in which the needs of the future are met through the family structure and a society in which the needs of the future are met through financial planning and saving. In our society it would be wrong for a father to neglect to save for his children's education, his own retirement, and old age on the grounds that he should ask only for one day's ration at a time. In our society part of this day's ration consists of the money to be laid aside for the next. Consequently, we are not to neglect our families by neglecting insurance policies, pension plans, or saving accounts. To do that would be to misinterpret Christ's teaching. At the same time, however, we are obviously not to become entirely wrapped up in these things as if our life and our future depended ultimately on them. Instead, we are to wrap ourselves in our confidence in God.

If you are a Christian, have you ever known God to be unfaith-

* William Barclay, *The Gospel of Matthew* (Philadelphia: The Westminster Press, 1958), Vol. I, p. 218.

ful to you? Have you lacked the necessities of life? I know that there are times when God does deprive us of things — sometimes to teach us something and at times merely to bring forth praise to Himself. We often are lacking in things we believe to be necessary but which are not. And yet, it is not the rule for God to permit His children to suffer great want. Is God faithful? Of course, He is faithful. Hence, you can trust Him both for your todays and your tomorrows.

SPIRITUAL NECESSITIES

We must not leave this request for our daily bread without pointing out that we need spiritual nourishment also. This is the third point. We need to feed spiritually on God.

Have you ever noticed that there is only one other place in the entire Bible where a request to "give us bread" is spoken? It is in the midst of Christ's sermon on the spiritual bread recorded in John 6. Jesus had said to His hearers, "Moses gave you not that bread from heaven; but my Father giveth you the true bread from heaven." They had answered, "Lord, evermore give us this bread." Jesus said, "I am the bread of life; he that cometh to me shall never hunger, and he that believeth on me shall never thirst" (John 6: 32-35). The Jews were thinking of physical bread, no doubt, just as the woman of Samaria had been thinking of physical water. But Jesus turned them away from these physical things to Himself as the One who could satisfy the far greater hunger of the soul.

What does it mean to feed spiritually on the Lord Jesus Christ? It means quite simply that He is the source of all spiritual life and that we will grow spiritually only as we draw close to Him and learn about Him. Moreover, unless we do this we inevitably will be starved spiritually and feel spiritually hungry.

It is tragic that so many Christians will allow things to intrude between themselves and Jesus and, therefore, go on being hungry. God says that this happened repeatedly during the Old Testament period, for the Bible says that the people of Israel desired "things" instead of Him. Consequently, He gave them "things" but sent leanness to their souls (Ps. 106:15). We do the same today. Far too many believers find themselves like those described in one of our hymns — "rich in things, but poor in soul." Have you known such leanness, such hunger? Perhaps you have filled yourself with all the means of satisfying your physical hunger, and yet you have not looked to God for spiritual feeding. You pray, "Give me my physical bread," but you have never prayed, "Give me that spiritual bread that comes down from heaven." All our hungers are useful in themselves, of course. They are right within their bounds. They have been put there by God, who made us. We have a hunger for achievement, for love, for happiness. All these things are good in themselves when they are used as God intends them to be used. But it is tragic that many Christians will satisfy these hungers, or attempt to satisfy them, at the expense of spending much necessary and truly satisfying time with God.

DISPENSING HIS FRAGRANCE

We have seen in John 6 that Jesus is the source and sustainer of life. But we must add to this that Jesus will fill us with abundance of spiritual life only as we give some of what we have received to others. We come to Christ for filling, but we must share some of what we have received if we are to receive more from His hands.

Our lives as Christians are like a bottle of rich perfume. The fragrance is Christ, and we are called to dispense His fragrance in the world. We cannot do it if the bottle is sealed or if the top is left on. But if we dispense it, if we break the seal, we shall find, not only that others will come to a knowledge of Jesus Christ through us, but also that Jesus will constantly refill us to overflowing by the same miraculous power that multiplied the loaves in Galilee or the wine at the feast of Cana.

Perhaps you are one for whom this word is particularly relevant. You have been raised in a church in which you have been amply fed with spiritual things or in a home blessed by Christian parents. You have been taught in the Word, but you have failed to share what you have learned. If so, that must be corrected. You must share your experience of Jesus. Suppose you do not. In that case there will come a moment when you will be full and unable to absorb any more. Then you will go on year after year knowing only the same things, believing only the same things, reliving the same old spiritual lessons, and you will be unable to advance in the Christian faith.

Perhaps God would have you to be a witness right where you are at this moment. Perhaps there is work for you to do that you have thought about but have put off, an opportunity to speak to a new family in the neighborhood and make them welcome, to befriend some poor secretary at work, to start a Bible class in your home, or some other such thing. If God has been leading you to do this, you must respond to His leading, for you will find that only as you share the fragrance of Christ in your life will God fill you again and again. Only then will you inevitably learn more about Him.

PRAYING FOR OTHERS

All this actually leads us back to the precise wording of the Lord's Prayer, for the final lesson is that we are always to pray also for others. Have you noticed that each of these last three requests — the requests for life's necessities, for forgiveness, for deliverance from Satan's temptations — are not given to us in the singular ("I" or "me") but in the plural ("we," "us," and "our")? What does this mean? Simply this: that we are not to pray selfishly; we are to pray collectively for ourselves along with others — "Give *us* this day *our* daily bread. And forgive *us our* debts, as we forgive *our* debtors. And lead *us* not into temptation, but deliver *us* from evil."

The next time you pray, stop right in the middle of your prayer and think whether you have prayed selfishly. You may not have, but it is likely, for many of us do. If you have, learn that you are to ask God to provide for others (as He has provided for you), to forgive others (as He has forgiven you), to deliver others from temptation (as He has delivered you). In that way you shall intercede for others. You shall be led to give to others. And you shall enter more fully into the mind of Jesus who prayed thus for all His followers.

Chapter 31

Forgiveness Guaranteed

(Matthew 6:12, 14, 15)

Once, as I was talking to a Christian psychiatrist, I touched on the problem of forgiveness and the need men have for it. The psychiatrist said, "As far as I am concerned most of what a psychiatrist does is directly related to forgiveness. People come to him with problems. They feel guilty about their part in these problems. They are seeking forgiveness. In effect, they confess their sins to the counselor and find that he forgives them. Then a pattern is set up in which they can show their change of heart in tangible ways toward the other person or persons." The psychiatrist concluded by observing that the great need to be forgiven by men that many persons feel is only a shadow of a far greater need that all men have to be forgiven by God.

It is true. In his book *Confess Your Sins* Dr. John R. W. Stott, minister of All Souls Church in London, quotes the head of a large English mental hospital as having said, "I could dismiss half my patients tomorrow if they could be assured of forgiveness." He cites the Scottish churchman George MacLeod as having written, "We live in a world where literally thousands of church members [not to mention others] are in need of . . . release. . . . We live . . . in a vacuum where men simply are not freed." * None of these statements is in the least exaggerated. For in our day, as in all ages of man, people are crying out for real forgiveness and an assurance of it.

TYPES OF FORGIVENESS

It is this, of course, that makes the second area of requests in the Lord's Prayer so important. It concerns forgiveness. However, if we are to understand this request accurately, we must realize that it is speaking of forgiveness in one sense only — the forgiveness that is given after justification of a disobedient child of God. And we must realize that before this forgiveness is possible it must be

* John R. W. Stott, *Confess Your Sins* (Philadelphia: The Westminster Press, 1964), p. 73.

226

preceded by another type of forgiveness by which one becomes a member of God's family in the first place.

The request given here is certainly not a prayer for forgiveness in the same sense that we ask for forgiveness when we first believe on the Lord Jesus Christ for salvation. That request involves the acceptance of Christ's death as the one sufficient sacrifice for our sin — past, present, and future — and it is something that is done once for all. If the fifth petition in the Lord's Prayer is referring to this initial forgiveness, then we can have no real security before God. We cannot say, as Paul does, that "he who hath begun a good work in you will perform it until the day of Jesus Christ" (Phil. 1:6). We cannot say with Jeremiah that God will "remember our sin no more" (Jer. 31:34). We cannot say, "As far as the east is from the west, so far hath he removed our transgressions from us" (Ps. 103:12). All these verses would be meaningless if that kind of forgiveness is meant.

No, the Lord is not speaking of the forgiveness we receive in the first moment of our salvation. He is speaking of forgiveness that comes later, that comes repeatedly, a forgiveness that restores a broken relationship with God.

FORGIVENESS FOR BELIEVERS

Most Christians will immediately see the need for a distinction between the two types of forgiveness. But, unfortunately, there are Christians who feel that sin can be eradicated in the Christian during this life; and since they generally apply this to themselves, they therefore come to believe erroneously that they no longer need this forgiveness. That is wrong, of course, and the fact that the Lord Jesus Christ directed all His disciples to seek forgiveness refutes it.

We need to get one great principle straight. When a sinful human being becomes a Christian he does not cease to be a sinner any more than he ceases to be a human being. Oh, he has a new nature planted within him by God. The new nature does not sin. The new nature will constantly lead him along the paths of holiness if he will yield to it. But the Christian also has a sinful, fallen nature that he will never eradicate in this life. This old nature will get him into trouble again and again, and every time it breaks out he will find that it also breaks the fullness of his fellowship with God. What is the Christian to do in these circumstances? The Bible teaches that he is to return to the Lord again and again to confess his sin and to ask for forgiveness and cleansing. If he neglects to do this, he will lose all the joy of salvation. If he asks for forgiveness, he will enter increasingly into the joy of a deepening fellowship with God.

Moreover, this will involve our attitude toward others. For we shall not experience the fullness of God's forgiveness toward us, according to Jesus, unless we extend the same forgiveness to those who have wronged us. Thus, Christ says, "For if ye forgive men their trespasses, your heavenly Father will also forgive you; but if ye forgive not men their trespasses, neither will your Father forgive your trespasses" (Matt. 6:14, 15).

Why is this so? Well, it is not because God waits for us to earn His forgiveness by forgiving others; we can never earn any of God's favors. It is simply because we cannot truly ask for forgiveness unless our heart is right regarding other people. God does not work by halves. He will not allow us to come to Him confessing half a sin while hanging onto the other half. It must be all or nothing. Thus, if we confess our sin, that confession must of necessity involve a forgiving attitude toward others. Dr. Harry Ironside, in his commentary on Matthew writes correctly: "In the government of God as Father over His own children our forgiveness of daily offenses depends upon our attitude toward those who offend against us. If we refuse to forgive our erring brethren, God will not grant us that restorative forgiveness for which we plead when conscious of sin and failure. This, of course, has nothing to do with that eternal forgiveness which the believing sinner receives when he comes to Christ. It is the Father's forgiveness of an erring child, which must of necessity take into account the attitude of the failed one toward other members of the family." *

Jesus tells us to pray, "Forgive us our debts, as we forgive our debtors." And this certainly means, among other things, that we are to pattern the scope of our own forgiveness upon God's.

Assurance

We cannot go on to consider other parts of the Lord's Prayer without pausing to see one other great truth about this matter of forgiveness. When a person comes to God through Jesus Christ confessing his sin and seeking forgiveness, he need not be uncertain of the outcome. Instead, he can be absolutely certain that God will provide the forgiveness which he asks for.

* H. A. Ironside, *Matthew* (Neptune, N.J.: Loizeaux Brothers, 1948), p. 65.

You may be saying, "How can I be sure of that?" In the only way that we can be sure of anything else of a spiritual nature. How can we be sure that the death of the Lord Jesus Christ was the one sufficient sacrifice for our sins? Because God says so. He says, "For by one offering he hath perfected forever them that are sanctified" (Heb. 10:14). How can we be certain that once we have believed on Jesus Christ we will never be lost? Because God says so. Jesus said, "My sheep hear my voice, and I know them, and they follow me. And I give unto them eternal life; and they shall never perish, neither shall any man pluck them out of my hand" (John 10:27, 28). How can we be certain that God will forgive our sin when we come to Him to confess it? It is the same answer: Because God says so. Thus, we read in 1 John 1:9, "If we confess our sins, he is faithful and just to forgive us our sins, and to cleanse us from all unrighteousness."

There cannot be a greater promise than that, that we can be absolutely certain of the forgiveness of sins and that we can be certain because the forgiveness is based upon the faithfulness and justice of God. To what is God faithful? To His promises. God has promised to forgive, and He does not break His word. What is more, He is just in His forgiveness. The Lord Jesus Christ has paid the full price for our sin. On the basis of that fact, the justice of God necessarily requires Him to grant us full forgiveness. Full forgiveness! It is a wonderful truth, for it means that God has made provision in advance for our daily and sometimes hourly cleansing from sin and that His faithfulness and justice stand behind these promises.

Forgiveness in Advance

Furthermore, God has assured us in advance of this full forgiveness. Why has He done so? Is it not precisely to keep us from sinning? Certainly it is. For no sooner has John written, "If we confess our sins, he is faithful and just to forgive us our sins, and to cleanse us from all unrighteousness" (1 John 1:9), then he goes on to say, "My little children, these things write I unto you, that ye sin not" (1 John 2:1). In other words, God says that the truth that will most keep us from sinning is the promise that we will be forgiven by God even if we do.

Many years ago an incident occurred in the life of Dr. Donald Grey Barnhouse that is the perfect illustration of this truth. Dr. Barnhouse had been holding a series of meetings on a college campus and had been approached by one of the young professors at the close of a meeting. He had a sad story to tell. During the war, before he had become a Christian, he had fallen in with bad companions and while in Paris had lived a life of great sin. Now he had returned home, become a Christian, and had fallen in love with a fine Christian girl who also loved him. However, he hesitated to tell her of his love because he feared that his proclivities toward sin might cause him to sin again and thus wound the heart of the girl he now loved. What should he do? He stated his problem and waited for an answer.

Dr. Barnhouse prayed silently for a moment and then, after he had assured himself that the young man was a believer, advised him to share the story of his past life with the girl. If they were to live their lives together, said Dr. Barnhouse, there should be no barriers between them. Furthermore, he argued, her knowledge of his weakness would help him at every turn of the road.

Dr. Barnhouse then began to tell a story of two other people who had found themselves in a similar set of circumstances. The man had lived a life of great sin but had been converted, and eventually had come to marry a fine Christian woman. He had confided to her the nature of his past life in a few words. As he had told her these things, the wife had taken his head in her hands and had drawn him to her shoulder and had kissed him, saying, "John, I want you to understand something very plainly. I know my Bible well, and therefore I know the subtlety of sin and the devices of sin working in the human heart. I know you are a thoroughly converted man, John, but I know that you still have an old nature, and that you are not yet as fully instructed in the ways of God as you soon will be. The devil will do all he can to wreck your Christian life, and he will see to it that temptations of every kind will be put in your way. The day might come — please God that it never shall — when you will succumb to temptation and fall into sin. Immediately the devil will tell you that it is no use trying, that you might as well continue on in the way of sin, and that above all you are not to tell me because it will hurt me. But John, I want you to know that here in my arms is your home. When I married you I married your old nature as well as your new nature, and I want you to know there is full pardon and forgiveness in advance for any evil that may ever come into your life."

As Dr. Barnhouse was telling this story to the college professor, the young man lifted his eyes and said reverently, "My God! If anything could ever keep a man straight, that would be it." *

God has given you full provision in advance for every sin that may ever come into your life, and He has done this precisely that you might be kept from sinning. Do not forget that there is nothing in you that can ever astonish God or take Him by surprise. He knows what you are. Moreover, He has recommended His love to you on the basis of the fact that it was while you were yet a sinner Christ died for you (Rom. 5:8).

DEBTORS

There is just one other point that comes to us from this great text in Matthew; it comes from the word "debts." In this context the word refers to our sin, and the verse is a prayer for forgiveness. In this sense, by means of confession and God's forgiveness, we cease to become debtors to sin.

After we have come confessing our sin and receiving forgiveness, however, we become debtors in another sense, the same sense that occurs in Romans 1:14, 15, where Paul says, "I am debtor both to the Greeks and to the barbarians; both to the wise and to the unwise. So, as much as in me is, I am ready to preach the gospel to you that are at Rome also." This is a debt on two levels. First, we become debtors to God. We were nothing before Him. We were going our own way. We were serving ourselves. We were not even understanding or "did not even understand" spiritual things. But God came to us first in Christ Jesus to redeem us from sin and then in the Holy Spirit to open our eyes to His truth and to lead us in His way. Because of these things we are debtors to God to serve Him with all our heart and soul and mind and to carry out His purposes in this life.

But we are also debtors to men. Have you known God's forgiveness? If you have ever come to Him confessing your sin and your need for His Son to be your Savior, you have confessed that you know the Gospel. If you have ever come to a communion service, eating the bread and drinking the wine that stand for the broken body and shed blood of the Lord Jesus Christ, you have declared your knowledge of God's forgiveness. Well, then, if you know this, you are also acknowledging your indebtedness to declare that same forgiveness to others. You must tell them, for Jesus said, "Unto whomsoever much is given, of him shall be much required" (Luke 12:48).

* Donald Grey Barnhouse, *God's Methods for Holy Living* (Kingsport, Tenn.: Kingsport Press, 1951), pp. 72-74.

Chapter 32

How To Defeat Temptation

(Matthew 6:13)

At the end of the sixteenth century, after the Protestant Reformation in Europe and the wars that followed it, an anonymous Christian wrote these lines about temptation:

> *In all the strife of mortal life*
> *Our feet shall stand securely;*
> *Temptation's hour shall lose its power,*
> *For thou shalt guard us surely.*
>
> *O God, renew, with heavenly dew,*
> *Our body, soul, and spirit,*
> *Until we stand at thy right hand,*
> *Through Jesus' saving merit.*

These lines summarize some of the truths that the Word of God contains about temptation. To some extent they are, therefore, a commentary on the references to temptation in the Lord's Prayer, in the verse to which we now come in our study. The Prayer says, "And lead us not into temptation, but deliver us from evil [or, as we should say, from "the evil one]."

TYPES OF TEMPTATIONS

If we are to understand what the Lord Jesus Christ was talking about in this suggestion of how we should pray, we need to understand that several distinct types of temptation are mentioned in the Bible — some from God and some from Satan — and that this is a prayer for deliverance from only one kind.

Words often have more than one meaning. For instance, I have often had to explain the double significance of the word "marry" to my young daughter, particularly after I have performed a marriage ceremony. My daughter loves weddings and loves to talk about them. But when I say something about marrying the couple,

232

this is very confusing to her. "How can you marry them?" she asks. "You already have a wife. You can't have two wives. And besides you can't marry the man anyway; you have to marry a woman." I am glad to see that she has all of the important rules and relationships right, but I have to explain that the word "marry" can be used in two senses.

Well, the word "temptation" also has two meanings. It can refer either to a direct temptation to do evil, or to a trial, an ordeal, a testing.

We see this most clearly in the first chapter of the book of James. In the second and third verses of that chapter we read, "My brethren, count it all joy when ye fall into various trials [KJV, 'divers temptations'], knowing this, that the testing of your faith worketh patience." It is obvious that the writer is referring to a kind of test that comes to a Christian from God. This is the kind of testing that came to Abraham when God asked him to sacrifice his son, or that comes to us in persecution, sickness, discouragement, or abuse by our family or friends. Through these experiences God strengthens the faith of the Christian. We are to rejoice in such testing, counting it an honor so to suffer.

Later on in the same chapter James speaks of another kind of tempting, however. This is not at all from God. In fact, James says of this temptation, "Let no man say when he is tempted, I am tempted of God; for God cannot be tempted with evil, neither tempteth he any man" (v. 13). This is a temptation to sin, of course. So James adds, "But every man is tempted, when he is drawn away of his own lust, and enticed" (v. 14). We are not to rejoice in this type of temptation. It comes from our own sinful natures, and we are urged to triumph over it.

Finally, in the fourth chapter, verse 7, James speaks of the assaults we receive from the devil. Only here he says, "Submit yourselves, therefore, to God. Resist the devil, and he will flee from you."

The temptation referred to in the Lord's Prayer is not the first or the second of these three temptations. It is not the temptation that comes from God as a trial to strengthen our faith. Nor is it primarily the temptation that comes from within our own sinful lusts. The temptation that Jesus meant is the last of these three temptations. It is the temptation that comes to the believer directly from Satan (the "evil one").

SUBMIT AND RESIST

What is the secret to resisting this type of temptation? The secret is found in the last verse quoted from James. We read elsewhere that the temptation that comes from the flesh is to be resisted by fleeing from it; Paul writes, "Flee also youthful lusts" (2 Tim. 2:22) and "Flee fornication" (1 Cor. 6:18). We are to resist the temptation that comes to us from the world by allowing God to transform us by the renewing of our minds, that we may prove His perfect will for us (Rom. 12:1, 2). But when it comes to the devil, Scripture says, "Submit yourselves, therefore, to God. Resist the devil, and he will flee from you."

I think that at this point we must be very clear about what James is saying. He says, "Submit . . . to God" and "Resist the devil." We are to *submit* and *resist*. But how do we do that? What does "submission" mean? And how can we "resist" the wisdom and superior cunning of Satan? We need to answer these questions clearly, for if we are sensitive to spiritual things we know that Satan is stronger than we are. We know that we are unable to resist him in ourselves, and that we are weak beside him. Therefore, we need to know how we are to seek deliverance from the One who has defeated Satan and who will one day imprison him for ever.

What does it mean to submit? Quite simply it means to surrender one's will to God; and since this cannot be done in isolation apart from a personal relationship to Him, it means that we must spend time conversing with God through prayer. It is certainly no accident, for instance, that the petition "Lead us not into temptation, but deliver us from evil" comes last in the Lord's Prayer, after the Christian has already prayed, "Hallowed be thy name. Thy kingdom come. Thy will be done." This means that although the believer is to resist the devil — although he is to fight against him — he is able to do this successfully only after he has first of all submitted himself to God.

And what does it mean to resist? How do we resist? The answer is: by God's Word, by means of the Bible. The Lord Jesus Christ said to His disciples, "Now ye are clean through the word which I have spoken unto you" (John 15:3), meaning that purity of life can be ours to the degree that we feed upon the Bible and study it. The psalmist said, "Thy word have I hidden in mine heart, that I might not sin against thee" (Ps. 119:11). Paul wrote specifically of our spiritual warfare saying, "And take . . . the sword of the Spirit, which is the word of God" (Eph. 6:17).

In *Pilgrim's Progress* there is a scene in which this is portrayed allegorically as a terrible battle between Apollyon (who is the devil) and Christian:

> Then Apollyon espying his opportunity, began to gather up close to Christian, and wrestling with him, gave him a dreadful fall; and with that Christian's Sword flew out of his hand. Then said Apollyon, I am sure of thee now; and with that he had almost pressed him to death, so that Christian began to despair of life. But as God would have it, while Apollyon was fetching of his last blow, thereby to make a full end of this good man, Christian nimbly reached out his hand for his Sword, and caught it, saying, Rejoice not against me, O mine Enemy! When I fall I shall arise; and with that gave him a deadly thrust, which made him give back, as one that had received his mortal wound: Christian perceiving that, made at him again, saying Nay, in all these things we are more than conquerors through him that loved us. And with that Apollyon spread forth his Dragon's wings, and sped away, that Christian for a season saw him no more." *

As I read this paragraph I realize that Bunyan knew the truth of James 4:7 personally, for he knew that it had reference to the use of the sword of the Spirit, which is the Word of God.

THE LORD'S EXAMPLE

One final example of how temptation can be resisted is the account of the temptation of Jesus Christ recorded in the fourth chapter of the gospel of Matthew.

At some point during the first year in which I was speaking on the Bible Study Hour, in a question and answer period, the announcer asked a question that I have heard many people ask in one form or another. He asked, "We have all heard the expression, Dr. Boice, that temptations come to us from the world, the flesh and the devil, but it seems that all three of Christ's temptations in the wilderness came to Him from the devil. Isn't that right? And if it is, how can we say Jesus 'was in all points tempted like as we are, yet without sin' (Heb. 4:15)?"

It was a good question. I pointed out the fact that there is a fine distinction here, on the basis of which it was necessary for

---

* John Bunyan, *Pilgrim's Progress*, Everyman's Library edition (London: J. M. Dent & Sons, 1954), p. 61.

Jesus to be tempted in all points directly by the devil. Jesus did not have a sinful nature as we do, so He could not be tempted by a sinful nature. Neither could He be tempted by the world directly because the sins of the world are pride, arrogance, a desire for dominance, and so on, and Jesus had no point of contact in Himself for these. If Jesus was to be tempted at all, the temptations had to come to Him from a direct encounter with the devil, just as Adam and Eve had to receive their temptations from the devil; for before their fall, Adam and Eve did not have a sinful nature either.

At the same time, however, we notice as we read the account of Christ's temptations that each of the temptations did relate to one of these three areas. The temptation to turn stones to bread was a fleshly temptation; the temptation to throw Himself from the top of the Temple in Jerusalem was a temptation to gain the world's esteem in the world's way; the temptation to worship Satan was an outright spiritual temptation that would have placed the Lord in direct opposition to God, His heavenly Father. Thus, although all the temptations came originally from the devil, they were nevertheless temptations to the sins of the flesh, the world, and the devil. They show us that Jesus was tempted in all the ways that we are. Of course, these temptations were far more subtle and stronger than our temptations because of their source.

Now, how did the Lord Jesus Christ come out on top of these temptations? The answer to this question is contrary to what most people think, for they think He did it by drawing on His divine nature. They believe that He had more power to resist temptation than we have. It is true, of course, that Jesus did have more power than we have. But there is nothing in the Bible to show that Christ ever resisted temptation by drawing on His divine nature. Jesus was both man and God. Yet He resisted temptation as a man. What is more, it is for this reason that He is an example for us when we are tempted.

So let me ask the question again. How did Jesus resist the temptations that are recorded in Matthew 4? Well, first, He had just spent forty days in fasting and in prayer. And, second, He replied to the devil in every instance by quoting Scripture.

Satan had come to Him saying, "If thou be the Son of God, command that these stones be made bread." This was a temptation to put physical needs above spiritual ones, and Jesus answered by saying, "Man shall not live by bread alone, but by every word that proceedeth out of the mouth of God." It was a direct quotation from Deuteronomy 8:3. Next, the devil took Him up to Jerusalem and, placing Him on a pinnacle of the Temple, challenged Him to throw Himself down trusting God to bear Him up. In this way Christ would appear, as it were, from heaven and thereby gain an immediate following. Jesus answered by quoting Deuteronomy 6:16, "It is written again, Thou shalt not put the Lord, thy God, to the test." In the final temptation Satan asked Christ to worship him in exchange for this world's glory. This was a spiritual temptation. Jesus replied, "Begone, Satan; for it is written, Thou shalt worship the Lord, thy God, and him only shalt thou serve." Once again Jesus had resisted the devil by a quotation from the book of Deuteronomy (Deut. 6:13).

Jesus overcame temptation just as we are to overcome temptation — by prayer and by the knowledge of the Bible, and He even had to learn His knowledge of the Bible. Certainly when we learn to pray as Jesus prayed and when we learn the Bible as Jesus knew the Bible, then we will experience victory over our temptations also.

OUR CONFIDENCE

Moreover, if we do these things we also will have great confidence before God even when we are faced with temptations. We will pray that God will keep us from Satan's temptations. I would rephrase this section of the Lord's Prayer to say, "Keep us from wandering into paths where we will be tempted by the devil; but if he comes, keep us out of his clutches." But even as we pray this we will pray knowing that "God is faithful, who will not permit you to be tempted above that ye are able, but will, with the temptation, also make the way to escape, that ye may be able to bear it" (1 Cor. 10:13).

Finally, the prayer ends with the words, "For thine is the kingdom, and the power, and the glory, forever. Amen." It does not ask that these things might become true. It acknowledges that they are true. Are they true? Then we ought not to worry about the future if we are God's children. All too often we find ourselves doubting that God really is able to take care of us, and we worry about our own little kingdoms, our power, and our glory. How foolish when we know that His kingdom is certain, that His power is sufficient for all situations, and that His glory ultimately will prevail.

Chapter 33

Fasting

(Matthew 6:16-18)

The first two examples of Christian piety that Jesus gives in the middle of the Sermon on the Mount do not seem particularly difficult. To most people, prayer and the giving of alms make sense and are familiar, even though they may not understand them completely or practice them. But that cannot be said of Christ's third example. The third example is fasting, which means abstaining from food for some spiritual end; and not only does fasting seem unnecessary to most persons, it may even seem quite foolish or absurd.

Unfortunately for these views, Jesus assumed that fasting would be practiced by His disciples. And, what is more, He even gave instructions about it. He said, "Moreover, when ye fast, be not, as the hypocrites, of a sad countenance; for they disfigure their faces, that they may appear unto men to fast. Verily I say unto you, They have their reward. But thou, when thou fastest, anoint thine head, and wash thy face, that thou appear not unto men to fast, but unto thy Father, who is in secret; and thy Father, who seeth in secret, shall reward thee openly" (Matt. 6:16-18).

Financial Reasons

The easiest (but also the most superficial) way to make fasting come alive to Christian living in our time is to tell stories of some who have practiced fasting for financial reasons.

One such story comes from the days I spent studying in Switzerland. There was an American couple in Switzerland, whom I got to know during the first year of my program, who were

238

probably the most financially pressed of any American family I encountered. They had an abiding concern about being able to complete their three-year program. And their concern was well justified, for their resources were very limited and if they had run out of money before the end of their three years there would have been no adequate grants or scholarships to fall back on. At one point, however, this couple learned of the far greater difficulties of an Asian student who was also in the theological program. He was so desperate for funds that he was on the verge of being forced to abandon his studies and leave Switzerland. When my financially pressed friends learned of it they began to marshall help from among the American community and then actually contributed themselves. Another person who knew of their situation asked them, "How are you going to find money to help the Asian student when you are so pressed for money yourself?" They answered, "We'll just fast one day a week."

I know of another case involving a girl who was a student at the University of Pennsylvania. She had been very impressed by a series of church services on missions and, as a result, wanted to contribute to the support of a girl her own age who was going to North Africa. She did not think it was right for her to take the money her father was giving her for her education to do this, however. So she skipped lunch twice a week and sent the lunch money. Later, in another school, she worked on the telephone exchange to maintain her commitment.

Both these stories tell of those who fasted for a specific reason. They make sense. But, unfortunately, they are not a great deal of help to us personally Many of us are so far from the level of need revealed in these stories that fasting does not even enter into the picture. We can generally meet out of our income, the needs to which we become sensitive, not to mention our investments or savings. Moreover, when we read of fasting in the Bible, as here in the words of Jesus, it is clear that financial reasons for doing without food for a period of time are not really under consideration.

OLD TESTAMENT TEACHING

The first real clue to what fasting should mean today comes from a study of the Bible. The clue is seen in the fact that in the Old Testament period fasting had an entirely different purpose from that in the New, and what is more, the pivotal text upon which this change takes place is the text we are studying in Matthew.

What was the purpose of fasting in Old Testament times? Fasting always was connected with mourning for sin and repentance of it. Thus, the entire Hebrew nation was to fast on the Day of Atonement, for this was the day in which they were to mourn for their sin and look for the reconciliation which God had provided through the sacrifices. This was the only occasion in the Old Testament on which Israel was specifically commanded to fast. From this the practice spread to occasions of national disaster or mourning. In the book of Joel it was part of God's call to the people to repentance (Joel 2:12). Nineveh repented with fasting after hearing the preaching of Jonah (Jonah 3:5). Israel fasted following the civil war with Benjamin (Judg. 20:26), the death of Saul and Jonathan (1 Sam. 31:13), and as part of a national revival under the prophet Samuel (1 Sam. 7:6). The Hebrew word for fasting suggests the repentant humbling of the soul before God.

If anyone doubts that this is the central characteristic of fasting in the Old Testament era, the definite proof is to be found in two other texts where it is mentioned. The first is Matthew 9:14, 15, where Jesus is speaking to the disciples of John the Baptist, who practiced fasting. These came to Jesus to ask why His disciples did not fast. Jesus answered, "Can the sons of the bridechamber mourn, as long as the bridegroom is with them?" In other words, the disciples did not fast because fasting implied sorrow, and the years of Jesus' earthly ministry were joyous.

The other text is a great one, for it is probably the most extensive discussion of fasting in the Old Testament. It occurs in Isaiah 58:1-7. Here the people of Israel reminded God that they had fasted but complained that fasting had not produced the results they were seeking. God answered by saying, "Behold, ye fast for strife and debate, and to smite with the fist of wickedness. . . . Is not this the fast that I have chosen — to loose the bands of wickedness, to undo the heavy burdens, and to let the oppressed go free, and that ye break every yoke? Is it not to deal thy bread to the hungry, and that thou bring the poor that are cast out to thy house? When thou seest the naked, that thou cover him; and that thou hide not thyself from thine own flesh?" In other words, God says that ceremonial fasting means nothing.

The only fasting that is of any value is that which involves repentance of sin resulting in a transformed and charitable life. This is what fasting implied before Christ's coming.

WAITING UPON GOD

After Jesus came, fasting was conceived of differently. The early Christians were aware that their sin had been forgiven so they did not mourn for it in the way men did before Christ's death and resurrection. They did not fast for their sin. They did not fast in sorrow. And yet, it is true that they did fast. What was the reason? The reason was their desire to set aside the normal distractions of this life in order to seek God's clear direction for their lives. It was a discipline by which they waited upon God while asking Him to reveal His will to them.

How do we know this? For one thing, by the way the Apostle Paul links fasting to "watching" in writing to the Corinthian Christians. Here he speaks of the apostles who conduct themselves "as the ministers of God, in much patience, in afflictions, in necessities, in distresses, in stripes, in imprisonments, in tumults, in labors, in watchings, in fastings" (2 Cor. 6:4, 5). He is saying that fasting was a spiritual exercise by which he waited upon God to reveal His will to him.

Someone may say, "Well, is there any evidence that God actually responded to the fasting of these early Christians by revealing His will to them? Did it happen? Is this theoretical purpose that you have mentioned borne out in practice?" The answer is Yes. What is more, the instances themselves show that fasting was linked to the two most significant advances of the Gospel in the ancient world following Pentecost.

What were the two major advances of the Gospel after it had been first proclaimed and the Holy Spirit had come on the believers? Certainly the first was the opening of the Gospel to the Gentiles through Cornelius by the ministry of Peter. Was fasting connected to that great opening? Yes, it was, according to the words of Cornelius. We read in the tenth chapter of Acts that after Peter had received his vision of the great sheet let down from heaven containing all kinds of animals and had gone on the basis of that vision to the home of the Gentile centurion, Cornelius spoke to explain the reason he had called Peter, saying, "Four days ago I was fasting until this hour; and at the ninth hour I prayed in my house, and, behold, a man stood before me in bright clothing, and said, Cornelius, thy prayer is heard, and thine alms are had in remembrance in the sight of God. Send, therefore, to Joppa, and call here Simon, whose surname is Peter; . . . who, when he cometh, shall speak unto thee" (Acts 10:30-32). It was while he was fasting that Cornelius received this important revelation.

The other great example is found in the thirteenth chapter of Acts, which recounts the start of Paul's missionary journeys. Here we read that as the church at Antioch "ministered to the Lord, and fasted, the Holy Spirit said, Separate me Barnabas and Saul for the work unto which I have called them. And when they had fasted and prayed, and laid their hands on them, they sent them away" (Acts 13:2, 3). In other words, out of that prayer meeting with fasting there came a revelation from God that resulted in Paul's lifelong ministry to the Gentiles throughout the Roman world.

Here is a great change in the use and purpose of fasting, a change which may be traced to the words of the Lord Jesus Christ that we are studying. He did not say that fasting was a form of outward piety. He did not consider it an exercise for the subjection of the body. It was not a means of social protest. He taught that it was to be a personal exercise between the soul of the individual and God. "But thou, when thou fastest, anoint thine head, and wash thy face, that thou appear not unto men to fast, but unto thy Father, who is in secret; and thy Father, who seeth in secret, shall reward thee openly." The reward is not money, of course. It is not an office promotion. It is the reward of the Father's presence and the revelation of His will. Jesus taught that fasting was valuable to that end so long as we do it before the Lord and not men.

FASTING FROM THINGS

Once this has been said, the truths about fasting may then be used to help us go on farther. If this is what fasting is — not an external religious exercise but a period of abstinence in which the Christian can seek God's will — then it also is true that the essence of fasting can be achieved also in other ways. It can be achieved by abstaining from things. What is more, for us this may be far more important than not eating.

In his classic book on prayer, Dr. O. Hallesby has written, "Fasting is not confined to abstinence from eating and drinking.

Fasting really means voluntary abstinence for a time from various necessities of life, such as food, drink, sleep, rest, association with people and so forth. . . . Fasting in the Christian sense does not involve looking upon the necessities of life, which we have mentioned, as unclean or unholy. . . . Fasting implies merely that our souls at certain times need to concentrate more strongly on the one thing needful than at other times, and for that reason we renounce for the time being those things which in themselves, may be both permissible and profitable." *

One thing for which we should lay aside our normal routine is Bible study — both individual Bible study and that with other Christians. This is much to the point. For it is in Bible study more than in other ways that God speaks to us and reveals His way to us. On this point I can speak personally, for it was out of such a study with other Christian friends that my wife and I were led to establish an English-speaking church in Basel, Switzerland. As the result of the Bible study, which met in our home every Friday evening, Christians began to grow spiritually, and others who were not yet believers began to be attracted to the Gospel. In time we felt the need for regular worship. A church service was established. To the regular Bible study in English was added another in German and a noon group for secretaries. Later on when I visited Basel again the group was still there, changed but growing, and the evidences of God's blessing were evident.

Sometimes our fasting will lead us away from such things as entertainment, perhaps from television. This was the experience of David Wilkerson whose story is told in *The Cross and the Switchblade.* Wilkerson had been the pastor of a small Assemblies of God church in Philipsburg, Pa. Although the church had grown and the congregation had been able to erect several new buildings, the pastor himself was restless. One night as he sat watching the "late show" on television the thought came to him that he might profit from spending the time which he usually spent watching television, praying. In other words, he might "fast from television" and then see what happened.

Immediately he came up with a number of excuses. He was tired at night; he needed the relaxation. It was good for him

* O. Hallesby, *Prayer,* trans. by Clarence J. Carlsen (Minneapolis: Augsburg Publishing House, 1960), p. 113.

to be in touch with the things most people were seeing and talking about. But his excuses were not entirely convincing. So he prayed, "Jesus, I need some help in deciding this thing, so here's what I'm asking You. I'm going to put an ad for that [television] set in the paper. If You're behind this idea, let a buyer appear right away. Let him appear within an hour . . . within half an hour . . . after the paper gets on the streets."

His wife was not very impressed with the idea when he told her about it the next morning, but he went ahead and put the ad in the newspaper anyway. It was a humorous scene in the Wilkerson home the next day after the newspaper appeared on the streets. Wilkerson sat on the couch with the TV set on one side, his wife and children on the other, and the clock and the telephone before him. After twenty-five minutes, just as he was saying, "Well, Gwen, it looks like you're right. I guess I won't have to . . . " the telephone rang.

"Do you have a TV set for sale?" a man's voice asked.

"That's right. An RCA in good condition. Nineteen-inch screen, two years old."

"How much do you want for it?"

"One hundred dollars," Wilkerson said quickly.

"I'll take it," was the reply. "Have it ready in fifteen minutes. I'll bring you the money."

Well, that was the beginning. Out of the times of prayer that followed, David Wilkerson was directed by God to the plight of the teenage gang members in the heart of New York City. Out of his efforts to help them came a work that God has blessed and is continuing to bless not only in New York but in many other cities also.

I do not know how all of this will apply to you. But whatever your daily routine or habits, there are undoubtedly some things that you may want to lay aside temporarily to spend time with God. Probably you will not tell people about it. That is all right, but you have the promise of Jesus that the Father, who sees in secret, will reward you openly.

Chapter 34

Who Owns Your Possessions?

(Matthew 6:19-24)

After the great teachings in the first half of Matthew 6 about the spiritual life of the Christian, the Lord Jesus Christ turned to warnings about the personal failures that most often deprive a believer of spiritual victories and nullify his witness. In these verses, beginning with Matthew 6:19 and continuing through Matthew 7:5, Jesus warns against a love of possessions, anxiety, and a judgmental attitude toward others.

LOVE OF MONEY

It is not really difficult to find examples of people who have allowed the love of money to ruin their spirituality and to nullify the effect of their witness. History is full of such examples, and they come from our time also. In the book of Joshua we are told of the sin of Achan that caused the defeat of the armies of Israel at Ai. Israel had just been victorious at Jericho and had dedicated the spoil of the battle to God, as God had indicated. But there was a scar on the victory. During the battle a soldier called Achan had come upon a beautiful Babylonian garment, two hundred pieces of silver and an ingot of gold. Because he coveted them, he took them and hid them in his tent. It was a small thing, but it was disobedience to God. Thus Israel was defeated in their next engagement, and judgment came upon Achan and his household.

Solomon allowed the love of money and women to ruin his spiritual life. Ananias and Sapphira lied to the Lord about money, pretending that they had given the full price of a sale to the church while actually keeping back a portion. They were struck dead. Paul wrote in one of his letters about a young man named Demas, who, he said, "hath forsaken me having loved this present world." We see the same problem today when people put their home and the care of it above the need for biblical teaching and mow the grass on Sunday when they should be at church, or when they direct all their efforts toward amassing a fortune (or part of one) while neglecting their families and the essential spiritual life of their home. No wonder that Paul wrote to Timothy to remind him that "the love of money is the root of all evil" (1 Tim. 6:10).

Remember that the Bible nowhere teaches that money itself is evil. It is not money or possessions that are at fault; it is the men who use them. Before God created men and women He created a vast world of pleasant and useful things for them. They were meant for man's use in every joyful and constructive way. But when man sinned, the things that were to be helpful to him came to usurp a place in his heart which they were never meant to have. Soon men began to fight and steal and cheat and do countless other things to possess them. Today, when a man surrenders to God and allows Him to redirect his life, a process begins in which money and things are removed from the center and God once again is reinstated on the throne.

There have been sensitive souls in the history of the Christian Church who have recognized the evils that accompany possessions and who have sought to eliminate the evils by doing away with the possessions collectively. Using the example of the early church in Jerusalem, which pooled its possessions and distributed to those who had need, these Christians have argued against the right of private property among believers and have sometimes even advocated a form of Christian communism. That is not right. If some Christians are led of the Lord to sell their possessions and give to others and they do so, particularly in a time of need, this is a great blessing. But it does not therefore follow that all Christians must follow their example.

Actually, if you examine the Bible carefully, you will see that far from condemning the possession of private property the Bible actually assumes the rightness of it. For instance, the eighth commandment says, "Thou shalt not steal" (Exod. 20:15). However, that verse teaches not only that I am not to take those things belonging to another person, but that neither is he to take mine. In the story of Ananias and Sapphira mentioned earlier, Peter said when speaking to the husband, "Ananias, why hath Satan filled thine heart to lie to the Holy Spirit, and to keep back part of the price of the land? While it remained, was it not thine own? And after it was sold, was it not in thine own power? Why hast thou conceived this thing in thine heart? Thou hast not lied unto men, but unto God" (Acts 5:3, 4). Peter was stating that God recognizes the right of private property and does not force any Christian to dispose of his money.

Now, someone will ask, "Didn't the Lord Jesus instruct the rich young ruler that he was to sell all that he had and give to the poor?" Yes, He did. But we must also note that He did not say it to Mary or Martha or Lazarus or to John the evangelist or to Zebedee. He said it to "the rich young ruler" because his chief obstruction to a life of following Christ lay in his possessions. He proved that by turning away. For such a person — and there are many today — the loss of their possessions would be the most significant blessing of their lives. The best thing they could do would be to give them away. This does not mean, however, that possessions in themselves are wrong or, for that matter, that poverty is a particularly blessed form of Christianity.

In this as in all other areas of the Christian life the true solution does not lie in abstinence or withdrawal. It lies in the proper use and proper estimate of the things which God has provided. In other words, we are not called upon to relinquish things but rather use them under God's direction. We are to use them for the health and well-being of our family, for material aid to others, and for the great task of proclaiming the Gospel and promoting Christian verities.

Treasure in Heaven

That is precisely what Jesus Himself was teaching in the verses concerned with money in the Sermon on the Mount. Jesus was not speaking against possessions. He was speaking against a ruinous preoccupation with them. He said, "Lay not up for yourselves treasures upon earth, where moth and rust doth corrupt, and where thieves break through and steal, but lay up for yourselves treasures in heaven, where neither moth nor rust doth corrupt, and where thieves do not break through nor steal; for where your treasure is, there will your heart be also" (Matt. 6: 19-21).

These verses also take us one step farther, for they contain the first of the reasons given by Jesus why worldliness in regard to our possessions is foolish and detrimental to our spiritual lives. The reason is that one day all earthly possessions will perish and will be gone forever, and since that is the case, a man who has spent his life accumulating them may himself be saved, but he will have nothing to show for what should have been a lifetime of profitable service. Thus, Paul wrote to the Corinthians, "Now if any man build upon this foundation [Jesus Christ] gold, silver, precious stones, wood, hay, stubble — every man's work shall be made manifest; for the day shall declare it. . . . If any man's work abide which he hath built upon it, he shall receive a reward. If any man's work shall be burned, he shall suffer loss; but he himself shall be saved, yet as by fire" (1 Cor. 3:12-15). This means that it is only as a man uses his possessions for spiritual ends that he is able to accumulate true treasure.

Then, too, there is another reason why a preoccupation with material things is foolish for the follower of Jesus Christ. Jesus said that if a man's treasure is on earth, his heart will be on earth also, and therefore things will rule him.

There is a great illustration of this in the linguistic development of the Hebrew word *mammon* which occurs several verses farther on in this chapter, where it says, "Ye cannot serve God and mammon" (Matt. 6:24, KJV). *Mammon* was a word for material possessions, but it had come into Hebrew from a root word meaning "to entrust," or "to place in someone's keeping." *Mammon* therefore meant the wealth that one entrusted to another for safekeeping. At this time the word did not have any bad connotations at all, and a rabbi could say, "Let the *mammon* of thy neighbor be as dear to thee as thine own." When a bad sense was meant an adjective or some other qualifying word was added. So we have the phrase "the mammon of unrighteousness" or "unrighteous mammon."

As time passed, however, the sense of the word *mammon* shifted away from the passive sense of "that which is entrusted" to the active sense of "that in which a man trusts." In this case, of course, the meaning was entirely bad, and the word *mammon* which was originally spelled with a small "m" came to be spelled with a capital "M" as designating a god.

This linguistic development repeats itself in the life of anyone who does not have his eyes fixed on spiritual treasures. Is that true of you? Have things become your god? Don't forget that these things are written to Christians, and that they are therefore meant to make you ask whether the Lord God Almighty occupies the central place in your life or whether things obscure Him. If you think most about your home, car, vacation, bank account, clothes, or investments, then you are building your treasure on earth; and, according to Jesus, "where your treasure is, there will your heart be also."

DISTORTED VISION

The third reason why Jesus Christ warns His followers about an improper concern for possessions occurs in verses 22 and 23. It has to do with our spiritual vision. Jesus said, "The lamp of the body is the eye; if, therefore, thine eye be healthy, thy whole body shall be full of light. But if thine eye be evil, thy whole body shall be full of darkness. If, therefore, the light that is in thee be darkness, how great is that darkness!"

William Barclay writes of these verses: "The idea behind this passage is one of childlike simplicity. The eye is regarded as the window by which the light gets into the whole body. The color and state of a window decide what light gets into a room. If the window is clear, clean, and undistorted, the light will come flooding into the room, and will illuminate every corner of it. If the glass of the window is colored or frosted, distorted, dirty, or obscure, the light will be hindered, and the room will not be lit up. . . . So then, says Jesus, the light which gets into any man's heart and soul and being depends on the spiritual state of the eye through which it has to pass, for the eye is the window of the whole body." *

Let me ask you a question. Do you see spiritual things clearly? Or is your vision of God and His will for your life clouded by spiritual cataracts or near-sightedness brought on by an unhealthy preoccupation with things? I am convinced that this is true for many Christians, particularly those living in the midst of Western affluence. Now and then people like this complain to me that they cannot understand the Bible, or that God seems far away. Sometimes they are confused about the Christian life or about God's will for them. Well, it is not surprising. And, what is more, it always will be this way for one who knows his way around a

* William Barclay, *The Gospel of Matthew* (Philadelphia: The Westminster Press, 1958), Vol. I, p. 245.

supermarket or a brokerage house more than he knows his way around the New Testament. Although Jesus did not direct us away from possessions themselves, He did warn us against losing our spiritual vision because of them.

There is another thought in this section, coming from the word which the King James' translators rendered "single" and the translators of the Revised Standard Version, Phillips, and the New English Bibles rendered "sound." It is the word *haplous,* related to the noun *haplotes.* In some texts the words mean "simple" or "simplicity," but there are other texts in which the only possible translation is "generosity." The translators of the New Scofield Bible recognized this truth when they came to the twelfth chapter of Romans, verse 8, for in that verse the word "simplicity" (used in the King James Version) is changed to "liberality" so that the text now reads: "He that giveth, let him do it with liberality." In James 1:5, we read, "If any of you lack wisdom, let him ask of God, who giveth to all men *liberally.*" The word occurs in this same sense at least three times in 2 Corinthians (8:2; 9:11, 13) and once in Colossians (3:22).

I believe that it is this sense of the word that is present here in Christ's teaching. The "single eye" is the "generous eye." And if that is the case, then Jesus is promoting a generous spirit in regard to our money. How can you tell whether riches have clouded your spiritual vision? The answer may be determined by the extent to which you are generous with the goods which you have been given.

Do not tell me that you cannot be generous this year because it is a bad year financially or because your stocks have declined. I once received a report of alumni giving to Harvard University for the fiscal year 1969-70. It was the second highest record of annual giving in the history of the university, and it occurred in a year in which the Dow Jones average dropped from a high near 1000 to below 700. No, liberality is not closely linked to affluence, unless it is an inverse relationship, and we all need to learn the secret of the Philippian Christians who out of "the abundance of their joy and their deep poverty abounded unto . . . liberality" (2 Cor. 8:2).

GOD AND MAMMON

The final verse of our section (verse 24) deals with the mutually exclusive nature of serving God and riches. "No man can serve two masters; for either he will hate the one, and love the other; or else he will hold to the one, and despise the other. Ye cannot serve God and money."

Nothing could be said more clearly, or be more obvious. It should be a heart-searching question for all Christians. Ask yourself this: Can anything be more insulting to God, who has redeemed us from the slavery of sin, put us in Christ, and given us all things richly to enjoy than to take the name of our God upon us, to be called by His name, and then to demonstrate by every action and every decision of life that we actually serve money?

In discussing this verse in *The Sermon on the Mount,* Dr. D. Martyn Lloyd-Jones tells the story of a farmer who one day reported to his wife with great joy that his best cow had given birth to twin calves, one red and one white. He said, "You know, I have been led of the Lord to dedicate one of the calves to Him. We will raise them together. Then when the time comes to sell them, we will keep the proceeds that come from one calf and we will give the proceeds that come from the other to the Lord's work."

His wife asked which calf he was going to dedicate to the Lord, but he answered that there was no need to decide that then. "We will treat them both in the same way," he said, "and when the time comes we will sell them as I have said."

Several months later the man entered the kitchen looking very sad and miserable. When his wife asked what was troubling him he said, "I have bad news for you. The Lord's calf is dead." "But," his wife remonstrated, "you had not yet decided which was to be the Lord's calf." "Oh, yes," he said. "I had always determined that it was to be the white one, and it is the white calf that has died."

It is always the Lord's calf that dies — unless we are absolutely clear about our service to Him and about the true nature of our possessions. Who owns your possessions? The Lord Jesus Christ tells us that either God owns them and you serve Him, or else your possessions own you, and you serve them. In any case, no one ever really possesses them himself, although many persons think they do. May God give us each the victory that comes when our gifts, wealth, time, friends, ambitions and talents are turned over to Him and we use them to establish indestructible riches in heaven.

Chapter 35

Are You Free From Worry?

(Matthew 6:25-34)

In 1961, *Time* magazine published a cover story on the presence of anxiety in America. The article was entitled "Guilt and Anxiety." It stated that the breakdown of faith in God (in the nineteenth century) and in reason (in the twentieth century) coupled with the accelerated pace and high tension of modern life have produced intense anxiety in many millions of people, so much so, in fact, that it would be correct to call worry one of the most widespread and debilitating ailments of our time.

Time wrote, "Not merely the black statistics of murder, suicide, alcoholism, and divorce betray anxiety (or that special form of anxiety which is guilt), but almost any innocent everyday act: the limp or overhearty handshake, the second pack of cigarettes or the third martini, the forgotten appointment, the stammer in mid-sentence, the wasted hour before the TV set, the spanked child, the new car unpaid for." The writers added that these symptoms are intensified for many of us by the dominant American myths that "the old can grow young, the indecisive can become leaders of men, the housewives can become glamour girls, the glamour girls can become actresses, the slow witted can become intellectuals" (March 31, 1961, pp. 44, 46).

In this analysis *Time* was, I believe, at its best. For it is true that worry *is* with us, and that millions of persons (many of them Christians) are troubled by it. It is not well defined. Perhaps the very vagueness of anxiety is its worst feature. Still it is quite real. Someone has called anxiety "fear in search of a cause." Kierkegaard once wrote, "No Grand Inquisitor has in readiness such terrible tortures as anxiety."

252

Is there a cure for anxiety? The only solutions that *Time* knew were sedatives and psychiatry. Fortunately, the Bible offers an entirely different and far more effective cure.

STOP WORRYING

The fact that there is a cure for anxiety is seen most clearly in the recognition that Jesus commanded His followers to avoid it. We see this clearly in the list of warnings (Matt. 6:19 - 7:5) that begin in the middle of the Sermon on the Mount. Jesus said, "Therefore, I say unto you, Be not anxious for your life, what ye shall eat, or what ye shall drink; nor yet for your body, what ye shall put on. . . . For after all these things do the Gentiles seek. For your heavenly Father knoweth that ye have need of all these things. But seek ye first the kingdom of God, and his righteousness, and all these things shall be added unto you" (Matt. 6:25, 32, 33).

The translators of the New Scofield Bible (as well as translators of most modern versions) did not retain the expressions of the King James Version, "Therefore . . . take no thought for your life" and "Take no thought for the morrow." This language has misled some persons into thinking that Jesus was warning against working for a living or against making proper provision for the future. He was not. Actually, we have a case here in which words have changed their meaning. In the Greek and in the English of the time of King James the meaning was just "stop worrying." Therefore, according to Jesus, Christians must not be anxious or worried about anything; for worry, as well as a love of money and possessions or a judgmental attitude toward others, will stifle our Christian life and ruin our witness.

THREE REASONS

It is very important, if we are to understand the essential point of these verses, that we recognize the clear outline found here. The clue is found in the repetition of the word "therefore" in verses 25, 31, and 34. It has been said that in your reading of the Bible whenever you come upon the word "therefore," you should not go on until you understand what it is "there for." And if that is true for just one instance of the word, it is much truer when the word is repeated several times over.

"Therefore" means "because" or "because of this." Thus, in these verses Jesus gives a conclusion based on three things which have been said previously. Because of the teaching in verse 24 the Christian is not to worry. Because of the truths in verses 26 through 30 the Christian is not to worry. Finally, because of the teaching in verses 32 and 33 the Christian is not to worry.

What are these three teachings? The first is found in verse 24, which is, properly speaking, the conclusion to Christ's words about money. In that section of the Sermon Jesus taught that a love of money was harmful because it is impossible for a person to serve God and money at the same time. Now He says that for the same reason His followers are not to be anxious about some future happening or provision.

I think we can see this truth in two ways. First, let us recall the first question of the Westminster Shorter Catechism which says, "What is the chief end of man?" Its answer is: "Man's chief end is to glorify God and to enjoy Him for ever." If that is an accurate description of our Christian service, then it is evident that we cannot be serving God by glorifying Him if we are constantly filled with doubt about His ability to take care of us.

The other way in which we can understand Christ's first point is by using the old cliche, "If you're worrying, you're not trusting; and if you're trusting, you're not worrying." That is literally true, and it is a proper restatement of Christ's warning that you cannot serve God and worry. Kenneth S. Wuest, in his *Word Studies in the Greek New Testament,* has written: "God commands us to 'Stop perpetually worrying about even one thing.' We commit sin when we worry. We do not trust God when we worry. We do not receive answers to prayer when we worry, because we are not trusting." *

HE CARETH FOR YOU

The second reason why we are not to worry (verses 26-30) is not so much a logical one, as is the first, but one that involves knowledge. It is a reminder of a fact which every Christian should know: the fact that God is both able and willing to care for those who trust Him. Jesus said, "Behold the fowls of the air; for they sow not, neither do they reap, nor gather into barns, yet your heavenly Father feedeth them. Are ye not much better than they? . . . And why are ye anxious for raiment? Consider the lilies of the field, how they grow; they toil not, neither do they spin, and

* Kenneth S. Wuest, *Wuest's Word Studies* (Grand Rapids: Wm. B. Eerdmans, 1966), Vol. IV, p. 43.

yet I say unto you that even Solomon, in all his glory, was not arrayed like one of these. Wherefore, if God so clothe the grass of the field, which today is, and tomorrow is cast into the oven, shall he not much more clothe you, O ye of little faith?" (verses 26, 28-30).

Do you see the importance of these verses? It is not merely that we are commanded not to worry. We also are given reasons why we are not to worry, reasons that have to do with the demonstrable ability of God to take care of us.

In the early days of his association with Jesus the Apostle Peter was worried about many things. Walking toward Jesus upon the water he began to look at the waves and became so worried that he began to sink (Matt. 14:30). He was worried that Jesus might not pay taxes (Matt. 17:24ff.). At one point he was worried about who might betray Him (John 13:24). He was worried that Jesus might have to suffer and so rebuked Him on one occasion (Matt. 16:22) and sought to defend Him with a sword on another (John 18:10). Peter was a great worrier. But after he came to know Jesus better he learned that Jesus was able not only to take care of Himself but also to take care of Peter. Thus, toward the end of his life in his first epistle he wrote to other Christians telling them how to live: "Casting all your care upon him; for he careth for you" (1 Peter 5:7).

In this verse the word "care" is the same word as that used in the Sermon on the Mount. The word "cast" is not the normal word for throwing something. It is a word that signifies a definite act of the will by which we stop worrying about things and let God assume the responsibility for our welfare. Finally, the word "care" in the phrase "he careth for you" is not the word "worry," but literally means "for he is mindful of you and your interests." "God thinks about you!" That is what Peter means. That is what he had learned, and that is what the Bible everywhere encourages us to learn also.

FIRST, HIS RIGHTEOUSNESS

The final reason given by Jesus to teach us not to worry is one that appeals to experience. Jesus said, "But seek ye first the kingdom of God, and his righteousness, and all these things shall be added unto you" (verse 33). In other words, make it your business to seek God's interests and follow His way and see if all of your physical needs do not come to you effortlessly and without any necessity on your part of being anxious about them.

Do you know the bliss of that statement? Do you know its truth? If you do not, it may be that you have never had that hunger and thirst after righteousness which Jesus speaks of earlier in the Sermon, or the poverty of spirit that Jesus asks for in those who should inherit God's kingdom. Remember Christ's teaching recorded just a few verses earlier: "Lay not up for yourselves treasures upon earth, where moth and rust doth corrupt, and where thieves break through and steal, but lay up for yourselves treasures in heaven, where neither moth nor rust doth corrupt, and where thieves do not break through nor steal; for where your treasure is, there will your heart be also" (verses 19-21).

THE MAN WHO NEVER WORRIES

Of course, we still may be saying, "I can see from these reasons that I ought not to worry. But still I do worry. Is there an answer? And if there is, what is the solution for me personally?" I believe that the answer to this question is a simple one. It has three parts.

First, we must recognize that all the promises Christ makes in the Sermon on the Mount are for Christians only. If you are not a Christian, or are uncertain whether you are a Christian or not, you must begin by straightening out this question. Every so often someone says to me, "If God has promised to take care of all our needs, why is there so much poverty and deprivation in the world?" But the answer is that the promises of God's care are for Christians only. They are for those who have accepted the death and resurrection of Jesus Christ as the one sufficient ground for their salvation. Unless you believe these things, the promises of God's care are not for you.

Second, if you are a believer, you need to add to your initial experience of salvation all you can learn about God's nature and His ability to care for His people. Most Sunday mornings in my church I begin the worship service with a passage that teaches this exactly. It is Matthew 11:28-30. "Come unto me, all ye that labor and are heavy laden, and I will give you rest. Take my yoke upon you, and learn of me; for I am meek and lowly in heart, and ye shall find rest unto your souls. For my yoke is easy, and my burden is light." In other words, you are to learn all you can about Jesus Christ, for as you learn about Him you will grow strong in faith, knowing that He is able to do the things He has promised.

Finally, you need to get into the habit of turning to God whenever you feel worry approaching. Your reaction in trouble should be something like a conditioned reflex. We all know what a normal reflex is. If you are working in the kitchen and accidentally get your hand too close to the stove, your body will jerk the hand back. You do not need to think about the action; it comes naturally. A conditioned reflex is exactly the same, except that it has to be learned. A conditioned reflex may be illustrated by your reaction in stepping on the brake when you see a red light suddenly while driving, or, in rising to your feet when someone begins to play the *Star Spangled Banner*. These reactions are almost automatic, but they do not result from instinct. They result from training or practice. In the same way, we need reflexes that will turn us to the Lord at the first sign of trouble.

Most persons have reactions of one sort or another. Some persons turn in upon themselves whenever they see trouble approaching. Others turn to some other person. Some turn to drink. Your task, as a Christian, is to supplant these or any other reactions with a behavioral pattern that turns you toward God. If you do not, you will end up worrying. If you do turn to God, you will increasingly come to know that divine tranquility that passes all understanding and is able to give peace in time of storm.

In one of the early Greek manuscripts from the first centuries of the Christian era there is a record of a man whose name was Titedios Amerimnos. The first part of that name is a proper name, but the second part is made up of the Greek word for "worry" plus the prefix meaning "not" or "never." In other words, the second name is a descriptive epithet like the second part of "Frederick the Great" or "James the Just." In this case many have thought that the man was originally a pagan who constantly worried but who, after he became a Christian, stopped worrying. He was then called Titedios Amerimnos — "Titedios, the man who never worries." Can you add that statement to your name? You should be able to write "John Smith," Betty Jones," "Charles Miller," "Susan Moore" (or whatever your name may be) and then add, "the one who never worries."

Chapter 36

Motes, Beams and Hypocrites

(Matthew 7:1-5)

A person once said to me, "If the devil is not able to destroy a Christian's witness by making him apathetic, he will try to do it by making him a fanatic." I believe that is true.

In the midst of the Sermon on the Mount Jesus talks about failures which will render a Christian apathetic in regard to Christian service. They are a love of money, and anxiety. Both of these will have a desensitizing effect in his witness, for if a Christian has his mind centered on things (either to accumulate them or to worry about them) he will not see God and, hence, he cannot serve Him. At this point, however, Jesus goes on to show that there is also a type of *zeal* that can ruin a believer's witness. That is a zeal for judging others. It is harmful because it will turn him into a sharp and unjust critic of his Christian brothers.

In warning against this failure, Jesus said, "Judge not, that ye be not judged. For with what judgment ye judge, ye shall be judged; and with what measure ye measure, it shall be measured to you again. And why beholdest thou the mote that is in thy brother's eye, but considerest not the beam that is in thine own eye? Or how wilt thou say to thy brother, Let me pull the mote out of thine eye; and, behold, a beam is in thine own eye? Thou hypocrite, first cast the beam out of thine own eye, and then shalt thou see clearly to cast the mote out of thy brother's eye" (Matt. 7:1-5).

It is a ludicrous picture. The word translated "mote" is a word the Greeks used for a speck of sawdust or a piece of chaff, while the word "beam" referred to a huge wooden rafter or log. Our equivalent would be a steel girder. Jesus is therefore saying, "And be careful that you do not become like the hypocrite who bustles up to another person and says, 'Oh, you poor Christian, you have a speck of soot in your eye; but he does not see the thing that everyone else can see and which is so obvious — that he has a steel girder protruding from his own.'"

GOSSIPS

There is a sense in which the text is so clear and so obvious that any attempt to explain it can only weaken its impact. And yet, we need to do more than explain it. We need to apply it. And, what is more, when we do this its impact should be felt even more strongly and be more personal.

What does Jesus Christ mean when He points up this hypocritical attitude which so many have toward others? Well, it is certain that He does not mean that we are not to exercise proper spiritual discrimination, for the very next verse (v. 6) says that we are to use true judgment when dispensing spiritual things. Moreover, He does not mean that we are to forego discipline in the Church or that we are not able to separate the truth of the Gospel from falsehood. We are told to do each of these things at several other places in the New Testament. No, Jesus is simply pointing to a general human tendency to see the faults of our neighbors while blithely overlooking our own.

The most obvious example in church life is gossip, for the one who is hunting motes in others is never fully satisfied unless he can talk freely about them. Here is a woman who marries the wrong man while in college and whose marriage ends in divorce. She marries again in disobedience to the Lord's commandments. Still, the Lord blesses the second marriage and gives her and her husband fine opportunities for Christian service. The mote-seeker finds out about it, and, although the fault was long in the past and long since confessed and forgiven, it is not long before the fault-finder has spread his discovery throughout the full range of his acquaintances. Or again, here is a man who is so afraid of not being accepted in the office that he puts on airs, actually lying about his past accomplishments and prospects. The mote-seeker digs for the truth, and when he has found it out he goes about to make sure that the fault is well-known.

Jesus said that this is wrong, adding not only that it is wrong but that it is actually a far greater sin than the one which has been uncovered. To be sure, remarriage was sin. But it was only a mote compared to talking about it; that was a girder. The lie was a mote; but making it known was a beam. Instead of this kind of judging, the Bible teaches that we are to bear with the one who has sinned, instructing him where necessary and in private encouraging him in God's way.

DOCTRINAL CRITICS

Another form of mote-seeking relates to doctrine, for there is always a type of person who listens to the minister, or to another Christian, only to find out where he deviates from the mote-seeker's personal standards. Often, because he comes to the situation filled with harsh prejudices, such a person does not even do a very good job of listening.

Like most ministers I have had experience with this sort of thing personally. Once a person called my church asking to speak to me on what she said was a "personal" matter. Actually, it concerned the National Council of Churches, and her question was whether my church belonged to this organization. I began to answer, trying to say that it is impossible for any individual church to belong to this ecumenical organization, although the United Presbyterian Church is associated with it as a denomination, and then trying to express my dissatisfaction with the National Council in those areas in which I believe it has been harmful to the Gospel and to the Church in America. None of this got through to the woman. She was so incensed at the Council that she denounced it for nearly ten minutes, reading me numerous quotations from others who also have denounced it. After trying to speak to her several times and getting nowhere, there was finally nothing left to do but to terminate the conversation.

The same thing also takes place with some ministers. Quite a few years ago I knew a minister who developed such a fixation about his church's need for money that there was seldom a sermon in which he failed to berate the congregation for their lack of adequate giving. Actually, because I had reliable knowledge about the state of the church's accounts, I knew that the giving was fairly good, and I knew that many of the parishioners were giving also to other worthwhile causes. It was not the attitude of the congregation toward money that was the problem. It was the minister himself. His fault was evident to everyone. And yet, because he could not see his failure, he eventually drove many of his best people from the congregation and thus greatly diminished his ministry.

Of course, these comments are not meant to encourage laxity in regard to sound doctrine. We *are* to discriminate. No congregation will ever be strong unless it is filled with persons capable of leadership who have drunk deeply at the fountain of God's Word and who are therefore able to be discriminating. We are not to support error. But we are to be most careful in regard to our attitude toward those who appear to us to be erring.

Dr. Barnhouse, in a booklet entitled "First Things First," helps us by asking these questions: "Does such criticism arise because there is profound grief over sin? Is the critic moved by the fact that God is outraged and that great wrong is done?" He answers that too often the critic "has no sensitivity for sin at all. If his accusations of his neighbor are discovered to be false, and the neighbor is innocent, the critic looks for something else to criticize. Nor is it because of a great love for the neighbor that the critic makes his accusations and carries his tales. Love covers a multitude of sins. Love does not expose sin. . . . Since we see that there are no positive motives for the criticism, and since the Lord says that the critic is a hypocrite, it follows that the critic is moved by envy, jealousy, selfishness, and all other evil motives that put the poison sac of the asp under the human tongue" (Rom. 3:13). *

"Well," you say, "suppose there are errors?" In that case our attitude is to be that which Paul set forth for his friends in Galatia. Do you remember what he told them at the start of the last chapter of that letter? He wrote, "Brethren, if a man be overtaken in a fault, ye who are spiritual restore such an one in the spirit of meekness, considering thyself, lest thou also be tempted" (Gal. 6:1). The Greek word that is translated "restore" in this sentence is a word that was used in antiquity for setting a broken bone. Therefore, the implication is that the restoring should be done gently and with kindness.

Our attitude in such matters should be the attitude of my dentist. I am one of those people in whose system novocaine diffuses so slowly that the discomfort that comes from drilling is often only fully eliminated after the teeth have been finished. I do not find it a great discomfort, but it bothers my dentist nonetheless.

---

* Donald Grey Barnhouse, *First Things First* (Philadelphia: The Evangelical Foundation, 1961), pp. 37, 38.

One day when he could tell that I was feeling the drilling, he asked, "Are you still feeling pain?" I said, "Oh, I feel it a little bit, but it doesn't bother me." "Well," he said, "it bothers me." Then he quit for another five or ten minutes until the anesthetic became more effective.

How fine it would be if the attitude of those in the Christian Church was always equally solicitous toward those who need a physician. How kind we would be! And how gentle!

GOD IS LOVE

All this really leads up to one great final point, and that is the need for love. We all need love. We need to love. And the reason is simply that when we are filled with love we will find ourselves uninterested in finding specks in the eye of the other person.

In the first place, we need to be aware of God's love and of the fact that we have been loved by Him. When did the Lord Jesus Christ love us? "Lord Jesus Christ, did You wait to love me until I had done something to make myself lovely? Did You wait until I loved you? Did you wait until I had removed those great girders of sin which blinded my vision and distorted my spiritual understanding?" "Of course not!" Christ answers. "I loved you when you were still a sinner and unlovely by all divine standards." I hear the answer, and I turn to the fifth chapter of Romans and read, "For when we were yet without strength, in due time Christ died for the ungodly. For scarcely for a righteous man will one die; yet perhaps for a good man some would even dare to die. But God commendeth his love toward us in that, while we were yet sinners, Christ died for us" (Rom. 5:6-8). "Lord Jesus Christ, did You really love me like that? Did You die for me when I was yet a sinner?" "Yes, I did." Well then, I ask myself, how can I be judgmental toward those whose sins, though small, are visible to me but for whom He also died?

Dr. H. A. Ironside wrote: "When our hearts are occupied with His wondrous love, we remember that He loved us when we were unlovely, and some of us are not very lovely now; we remember that He loved us when we were unlovable, and some of us are not very lovable yet. If He could do that when we were rebellious, and if that same love is now shed abroad in our hearts, we ought to be able to love those who are sinful and unkind and selfish." *

* H. A. Ironside, *Addresses on the Epistles of John* (New York: Loizeaux Brothers, n.d.), p. 179.

Then, too, we do not only need to be aware of God's love and of the fact that He loved us. We need this love *in* us. And this means that we need the kind of close, personal fellowship with Him that will make it possible.

The Apostle John was one who had learned a great deal about this love. Most of us tend to think of the Apostle John as rather quiet and loving, perhaps even effeminate, as so many works of church art have pictured him, but this is a wrong idea. When he first met Christ in the company of his brother James, Jesus had said, "I am going to call the two of you by another name. You are going to be called Boanerges, the sons of thunder." Certainly there is nothing effeminate about that.

Sometime later in the midst of Christ's ministry as they were passing through Samaria, James and John were so incensed by the attitude of the Samaritans that they said to Jesus, "Lord, wilt thou that we command fire to come down from heaven, and consume them, even as Elijah did?" (Luke 9:54). That was not very loving or effeminate either. Earlier in His ministry the Lord had been received in Samaria; but at this time, knowing that the time of His death was at hand, Jesus was determined to push on to Jerusalem. When the Samaritans learned this, however, all the social prejudice they possessed had come out and they refused to let Jesus and His followers even spend the night in their city. So John, along with his brother James, wished to destroy the Samaritans. It was a clear case of John, with a beam in his eye, jumping up to judge a mote in the eye of the Samaritans.

But John soon learned differently. Jesus had said then, "Ye know not what manner of spirit ye are of." Later, as John came to know his Lord better, he learned his need for love and became one noted for love. He then wrote, "Beloved, let us love one another; for love is of God, and everyone that loveth is born of God, and knoweth God. He that loveth not knoweth not God; for God is love" (1 John 4:7, 8).

CLEAR CHANNELS

I do not know where you stand in this matter of motes and beams, but I know that few of us are ever entirely free from this fault. What is more, I know that the beams (if there are any) must be removed from our lives first if the love of God is to flow freely through our lives to help others.

In the summer of 1970, when I was in Europe, I visited a

friend in one of the new high-rise apartment buildings in France
that line the mighty Rhine River just across the water from Germany. From my friend's apartment I looked down on an old-
fashioned lock that existed at one time to direct the water from
the Rhine across the flatlands of France. At one time the channel
was undoubtedly useful. But as I looked down upon it I saw that
large beams had been used to choke the flow of the river. It was
true that the power of the river was still present. It was running
on to the north through Germany. But the beams were blocking
the channel, and now there was nothing coming through but a
trickle. The lock itself was closed by refuse that had entered the
cul de sac and had no outlet.

If you discover that a beam is blocking the flow of God's love
in your life, as these beams were blocking the river, then you must
know that the only solution is Jesus. He is the Great Physician,
and He is able to extract both motes and beams because He can
see clearly to do it. There is no mote in His eye to hinder His
vision. Besides, He will give you a vision of His glory, as you
look to Him, that will then be reflected from your purified eye to
others.

Chapter 37

Spiritual Discernment

(Matthew 7:6)

It is a characteristic of the Christian religion that most of its doctrines are totally unacceptable to most men, or, to put it another way, that most of what the Bible teaches is offensive.

Not long ago I heard of a young minister who went to a small church in one of the more fashionable denominations. It was not an evangelical church, nor was it particularly active. But he was both. As a result, through his preaching of the Gospel, the church began to grow and much happened. It also turned out that many who had been in the church when he had first come were offended. They disliked his teaching. They loved their old ways and opposed him. Finally, a crisis arose in which the young man was forced to resign and to seek service elsewhere. I know, of course, that there are other reasons for this kind of friction in churches, but in this case, the offensive was truly the offensive of the Gospel. The story illustrates the truth that for many men Christian teachings are objectionable.

In Matthew 7:6 there is a teaching that is particularly offensive even to some Christians. In the previous verse Jesus has been talking of judgment and of why Christians must not judge each other hypocritically. But then He adds, as if to correct the possible impression that a follower of His is barred from judging at all, "Give not that which is holy unto the dogs, neither cast your pearls before swine, lest they trample them under their feet, and turn again and lacerate you." To most persons this verse implies the worst

265

kind of intolerance or prejudice. And, while it is true that it does not actually teach prejudice, it is also true that it does teach the need for the utmost spiritual discernment and true discrimination on the part of Christians. In the simplest terms it means there are some persons with whom Christ's followers must not share some parts of spiritual truth.

NOT ALL TO BE SAVED

There is something in that statement that somehow goes against the highly permissive spirit of our age. For this reason, if for no other, it is necessary to place the teaching in the widest possible spectrum of biblical truth. What is the context into which the verse fits? Quite clearly it is the teaching that some, but not all, will be saved and that among those who will not be saved there will always be some who are so opposed to God's truth that the Christian should have no dealings with them.

Let me give some texts. In Matthew 15:14 Jesus said of the Pharisees, "Let them alone; they are blind leaders of the blind. And if the blind lead the blind, both shall fall into the ditch." In other words, the disciples were to make no attempt to convert them. The Apostle John, who is noted for his great emphasis on love, nevertheless said that if a person who does not believe in Christ's divinity should come preaching a gospel which is therefore not the Christian Gospel, the Christian should not even welcome him into his house. He writes, "If there come any unto you, and bring not this doctrine, receive him not into your house, neither bid him Godspeed; for he that biddeth him Godspeed is partaker of his evil deeds" (2 John 10, 11). Jude wrote, "And of some have compassion, making a difference" (v. 22). That is discrimination. Paul added, "As we said before, so say I now again, If any man preach any other gospel unto you than that ye have received, let him be accursed" (Gal. 1:9). He did not say, "Let him be converted."

In the light of these texts it is obvious that Christ's call in the Sermon on the Mount for discernment is not as unique as it seems. In fact, it reminds us of a whole area of teaching that is quite easily forgotten and recalls us to the stern duties of discipline and understanding in the task of advancing God's claims through the Gospel.

TRUTH AND THE UNBELIEVER

What does the following statement mean practically — "Give not that which is holy unto the dogs"? What does it have to do with you? With me? What does it have to do with the Church of Jesus Christ generally?

The first thing it means (also the easiest to understand) is that all the truth of the Bible is not for the unbeliever. In fact, the only truth that *is* for him is the truth of his own sinfulness coupled with the offer of salvation through the death and resurrection of the Lord Jesus Christ. I know that some will answer, "Do you mean to tell me that the ethics of Christianity are not for unbelievers, that we are not to preach love, sacrifice, mercy, and other things to everyone?" That is exactly what I mean. We saw at the beginning of these studies that it was for the poor in spirit (not the proud), those who mourn for their sin (not the carefree), the ones whom God has made meek (not the boastful) to whom these teachings are given. You must have the Spirit of Christ within before you can take up His ethics.

Someone else will say, "But what about prayer? Can't you teach the non-Christian about prayer?" Again the answer is No. There is not a line in the Bible to support the idea of the value of prayer for any unbeliever. In fact, the Bible explicitly states that God will not hear the prayer of unbelievers. "When ye spread forth your hands, I will hide mine eyes from you; yea, when ye make many prayers, I will not hear" (Isa. 1:15). The only prayer that God will ever hear from an unbeliever is the prayer that asks for salvation on the basis of the death of the Lord Jesus Christ. And this doctrine is the only one that we have authority to preach to anyone who has not already become a child of God by believing it.

Moreover, isn't this precisely what we have in the example of the Lord Jesus Christ? There are persons who think of Jesus as going about the countryside preaching the Gospel to everyone who would listen and telling them all about His kingdom. It is probably closer to the truth to say that Jesus was the most discriminating of all preachers in terms of what He taught and to whom He taught it.

Take the case of the woman of Samaria, which John records in his gospel. Here was a woman who had a keen interest in religious questions. Jesus could have spoken to her either on the basis of her theological understanding or her ethics. Instead, He resisted her efforts to turn the conversation to those things and constantly redirected her thoughts to Himself. He offered to give her spiritual water, and she asked whether He was greater than her great ancestor, Jacob. Jesus directed her back to the spiritual nature of that which He was giving. She wanted to talk about the proper place for worship. We might call it liturgies. Jesus pointed to the fact that salvation was of the Jews and that the Messiah was to come through Judaism. Finally, when she began to debate about the coming of the Messiah, Jesus said firmly, "I that speak unto thee am he." For this woman, as for all unbelievers, there was to be no solution to religious or theological questions until there was an acceptance of Christ and a true understanding of His person.

Communion and Church Membership

There is also an important application of this principle to the standards for membership within the Christian churches. If it is true, as I have just indicated, that all the truths of the Bible are not for the unbeliever, then it is readily apparent that church membership is not for him either. For membership in the local church implies membership in the Body of Christ. And one becomes a member of Christ's Body only by believing in the Gospel.

Unfortunately, there are thousands of persons in the churches today who have been received by transfer of letter without a clear statement of faith or by committees who were more interested in the applicant's social position than in his position before Almighty God. These ought never to have been admitted to church membership. It is a scandal and a great weakness. For such persons and for churches that permit it, church membership has become a partial fulfillment of Malachi 2:1, 2 which says, "And now, O ye priests, this commandment is for you. If ye will not hear, and if ye will not lay it to heart, to give glory unto my name, saith the LORD of hosts, I will even send a curse upon you, and *I will curse your blessings;* yea, I have cursed them already, because ye do not lay it to heart." In such cases membership in the Church of Jesus Christ, which should be a thing of great blessing, has become a curse under which many a church and many a denomination are laboring.

I am afraid, too, that there are many persons in our day for whom the Lord's table has become a curse, for it has led many a person to think that he is right with God merely because he has followed some rite of the Christian religion.

Dr. Barnhouse writes, "How terrible it is for an individual to go to the Lord's Supper and think that he is in a place of special privilege when he has no true fellowship with the Lord God who is the only giver of blessings! Must it not be said of many today, 'Let their table be made a snare'? The Communion table is not to be the table of just any professing Christian; it is the Lord's table. . . . The table can be a snare that hardens the heart and makes a man think that he has satisfied God's demands for inward justice and righteousness because he has allied himself with the outward rites of some form of the Christian religion." *

Let every man examine himself. An early church writer once said, "Let no man eat or drink of your Eucharist except those baptized into the name of the Lord; for, as regards this, the Lord has said, 'Give not that which is holy unto dogs.'" The Lord's table is for Christians only. Let those who are responsible for admitting non-believers into church membership take warning.

PREACHING THE GOSPEL

The final application of this text is the clearest and yet the most difficult to speak of, for it relates to those persons who are more than mere unbelievers. They are those whom Jesus Christ called "children of the devil." According to the full teaching of the Word of God, we are to preach the Gospel to mere unbelievers. But to those who have heard the Gospel and who, in the hardness of their hearts, actually despise and mock it, we are to say nothing. Instead, like Jesus Himself, Paul, and all the other disciples, we are simply to shake the dust from our feet and go elsewhere.

I know that there will be some who find this thought unacceptable and who refuse to admit that any man can be like this. But the truth is of God, and all history provides examples. In the Middle Ages one of the most decadent of the Roman pontiffs said of Christianity, "What profit this farce has brought us." A Protestant king wishing to rule France by gaining the esteem of the populace once followed his own instincts and took a Roman mass saying, "Paris is well worth a mass." In our time the same spirit

*Donald Grey Barnhouse, *God's Covenants* (Grand Rapids: Wm. B. Eerdmans, 1963), p. 120.

makes light of the most holy of spiritual teachings. Thus, in the name of wit they write, "Custer died for your sins," "Jesus is the answer (but what is the question?)," or "Jesus saves green stamps." Don't laugh. The words are the barkings of dogs or the grunting of swine, and the Christian is disobeying God when he casts his pearls before them.

Is there hope for such men? We cannot say. But if there is, it lies in the sovereignty of God and in the demonstrable reality of true Christian living, not in words. William Barclay, the great British devotional commentator, in *The Gospel of Matthew,* writes, "It is often impossible to talk to some people about Jesus Christ. Their insensitiveness, their moral blindness, their intellectual pride, and cynical mockery, the tarnishing film, may make them impervious to words about Christ. But it is always possible to show men Christ; and the weakness of the Church lies not in lack of Christian arguments, but in lack of Christian lives." *

GOD'S PEARLS

We have really dealt with the problem of spiritual discrimination, unpleasant as it may have been, but before we end this study we can note a few entirely different but very pleasant things suggested by the word "pearls."

First, it suggests to us what we ought wisely to regard as our true riches. Just a few verses previous to this in His sermon, Jesus had spoken of those who were overly preoccupied with earth's riches. Now He reminds us that the Christian's riches are actually found in God's Word. The truths of the Word are our treasure.

> *Thy Word is like a deep, deep mine;*
> *And jewels rich and rare*
> *Are hidden in its mighty depths*
> *For every searcher there.*

Second, the verse suggests that we should be content with this treasure, which the world despises, even though on the physical level we should be asked to endure the most serious calamities of life. The great Australian commentator, Arthur W. Pink, writes on this point: "We may lose our health and wealth, our friends and fame, yet this treasure remains. Here is a lamp for the darkest night (Ps. 119:105). Here is to be found comfort in the sorest

---

* William Barclay, *The Gospel of Matthew* (Philadelphia: The Westminster Press, 1958), Vol. I, p. 273.

affliction (Ps. 119:50). Here are to be obtained songs for our pilgrimage (Ps. 119:54)." * No Christian is ever poor or destitute who has these riches.

Finally, the verse intimates how we are to use this treasure. Pearls have high value, and a wise man should take great pains to secure them. God's Word is truly a pearl of great price. Do you so value it? Do you dig for the pearls? Do you cultivate the mine? When you have uncovered these truths, do you preserve them, committing them to memory and thus locking them forever in your heart? David did this, for he wrote, "Thy word have I hidden in mine heart, that I might not sin against thee" (Ps. 119:11). Mary did it; so did Martha. So have countless others. May this be your practice also.

* Arthur W. Pink, *An Exposition of the Sermon on the Mount* (Grand Rapids: Baker Book House, 1969), p. 294.

Chapter 38

Our Gracious God

(Matthew 7:7-11)

If a young man wants to ask his father for something, he will pattern his request on the nature and the temperament of his father. If the father is ill-tempered and stingy, the young man will ask for little. He will take care to present his need in the most winsome and unobjectionable manner. If the father is good-natured and generous, the child will present his need openly and with great confidence.

It is the same spiritually. If a man prays, he will pray in harmony with his view of the god to whom he is praying. If the gods are capricious, as the Greeks believed, then men will come warily and will be on their guard. If the god is vengeful, a man will be fearful. If God is gracious, as Jesus Christ declared the true God to be, then the one who believes in Him can come boldly. And he will not fear to ask for good gifts of the One who is declared to be his Father.

It is this that gives the full measure of importance to the verses which form the next section of the Sermon on the Mount, for the verses contain the Lord's declaration that God is indeed gracious to those who are His spiritual children. He declared, "Ask, and it shall be given you; seek, and ye shall find; knock, and it shall be opened unto you; for every one that asketh receiveth; and he that seeketh findeth; and to him that knocketh it shall be opened. Or what man is there of you whom, if his son ask bread, will he give him a stone? Or if he ask a fish, will he give him a serpent? If ye then, being evil, know how to give good gifts unto your children, how much more shall your Father, who is in heaven, give good things to them that ask him?" (Matt. 7:7-11). According

272

to these words, God is not harsh, revengeful, or stingy. On the contrary, He is loving, gracious, and merciful; and He is anxious to give the very best gifts to His children.

GOD'S CHILDREN

This passage may be summarized by a few simple propositions. First, it applies only to those who are really God's children.

This means, of course, that these verses (as well as all others in the Bible that refer to prayer) do not include everyone. They say, "Ask, and it shall be given you; seek, and ye shall find; knock, and it shall be opened unto you." Who are the "you's" in this text? The answer is in the full context, for it is clear that they are only those who have God, the Father of the Lord Jesus Christ, for their Father. The promises do not concern Buddhists. They do not concern Mohammedans. They do not concern nominal Protestants or nominal Roman Catholics. They are promises only for those in whose hearts God has performed the miracle of the new birth, so that while at one time they were without Christ, were aliens to Israel and strangers to the covenants of promise, having no hope, and without God in the world, they are now seen to be fellow citizens and members of God's spiritual household (Eph. 2: 12, 19).

Moreover, the promises of this section are additionally restricted to those who are obedient children. This is implied in the context of the Sermon on the Mount, and it is seen more clearly in other passages. Take 1 John 3:22, for example. This verse says, "And whatever we ask, we receive of him, because we keep his commandments, and do those things that are pleasing in his sight." Why does John say that his prayers are always being answered? It is because he is a member of God's family, of course. But it is also more than that. John says that it is because he keeps God's commandments and because he seeks to please Him. The person who does that can be certain that his prayers will be heard and that all of them will be answered.

I know that someone will say, "But isn't God the Father of all men? And doesn't He hear all prayers?" The answer to that is, "No! He is not the Father of all men. And He does not hear the prayers of those who are not in His family."

Do you know what the Lord Jesus Christ taught in the thirteenth chapter of Luke, verses 24-30? It is almost the exact counterpart of the text we are considering, and the point of Luke's passage is that there can be no answer to those who are not in God's family. Jesus had just taught that the only ones who would be saved were those who entered in by the narrow gate. He was referring to faith in Himself. He added that many would seek to enter in by other means but would not be able to. He then uttered this great sentence, "When once the master of the house is risen up, and hath shut the door, and ye begin to stand outside, and to knock at the door, saying, Lord, Lord, open unto us; and he shall answer and say unto you, I know you not from where ye are; then shall ye begin to say, We have eaten and have drunk in thy presence, and thou hast taught in our streets. But he shall say, I tell you, I know you not from where ye are; depart from me, all ye workers of iniquity." In both cases there is an asking. In both cases there is a knocking. But in Matthew it is the born-again child of God who is knocking and asking; in Luke it is the unbeliever.

If we are to exercise the spiritual discrimination and judgment that Christ was talking about in verse 6 ("Give not that which is holy unto the dogs, neither cast your pearls before swine"), then we must apply verses 7-11 to believers in the Lord Jesus Christ only. And we must read the verse this way: "Ask [you who are born again], and it shall be given you [who are born again]; seek [you who are born again], and ye [who are born again] shall find; knock [you who are born again], and it shall be opened unto you [who are born again]."

ASKING

The second obvious teaching of these verses is this: even if we are Christians, we must *ask* for the things that God promises. This section of God's Word contains the positive statement of the principle ("Ask, and it shall be given you"). James 4:2 contains the negative statement ("Ye have not, because ye ask not"). But the teaching of both texts is identical. God delights to give good gifts to His children. Hence, if we do not receive them, the fault does not lie in God. It lies in our failure to ask things of Him.

I believe that these texts contain the explanation of the weakness and irrelevance of much Christian living and of much contemporary Christianity. Every now and then a minister is asked by some Christian, "Why is it that I cannot seem to find victory in the Christian life? Why does the Bible seem difficult to understand? Why do I still seem in bondage to some besetting sin? Why am I such a poor witness? Why do the high principles of Christian conduct have such little effect on my job and on the affairs of my family?" The answer is that you do not ask God for these blessings. You do not have because you do not ask.

"Why is it," many a minister is asking, "that I do not have the power of God in my teaching? Why is the Bible so dead? Why are there so few persons being converted? Why are there no leaders to expand and reinforce the ministry?" Again the answer is simply that you are not praying.

"Why are there so few outstanding candidates for the Christian ministry?" many Christian laymen are asking. "Why is the church so weak, the preaching so poor, our impact upon our society so ineffective, our goals so unrealized?" Again God answers, "You are neglecting your prayer life." You do not have because you are not asking.

Don't these words describe the churches as we know them today? Don't they describe many of us personally? Dr. Reuben A. Torrey, who makes many of these points quite eloquently in his book *The Power of Prayer,* writes correctly, "We do not live in a praying age. We live in an age of hustle and bustle, of man's efforts and man's determination, of man's confidence in himself and in his own power to achieve things, an age of human organization, and human machinery, and human push, and human scheming, and human achievement; which in the things of God means no real achievement at all. . . . What we need is not so much some new organization, some new wheel, but 'the Spirit of the living creature in the wheels' we already possess." *

What do we lack in our own lives and in the Church generally? Is it wisdom to deal with this sophisticated and godly world, to distinguish good from evil, right from wrong, to present the claims of Christ intelligibly and with success? If it is, then we should ask wisdom of God. Jesus says, "If any of you lack wisdom, let him ask of God, who giveth to all men liberally, and upbraideth not, and it shall be given him" (James 1:5).

Do we lack suitable candidates for church office, for missions? Do we lack Sunday school teachers or church workers? If so, it is because we are not asking. Jesus said, "The harvest truly is plenteous, but the laborers are few. Pray ye, therefore, the Lord

* Reuben A, Torrey, *The Power of Prayer* (Grand Rapids: Zondervan, 1955), p. 16.

of the harvest, that he will send forth laborers into his harvest" (Matt. 9:37, 38).

Moreover, isn't it significant that these great remarks about prayer occur toward the end of the Sermon on the Mount after the long list of things that should characterize our lives as Christians? We read of purity of heart, and we lack it. We read of meekness, and we lack that. We lack integrity, love, trust in God, humility, discrimination, and all the other things Christ mentions. Isn't it true that Jesus mentions prayer again precisely at this point just so that we may be encouraged to ask God for these things? Prayer has not changed. God has not changed. His ear is as quick to hear and His arm as strong to save as ever. Then, let us ask!

Torrey writes, "Prayer can do everything that God can do, and as God can do anything, prayer is omnipotent. No one can stand against the man who knows how to pray and who meets all the conditions of prevailing prayer and who really prays." He adds that this is true because "the Lord God Omnipotent works for him and works through him." *

PREVAILING PRAYER

This brings us to our next point. Christ did not only say that we were to ask for God's blessings; He also said that we were to go on asking.

In the Greek language, which lies behind our New Testament, there are two basic kinds of imperatives. There is the aorist imperative which is a command to do one particular thing at one specific point in time, and there is a present imperative which is a command not only to do that thing once but to go on doing it indefinitely. For example, if we were to say to a person driving a car, "Stop at that light," *stop* would be an aorist imperative; it would refer to only one action. However, if one were then to say, "And don't forget, always stop for the red lights," in this sentence *stop* would be a present imperative; for it would refer to something to be done repeatedly. The imperatives in this section of Christ's sermon — "ask," "seek," and "knock" — are present imperatives. Hence, they are a command to pray repeatedly, to persist in prayer. They are a command not to become discouraged.

I know that there is something about the idea of prevailing prayer that on the surface at least seems contrary to a Calvinistic

* *Ibid.*, p. 17.

way of thinking, but the conflict is only superficial. In two of Jesus' parables there is the story of a person who prevailed in a request by means of perseverance. In Luke 11:5-10, there is the story of a man who lacked food to feed a guest who arrived at his home at midnight. He went to his neighbor. At first the neighbor did not want to be bothered, but at last he gave the things which were needed because of the man's persistence. Jesus then repeated His teaching from the Sermon on the Mount, saying, "Ask, and it shall be given you; seek, and ye shall find; knock, and it shall be opened unto you." In Luke 18:1-8 Jesus told of a widow who gained justice from a dishonest judge through a similar course of action. He then added, "And shall not God avenge his own elect, who cry day and night unto him, though he bear long with them?" (v. 7). Paul wrote to the Thessalonians, "Pray without ceasing" (1 Thess. 5:17). He wrote to the Romans, "I beseech you, brethren, for the Lord Jesus Christ's sake, and for the love of the Spirit, that ye strive together with me in your prayers to God for me" (Rom. 15:30).

In all these texts the emphasis falls on the discipline of prayer and persistence. Persistence! That is the thing. We are to realize our need and then have persistence in seeking its fulfillment.

GOD'S SPIRIT

As we do this we are also to pray knowing that God sees our needs more than we do and is actually far ahead of us in fulfilling them. In fact, this is one ministry, perhaps one of the greatest ministries, of the Holy Spirit. Paul writes, "Likewise, the Spirit also helpeth our infirmity; for we know not what we should pray for as we ought; but the Spirit himself maketh intercession for us with groanings which cannot be uttered. And he that searcheth the hearts knoweth what is the mind of the Spirit, because he maketh intercession for the saints according to the will of God" (Rom. 8: 26, 27).

Do you see what this means? It means that God the Holy Spirit not only dwells within us, hearing what we say and then responding to it. He also takes an initiative in prayer, probing our hearts to see our greatest needs, and then interpreting our prayers in that light to God our heavenly Father. God loves us. He wants to help us. Thus, He searches us out to see what He can do for us.

When my sisters and I were very young I remember what great difficulty we had in our home to discover before Christmas or before my father's birthday what we could do for him. I am sure he had obvious needs, but to us at the time it seemed as if he were the only man in the world who had everything. He liked to fish, but he seemed to have all the equipment he needed for fishing. He liked to hunt, but we could not help him there. We were always at great pains to discover some need that we could fulfill for him. If he would ever drop a hint of some need, we were then quite delighted if we could respond to the need and give him the thing he desired.

In exactly this way we are told that our gracious God and heavenly Father searches our hearts to see what we need, and then He delights to answer the need out of His inexhaustible storehouse of blessings.

Chapter 39

God's Straightedge

(Matthew 7:12)

During the first quarter of the nineteenth century, toward the end of Beethoven's life, an unknown musician made a small alteration in the construction of the harpsichord that subsequently altered the whole development of western music. Before his time most of what we call piano music was composed for that instrument, but because of its design the music itself was quite limited. The strings of a harpsichord are plucked by a small hook, producing a sound even in intensity and similar to that of a harp. In this change the hook was replaced by a hammer, so that the string was struck rather than plucked. This minute alteration made all the difference musically, for the dynamic range of the instrument was greatly increased. The harpsichord became a piano. And the way was paved for the dramatic and thrilling compositions of Rachmaninoff, Schumann, Brahms, Liszt and Chopin. The development of music then revolved to a large degree around the piano, just as it had previously revolved around the organ during the Baroque era.

This story illustrates the kind of change that was brought into the realm of ethics by the teaching of Jesus Christ, and in particular the change that is embodied in the so-called Golden Rule, to which we now come in our studies. The Golden Rule, which is found in the seventh chapter of Matthew, verse 12, is probably the most universally praised statement that Jesus ever made. It has been called "the topmost peak of social ethics . . . the Everest of all ethical teaching." But anyone who knows the history of ethics knows that this has resulted from the most minute change over the teachings of countless other religious teachers, philosophers, and rabbis.

What I mean is this. It is not at all difficult to find praiseworthy parallels to this saying in its *negative* form. Hillel, the renowned Jewish rabbi, once said to a follower, "What is hateful to yourself, do to no other; that is the whole Law, and the rest is commentary. Go and learn." In the book of Tobit (which was probably composed in the third century before Christ) there is a section in which the hero of the book tells his young son, "And what thou thyself hatest, do to no man." There is a story in *The Letter of Aristeas* of a Jewish scholar who instructed an Egyptian king, "As you wish that no evil should befall you, but to be a partaker of all good things, so you should act on the same principle towards your subjects and offenders, and you should mildly admonish the noble and good."

There are many other examples. William Barclay, who lists these examples among others in his commentary, also cites parallels in the teachings of Confucius, Epictetus, the Stoics, and in the *Hymns of the Faith* of Buddhism. They are similar. But the point is that all these sayings are negative. They say, "Do not do anything to anyone that you would not want them to do unto you." Jesus presented the same truth positively, thereby inverting the saying and, of course, changing its scope immeasurably. Jesus said, Therefore, all things whatever ye would that men should do to you, do ye even so to them; for this is the law and the prophets."

Because of this apparently small change, it is correct to say that there is no real parallel to this saying. It is unique and altogether sublime. Barclay says, "This is something which had never been said before. It is new teaching, and a new view of life and of life's obligations." *

AN IMPOSSIBLE STANDARD

It is clear above all else that to express the Rule in a positive form is to make it extremely more difficult. In fact, it makes it impossible for normal human beings to keep.

It always has been possible for men to keep the negative side of this saying. In its negative form the Rule is a legal principle, and the law always has self as center. Thus, it is possible for a man to discipline himself so that he does not hurt others, primarily because he does not want them to hurt him. He can stop at stop signs, pay his bills, obey the law, and many other things. To give

* William Barclay, *The Gospel of Matthew* (Philadelphia: The Westminster Press, 1958), Vol. I, p. 277.

a timely example, a man can avoid overt acts of prejudice because he does not want to alienate another person and so thereby suffer retaliation from him. He wants to keep peace, but he wants to do so primarily so that he will be able to keep on with the work of satisfying his own selfish needs and desires. Actually, as C. S. Lewis in *Mere Christianity* notes, he is much like the honest man paying his taxes. He pays them all right, but he hopes that there will be enough left over for him to live on. And this is true because he is actually taking his old, natural self as the starting point.

On the other hand, if a man is trying to keep the positive form of this saying, it becomes evident early that this is precisely what he cannot do. And he cannot do it precisely because he is taking himself as the starting point. The law tells us what we must not do. The saying of the Lord Jesus Christ tells us what we ought to do. But a man can do what Jesus says only if his mind is entirely off himself and fixed at all moments on the needs, cares, loves, joys, hopes, and dreams of other people. In this expression, Jesus is therefore actually outlining the true nature of morality. And He is asking us to see that the way into heaven is either by supplying an inward perfection equal to God's own love and grace and holiness, which no one can do, or else by turning from the demands of the law entirely in order to receive a new life from God which alone is capable of doing the things that God requires.

THE STANDARD CONDEMNS

At this point, then, we have actually reached the first great statement of the solution to the problem of human morality. But before we pursue it, it is necessary to see that the major effect the Golden Rule was intended to have on human goodness was to condemn it. It wipes it out. By this standard all natural, human goodness is condemned and, being weighed in the balances, is found wanting.

Perhaps we can see this most clearly if we substitute a very good British expression for the word "rule." The rule as we have it in the phrase "the Golden Rule," is a ruler, a twelve-inch measuring stick. But in England a ruler is called a straightedge. If this expression is transferred over to the phrase "the Golden Rule" so that it becomes "the Golden Straightedge," we could accurately say that Matthew 7:12 is God's straightedge by which a man may know how morally crooked he really is.

That is the purpose of the whole law of which the Golden Rule itself is only a partial summary. What does Paul teach us about the purpose of the law in Romans? He says, "Therefore, by the deeds of the law there shall no flesh be justified in his sight; for by the law is the knowledge of sin" (Rom. 3:20). Phillips, who is an Englishman and who knows the word "straightedge," has paraphrased the text, "No man can justify himself before God by a perfect performance of the Law's demands — indeed it is the straightedge of the Law that shows how crooked we are."

Imagine a group of children sitting at their desks in an elementary school. The teacher says to the children, "We are going to draw a picture today, and I want you to begin by drawing a straight line down the center of your paper." At this moment the principal sticks his head in at the door, and the teacher has to step out for a moment. The children go on drawing, some very carefully and others with carelessness. The teacher is delayed, and in a few minutes the children are comparing their lines. "My line is straighter than yours," one child says. "No it's not," the other child answers. Pretty soon the lines are compared, and it is soon clear that some lines are better and others are much worse. Some of the children say, "Well, Suzie has drawn the best line." Most of them agree except for George and Arthur who say, "But she had a better pencil than we did."

That is how it is when the teacher returns. Some of the children think their lines are quite straight. But if the teacher were then to take the straightedge and draw a second line on the paper of each child, even the best of the children's lines would seem wavering and very inadaquate.

That is exactly what we have in human morality. Men draw the lines of human character and then compare the lines to see whose line is straightest. "I'm straighter morally than you are." "No, you're not, I am." "Arthur's the best." But then God enters and produces His straightedge, and we see that all human lines of character are crooked.

If a man could keep the Golden Rule — if, if, if, if, if, if — then he could step into heaven and say, "Move over, God, and let me sit down on the throne with You. You gave Your standard, and I've kept it. Therefore, I am as perfect as You are. It's You and I from here on in." If a man could keep that standard, he could take over heaven. But on the other hand, if a man sees that he has not kept it and that indeed in his own strength he will never be able to keep this standard, then he must take his place with all lost humanity, admitting that he has fallen short of the glory of God and deserves God's judgment. To such men God comes with the offer of salvation, revealing that He has set forth His own Son to be their righteousness and to provide them with a heavenly life that alone of all lives is capable of pleasing Him.

> *Jesus, thy blood and righteousness*
> *My beauty are, my glorious dress;*
> *'Midst flaming worlds, in these arrayed,*
> *With joy shall I lift up my head.*
>
> *Jesus, be endless praise to thee,*
> *Whose boundless mercy hath for me —*
> *For me a full atonement made,*
> *An everlasting ransom paid.*

With such righteousness — and not a righeousness of our own making — we shall be accepted before God forever in the Beloved.

NEW MEN

At this point many very good studies would stop. For this is the Christian Gospel and it lies at the heart of all Scripture. It is a good place to end. However, I believe that if we were to end here, we would be untrue to this text before us. For the Sermon on the Mount was given, as we saw in one of our earlier studies, not merely to drive a man to Christ (although that is the first thing necessary), but also to set forth that standard of morality to which God is constantly leading the Christian.

William Barclay says, "To obey this commandment [he is referring to the Golden Rule] a man must become a new man with a new center to his life." * But when we understand the Gospel in its fullness we realize that it is precisely to make us new men that God has redeemed us. He did not save us so we would remain in our sin. He saved us to make us like Jesus, and that means to live out this standard. In *Studies in the Sermon on the Mount,* Dr. D. Martyn Lloyd-Jones observes correctly, "After all, the law was not meant to be praised, it was meant to be practiced. Our Lord did not preach the Sermon on the Mount in order that you and I might comment upon it, but in order that we might carry it out." **

* *Ibid.,* p. 281.
** D. Martyn Lloyd-Jones, *Studies in the Sermon on the Mount* (Grand Rapids: Wm. B. Eerdmans, 1967), Vol. II, p. 211.

Someone will say, "But how can I carry it out? Didn't you just say that the Golden Rule is impossible, in fact, that it condemns me?" Yes, I did. "Then how can I do it?" The answer is that *you* cannot do it; but when God enters your life at the moment of your conversion a new life is created by which the new you — fed and nourished by the Spirit of God — is made capable of attaining increasingly to all that God requires. That is why there are so many commandments for the Christian in the Bible. Take Romans 12: 1, 2, as an example. "I beseech you therefore, brethren, by the mercies of God, that ye present your bodies a living sacrifice, holy, acceptable unto God, which is your reasonable service. And be not conformed to this world, but be ye transformed by the renewing of your mind, that ye may prove what is that good, and acceptable, and perfect, will of God." If we are to approach this commandment as natural men, we find it impossible. But when we come as Christians, with the life of God Himself within, we find it attainable. And we find that the Spirit of God constantly urges us to do it.

Moreover, it is also true that God will continue to do this with us even though we may grow tired of the process and want to settle for less.

We find an excellent illustration of this principle in *Mere Christianity* by C. S. Lewis: "When I was a child I often had a toothache, and I knew that if I went to my mother she would give me something which would deaden the pain for that night and let me get to sleep. But I did not go to my mother — at least, not till the pain became very bad. And the reason I did not go was this. I did not doubt she would give me the aspirin; but I knew she would also do something else. I knew she would take me to the dentist next morning. I could not get what I wanted out of her without getting something more, which I did not want. I wanted immediate relief from pain: but I could not get it without having my teeth set permanently right. And I knew those dentists; I knew they started fiddling about with all sorts of other teeth which had not yet begun to ache. They would not let sleeping dogs lie; if you gave them an inch they took an ell.

"Now, if I may put it that way, Our Lord is like the dentists. If you give Him an inch, He will take an ell. . . . That is why He warned people to 'count the cost' before becoming Christians. 'Make no mistake,' He says. 'If you let Me, I will make you perfect.

The moment you put yourself in My hands, that is what you are in for. Nothing less, or other, than that. You have free will, and if you choose, you can push Me away. But if you do not push Me away, understand that I am going to see this job through. . . . I will never rest, nor let you rest, until you are literally perfect — until my Father can say without reservation that He is well pleased with you, as He said He was well pleased with Me.'" *

What Lewis, the great twentieth-century apologist, says in that quotation is absolutely right. It is an expression of Philippians 1:6. "He who hath begun a good work in you will perform it until the day of Jesus Christ." God will not quit. Hence, the Golden Rule (as well as all of the Sermon on the Mount) is as much a statement of where God is taking the Christian as it is a standard by which the goodness of the natural man is judged. What will it be? Will you flail away at that or some other standard, and be judged by it? Or will you surrender to Christ, letting God enter your life and re-make you into His image? If you let Him, He will turn you into the kind of being who really will think first of others and will reflect back to God, like a pure mirror, some of His own limitless glory, power, love, and goodness. The process may be painful at times, but it will be certain. And you will not miss the goal.

* C. S. Lewis, *Mere Christianity* (New York: The Macmillan Company, 1958), pp. 157, 158.

Chapter 40

The Need for Decision

(Matthew 7:13, 14)

The Golden Rule is the concluding verse of the major part of the Sermon on the Mount, for all the verses that follow it are but a long, although significant, postscript. Like Matthew 5:48, the verse that concludes the first chapter of the Sermon, the Golden Rule aptly summarizes all that has gone before it and then lifts the eyes of the reader to Jesus Christ who is the only possible source of such goodness. From this point on Jesus turns to a series of warnings designed to keep His listeners from falling by the wayside through unbelief, apathy, deceit, hypocrisy, or discouragement.

CHRIST'S WARNINGS

That does not mean, of course, that the verses that follow are unimportant. Because, although they are largely in the nature of a postscript, for some persons — perhaps yourself — they could be the most important verses of all. For instance, we may imagine a man who has agreed with the bulk of this teaching but who thinks he can put it into practice merely by exerting a little more effort while continuing in the same general direction in which he is going. To such a man these verses are a reminder that the Christian life must begin with an about-face and that it cannot be carried on without a personal commitment to the Lord Jesus. Another man finds himself thinking that religion is a good thing, and he determines to go on listening to other teachers. Jesus warns that there are many false prophets who have gone out into the world, and that religion from these sources will not save him. In the same way He warns against settling for an outward profession of Christianity without experiencing a change of heart, and He cautions that the

286

only valid religious life must be built upon Himself as the only firm and, therefore, adequate foundation. Obviously, these warnings apply to many who are grappling with the claims of the Gospel in the twentieth century.

We must see, however, that these concluding thoughts also had a particular poignancy for those who listened to this Sermon for the first time, those who heard the Sermon in Galilee presumably during the earliest months of Jesus' ministry.

We must remember here that Jesus was speaking of ultimate things to those who as yet had no knowledge of His coming death and resurrection. Those events, on which salvation through faith depended, were yet years away, while in between there would be days in which the popularity of the Galilean ministry would give way to insults, trials, scorn, and danger. What was to happen to His hearers during the intervening years? Was the teaching of the Sermon on the Mount to become for them only a beautiful dream buried somewhere in their memories of the past? Was it to be enshrined as something very lovely but totally impractical? Or, on the contrary, would it challenge them to keep on? Certainly, Jesus was calling for the latter. He was telling His hearers, "Keep on. Do not fall by the wayside. If you do keep on, one day you will see the gate clearly, and you will pass through to life everlasting."

THE NARROW WAY

If all this is true — that is, if these verses (Matt. 7:13-27) are primarily a warning to those of Christ's time to keep on until His death and resurrection brought His ministry to completion — then it is also clear how we must understand the first of these four warnings.

Jesus said, "Enter in at the narrow gate; for wide is the gate, and broad is the way, that leadeth to destruction, and many there be who go in that way; because narrow is the gate, and hard is the way, which leadeth unto life, and few there be that find it" (Matt. 7:13, 14). What does this mean? In this context the verses can mean only that there is a broad way of life leading to a broad gate which in turn leads to destruction, upon which all men naturally are traveling. And there is a narrow way leading to a narrow gate, which is Jesus Christ and which leads to eternal life, upon which some of His hearers may be about to be traveling. Therefore, Jesus is saying, "Keep on the narrow way until you pass through Me to salvation."

We must understand this idea clearly if we are to avoid the most common and most dangerous misinterpretation of these verses. If we are to assume that Christ's hearers are Christians at this point (which, of course, they could not be but which many persons have easily assumed), then this verse is really a warning to keep on working at the Christian life in order that one does not lose his salvation eventually. In this case, of course, the verse would contradict the doctrine of eternal security of the believer which is everywhere apparent in Scripture. Unfortunately, some Bible teachers have taught that this is true, and others have implied it by stressing in this context that the Christian life is a narrow life and that only he who perseveres to the end shall be saved.

The warning does not mean that. On the contrary, it means that if you are an unbeliever who has been exposed to the Gospel, you must not stop short of salvation by imagining that you can simply continue along the same path you are following. If you are not on the way to Christ, you are on the way from Him. Thus, you will either come finally to a perfect salvation by the grace of God through the Lord Jesus Christ or to the lake of fire withou. Him. That is the heart of Christ's warning.

"I Am the Way"

Another truth also lies at the heart of His warning, the truth that salvation is by faith in the Lord Jesus Christ only. What is the gate? What is the way that leads to life? The answer is: the Lord Jesus Christ. Jesus said, "I am the door; by me if any man enter in, he shall be saved" (John 10:9). He said, "I am the way, the truth, and the life; no man cometh unto the Father, but by me" (John 14:6). These verses throw only proper light upon our text. For they show that Jesus was speaking of faith in Himself when He told the Galileans, "Narrow is the gate, and hard is the way, which leadeth unto life, and few there be that find it." The way to heaven is as narrow as Jesus.

When I was in college I was taught that one of the things a student should never do when writing a paper was to make a value judgment. Since my college days I have come to doubt the wisdom and correctness of that axiom. But I accepted it then. For I was taught that you could describe the subject matter, you could contrast it with something else, you could dissect it; but you could not say that the thing itself was either good or bad — inherently worse or better than something else.

The same idea that was present in the classroom then, today pervades our entire American culture. The result is that for most people nothing is to be received as absolute truth, and nothing is inherently better than anything else. Right here Christianity takes issue. Christianity is unique in claiming to have absolute truth, since it presents Jesus Christ as the sole way to God. Jesus' words about Himself, as in the texts I have mentioned, are unqualified; and this means that if Jesus is right, as He is, then there are no other ways to God for men to follow.

Let me make this point clearly. First, it means that no man will be able to come to God through nature. That is a popular thought among many people who are dissatisfied with the Christian churches. But the idea that God can be found in nature is an illusion and leads to idolatry.

Several years ago, after I had spoken on this subject in my church, a woman came up to me and told me of her experiences working with Campus Crusade for Christ in California. She said that she had worked on the beaches with surfers. In many cases she was told by the surfers that they worshiped God in nature. She soon learned to ask, however, "What is God?" And often she was told, "My surfboard is my god," or something similar to it. Well, the statement may be honest. But the view is pure paganism, and it is nothing but a delusion to think that this attitude has anything to do with the worship of God Almighty, Father of the Lord Jesus Christ. A man is deluding himself if he thinks that he is worshiping God in nature as he plays golf on Sunday mornings or goes for a drive in the country. If you are doing this, you are not worshiping God in nature. You are either not worshiping at all (which is probably most often the case) or you are worshiping nature, and nature is not God. That belief is pantheism.

Let me ask this: Do you know what the revelation of God in nature is for? The Bible says that it is to condemn men for failing to recognize God. Romans 1:20 says that the wrath of God is revealed from heaven against all men, for "the invisible things of him from the creation of the world are clearly seen, being understood by the things that are made, even his eternal power and Godhead, so that they are without excuse." No man has ever come to the God of our Lord Jesus Christ through nature.

In the same way, men cannot find God in mere pious thoughts or religion. That is, they will not find God in the mere performance of certain religious duties, whether this is the following of the fourfold or sevenfold path to Nirvana, whether it is a life of meditation, whether it is the religion of "speed," LSD, or heroin, or even whether it is the ceremonial aspects of Christianity. God has written a No over all human efforts to be religious in order that He might write a Yes over all who abandon religion and turn to Him in Christ. Religion is the seeking after a god in your own image. Christianity is God's seeking you and moving to redeem you by the death of His Son, the Lord Jesus.

Neither can men find God through morality, either by attempting to live up to God's standard or by attempting to live up to their own. Men fell short of all standards. The first three chapters of Romans are written to show that no man will find God in any way but through Christ, and the man with high moral standards is included along with the rest. Paul describes three different types of persons — the pagan man, the moral man, the religious man — but he concludes with a word of condemnation against all human goodness. "There is none righteous, no, not one: there is none that understandeth, there is none that seeketh after God. They are all gone out of the way, they are together become unprofitable; there is none that doeth good, no, not one" (Rom. 3:10-12). Our natural ways will not lead us to the Father.

And yet, there is a way. The way is Jesus. You and I have sinned, in little ways or in big ways (it does not matter which), and sin keeps us from God. Unless sin is removed we shall never get into God's heaven. In fact, God will not even let us get close to it. On the other hand, even if we ourselves bear a just punishment for sin, we cannot get to heaven either. For the punishment of sin is to be separated from God. What is the solution? The solution is that God provided Jesus Christ as a substitute for us, that He died, not for His own sin (because He did not have any), but for your sin and mine. God will not punish the same sin twice. Consequently, if you will believe that Jesus died for you, if you will acknowledge Him as your substitute, then God will remove your sin forever, and it will be correct to say that you have passed over the narrow way through the narrow gate into salvation.

Do not make the mistake of counting upon your moral record as a way of coming to God. It is your record that gets you into trouble in the first place. Your record will condemn you, no matter how good you think you are or how good you appear in other men's eyes. Count on the fact that Jesus paid the penalty for your sin, that He did what no other person could do. Accept the fact that He by His death provided the way for simple, sinful people like you and me to enter heaven.

> *Thou art the Way: to Thee alone*
> *From sin and death we flee;*
> *And he who would the Father seek*
> *Must seek Him, Lord, by Thee.*
>
> *Thou art the Truth: Thy Word alone*
> *True wisdom can impart;*
> *Thou only canst inform the mind,*
> *And purify the heart.*
>
> *Thou art the life: the rending tomb*
> *Proclaims Thy conquering arm,*
> *And those who put their trust in Thee*
> *Nor death nor hell shall harm.*
>
> *Thou art the Way, the Truth, the Life:*
> *Grant us that Way to know,*
> *That Truth to keep, that Life to win,*
> *Whose joys eternal flow.*

A NEED FOR DECISION

We need to see one more great truth from this passage. Jesus said, "Enter in at the narrow gate," or, as the parallel saying in Luke's gospel puts it, "Strive to enter in" (Luke 13:24). Clearly it is not enough merely to listen to preaching about this gate or to study its architecture. It is not enough to praise it. It is not enough to stand by it. It must be *entered*. That means that everyone who comes under the preaching of the Gospel must make a personal decision to enter into Christ.

The idea that a decision is necessary in order to become a Christian is strange to many people today chiefly because they imagine that they already are Christians. Some think they have inherited Christianity from their parents, who may or may not actually have been believers. Some think they are Christians simply because they have been born in a so-called Christian country. Others consider themselves Christians because they are not Jews, Mohammedans, or "pagans." But none of these assumptions is adequate. No one is automatically a Christian. You cannot be neutral, for Jesus teaches that you are either on the broad way or on the narrow way. You cannot just drift into Christianity. The true gate is narrow and the way that leads to it is hard. If you are to become a believer, you must make a decision. No one else can settle the matter for you.

That always has been the case. Moses told the people of his day: "See, I have set before thee this day life and good, and death and evil. . . . Therefore, choose life, that both thou and thy seed may live" (Deut. 30:15, 19). Joshua spoke to the people, saying, "Choose you this day whom ye will serve" (Josh. 24:15). Jeremiah wrote on behalf of Jehovah: "Unto this people thou shalt say, Thus saith the LORD, Behold I have set before you the way of life, and the way of death" (Jer. 21:8). Peter declared, "Repent, and be baptized, every one of you, in the name of Jesus Christ for the remission of sins, and ye shall receive the gift of the Holy Spirit" (Acts 2:38). That is what God calls you to do.

What is the state of your heart? Perhaps you are one who has responded to many of these studies on the Sermon on the Mount, saying, "Yes, all those things are true." But they have never become true for you personally. If so, Jesus is warning you against that stance, for He is saying that that is not good enough. He is saying that there must come a point in your life at which He becomes *your* Savior. John Stott, minister of All Souls Church in London, is one who knows this, for he writes, "I remember how puzzled, even indignant, I was when it was first suggested to me that I needed to appropriate Christ and His salvation for myself. Thank God, I came to see that, though an acknowledgment that I need *a* Savior was good, and a belief that Christ was *the* Savior of the world was better, best of all was a personal acceptance of Him as *my* Savior." *

Jesus said, "I am the way, the truth, and the life." But He must be the way for you. He said, "I am the door." But you must enter it.

* John R. W. Stott, *Basic Christianity* (Chicago: Inter-Varsity Press, 1968), pp. 122, 123.

Chapter 41

Wolves in Sheep's Clothing

(Matthew 7:15-20)

Someone once said, "If you are going to place poison on a shelf where you have healing medicines, you had better label it clearly." He was discussing the presence of false teaching and false teachers in the Church; and he was recognizing the fact that if false teachers are going to be present in the Church (as the Bible teaches they will be), then they must be clearly identified before they do harm.

That is not just human wisdom; it is precisely the point of Christ's teaching in the Sermon on the Mount. In the last verses of the Sermon on the Mount (Matt. 7:13-27), Jesus warns against four things that can keep a person who has heard the Gospel from ultimately committing his life to the Lord. The first, which we looked at in the preceding study, is the false idea that a person can drift into salvation without having to make a personal decision concerning the Lord Jesus Christ. The second, which we come to now, is the error of the man who would hear Christ, decide to become religious, and then spend all his time listening to every teacher he can find. Jesus warns that there are false prophets in the world and that if a person turns from Christ to such teachers, these teachers will actually lead him away from the truth and from the source of salvation.

Jesus said, "Beware of false prophets, who come to you in sheep's clothing, but inwardly they are ravening wolves. Ye shall know them by their fruits. Do men gather grapes of thorns, or figs of thistles? Even so, every good tree bringeth forth good fruit, but a corrupt tree bringeth forth bad fruit. A good tree cannot bring forth bad fruit, neither can a corrupt tree bring forth good fruit. Every tree that bringeth not forth good fruit is hewn down, and cast into the fire. Wherefore, by their fruits ye shall know them" (Matt. 7:15-20).

FALSE PROPHETS

The practice of describing the enemies of God's people as wolves was common in Christ's day. For one thing, it was a natural image in a country where a large proportion of the people were either in the employ of herdsmen or were shepherds. For another, it was an image well-known from the Scriptures. For instance, Ezekiel had written of Israel's unrighteous rulers, "Her princes in her midst are like wolves ravening the prey, to shed blood, and to destroy souls, to get dishonest gain" (Ezek. 22:27). Zephaniah wrote, "Her princes within her are roaring lions; her judges are evening wolves . . ." (Zeph. 3:3). Paul used similar terms when he warned the Christians at Ephesus, "For I know this, that after my departing shall grievous wolves enter in among you, not sparing the flock. Also of your own selves shall men arise, speaking perverse things, to draw away disciples after them" (Acts 20:29, 30).

In our text in the Sermon on the Mount, these familiar ideas are given a slight twist which reveals the main thrust of Christ's teaching. According to Jesus the danger is not so much in the fact that there are going to be wolves in the *world* — although that is perfectly true — but that there are going to be wolves who have disguised themselves as *sheep*. In other words, the danger lies in the fact that there are going to be agents of the devil in the *Church*.

Someone will say, "Do you mean to tell me that God will allow men who are influenced by Satan to become church members?" The answer is, "Yes, indeed." And not only that, He also will allow them to become ministers and speak from the pulpit. This is the real meaning of 2 Corinthians 11:14, 15 which says, "For Satan himself is transformed into an angel of light. Therefore, it is no great thing if his ministers also be transformed as the ministers of righteousness, whose end shall be according to their works."

What is a prophet? Today the word usually means one who is able to tell what is coming in the future. In biblical times it had a much broader meaning. A prophet was one who spoke for another and particularly one who spoke for God. The true sense of the word is seen most clearly in a story from the fourth chapter of Exodus involving Moses. God had told Moses that he was going to send him to Egypt to lead His people out of that country into Palestine. Moses complained that he was not eloquent. Then "the anger of the LORD was kindled against Moses, and he said, Is not Aaron, the Levite, thy brother? I know that he can speak well. And also, behold, he cometh forth to meet thee. . . . Thou shalt speak unto him, and put words in his mouth; and I will be with thy mouth, and with his mouth, and will teach you what ye shall do. And he shall be thy spokesman unto the people" (Exod. 4:14-16). In this account Aaron is placed in the role of a prophet. Thus, we find God saying three chapters later, "See, I have made thee a god to Pharaoh; and Aaron, thy brother, shall be thy prophet" (Exod. 7:1).

When we carry this understanding of the word over into Christ's teaching, we see that Jesus actually is warning against men who will appear in the churches and pretend to speak for God when their teaching is really of the devil. These are the men spoken of in Jeremiah: "I have not sent these prophets, . . . I have not spoken to them, yet they prophesied. But if they had stood in my counsel, and had caused my people to hear my words, then they should have turned from their evil way, and from the evil of their doings" (Jer. 23:21, 22).

Do we have false prophets today? Do we have wolves in sheep's clothing? We certainly do. Moreover, we do not only have them in the pews and the pulpits. We have them in the denominational structures, in the seminaries, and in the church-related colleges. I find it amusing, in the light of our text, that today we call an academic degree or diploma a sheepskin. For some professors and ministers clearly cover their intentions with the sheepskins of higher learning while using their knowledge of the Bible and church history to damage the faith of those who listen to them. We are to be warned against such teachers.

No Straight Gate

All this brings us to the main point of Christ's teaching! How can we recognize false teaching? How can we detect a wolf in sheep's clothing? There are several answers.

First, there is no "straight gate" in the teaching of a false prophet. There is no "narrow way." This point comes from verses 13 and 14, the two verses that immediately precede Christ's warning about the false prophets. The verses of the Sermon on the Mount are not arranged as they are by accident. Thus, we are right to see a connection between verses 13 and 14 and Christ's warning about false prophets. He is saying that one of the ways you can detect the false prophet is by noticing that, although he says many things that seem probable, nevertheless he does not set forth the Lord Jesus Christ Himself as the only solution to man's need and the only door to salvation. Learn to apply this. When you hear preaching or teaching, or read about religion in books, ask yourself, "Does this system of thought have the Lord Jesus Christ as its center?" If it does, well and good. If not, then be warned against it.

Moreover, if you do this, you will not be led away from the truth by appearances. You will not be taken in by a polished but false proclamation. Likewise, you will not be turned off by a viewpoint that is true, even though it may be presented in an unusual fashion. This second point is particularly important because some Christians are too quick to assume that an unfamiliar vocabulary, or some other unusual aspect of a minister's preaching, marks him as a false prophet. They look for false teaching so intently that they fail to recognize true teaching.

An example of such a situation is found in the many youth workers of our day. Some of these Christian workers have the outward appearance and manners of the hippy community, but their purpose is to win these young men and women for Christ. Several years ago, when there was a general student strike on the University of California Berkeley campus, Campus Crusade immediately poured several hundred of their staff into the Berkeley area. Hippy-style workers mixed with students who were chanting, "Hell, no, we won't go," or "Out of Vietnam," and who were making the two-fingered peace sign. But the Campus Crusade workers held up their index finger only and chanted, "One way, one way, one way," meaning Jesus. That is Christianity. The first test of what is false or true teaching is whether or not Jesus Christ is proclaimed as the one way to God.

No Disturbing Doctrines

The second test for identifying false prophets is best seen in the writings of Jeremiah. It is this: False prophets do not have disturbing doctrines in their messages, even though the true state of man demands it. Their message is one of false peace. Jeremiah says, "They have healed also the hurt of the daughter of my people slightly, saying, Peace, peace; when there is no peace." Apparently Jeremiah thought that this truth was important enough to state more than once, for the identical verse occurs both in Jeremiah 6:

14 and 8:11. And he would undoubtedly say of all false prophets, as Arthur Pink does in *An Exposition of the Sermon on the Mount,* "There is nothing in their preaching which searches the conscience and renders the empty professor uneasy, nothing which humbles and causes their hearers to mourn before God; but rather that which puffs up, makes them pleased with themselves and to rest content in a false assurance." *

It is obvious that Jeremiah knew this situation in his own day, for he had a message of judgment upon the city of Jerusalem because of the sin of the people and, every time he preached it, there were false prophets saying that his words were untrue. They said that God loved His people so much He would not let evil come upon them (Jer. 23:16-22). But they were wrong, and Jeremiah was right. God allowed the Babylonians under King Nebuchadnezzar to destroy the city.

This can be applied to America. We have preachers and teachers in our day who are saying that all is well with America. Their message is one of peace, but there is no peace. There is a kind of false patriotism in our day that is wrapped up with the Gospel and that says, "America is a Christian country. God will not let anything happen to America." That is absolutely untrue. America is a pagan country today, and it is certainly every bit as materialistic as Soviet Russia. We must not preach false doctrine. Sin has its consequences; evil will be judged. Judgment will come, and it will come to America as much as to any other country. Moreover, it will come to you and me personally, unless our sin is covered by the blood of the Lord Jesus Christ.

True teaching involves the realities of man's depravity and sin, God's wrath and coming judgment, the need for repentance, and the answer to man's sin in Christ's vicarious atonement. Any teaching that omits these elements is erroneous.

THE TEST OF GOOD WORKS

Finally, there is the test of good works, which is the test that Jesus Himself gives in this sermon. He repeats it twice, once at the beginning of this section, once at the end: "Ye shall know them by their fruits . . . by their fruits ye shall know them" (vv. 16, 20). He shows that men are like fruit trees. Good ones only produce good fruit. Bad ones produce fruit that is bad.

* Arthur W. Pink, *An Exposition of the Sermon on the Mount* (Grand Rapids: Baker Book House, 1969), p. 339.

That means two things. First, it means that there must be fruit if the Christian life is genuine. On the one hand, it is certainly wrong to teach that salvation comes by works. Salvation is by grace through faith. Paul defends this doctrine in the book of Galatians. But then, it is equally wrong to imply that salvation can be real *without* good works. It is true that salvation may not produce good works as fast as we would like to see them. They may not appear in the same terms in which we are accustomed to see them. Nevertheless, there must be good works, and the evidence of them or the absence of them can be a very good test of false doctrine.

Second, fruit must be satisfying fruit. It must be spiritual fruit and not just the good works of which the world is capable. To put it practically we may ask, "Does the teaching really strengthen and encourage the hearer? Is it matched by blessing and true Christian character in the life of the teacher?"

This is suggested quite clearly by the meaning Christ's words must have had for those who heard them originally. For they must have related His words about grapes from thorns and figs from thistles to plants they knew personally. On this point William Barclay writes in *The Gospel of Matthew,* "There was a certain thorn, the buckthorn, which had little black berries which closely resembled little grapes. . . . There was a certain thistle, which had a flower, which, at least at a distance, might well be taken for a fig. The point is real, and relevant, and salutary. There may be a superficial resemblance between the true and the false prophet. The false prophet may wear the right clothes and use the right language; but you cannot sustain life with the berries of a buckthorn or the flowers of a thistle; and the life of the soul can never be sustained with the food which a false prophet offers. The real test of any teaching is: Does it strengthen a man to bear the burdens of life, and to walk in the way wherein he ought to go?" *

If we put these three things together — whether or not there is a straight gate in the message, whether or not the unpleasant themes of sin and judgment are dealt with along with the message of God's great love and grace, whether or not there is real and satisfying fruit as a result of such teaching — then we have a way of discerning truth from falsehood and of giving attention only to that message which comes from the Lord.

---

* William Barclay, *The Gospel of Matthew* (Philadelphia: The Westminster Press, 1958), Vol. I, p. 288.

Chapter 42

Nominal Christians

(Matthew 7:21-23)

In the final verses of the Sermon on the Mount, the Lord Jesus Christ has been warning His hearers against the things that can hinder a listener from going on to that full commitment to Chris that is the true gate to salvation. He has warned against the idea that salvation can come to a man in the normal course of things, that is, without true personal decision and conversion. He has warned against the false teachers and their doctrines. Now Jesus turns to a danger that lies within the heart of the individual himself. It is self-delusion, or deception.

Jesus said, "Not every one that saith unto me, Lord, Lord, shall enter into the kingdom of heaven, but he that doeth the will of my Father, who is in heaven. Many will say to me in that day, Lord, Lord, have we not prophesied in thy name? And in thy name have cast out demons? And in thy name done many wonderful works? And then will I profess unto them, I never knew you; depart from me, ye that work iniquity" (Matt. 7:21-23). This means that the listener to the Gospel must not count on a mere belief in Christ's person on the one hand, or the performance of great works in His name on the other hand as proof of his own salvation. These things will not save him. Rather, he must assure himself of his relation to Jesus Christ personally.

CHEAP GRACE

Dietrich Bonhoeffer knew the reality of this kind of self-delusion in the Lutheran Church in Germany in his day, and "cheap grace" was his term for describing it. Here was a church, like many of the denominations in America, in which the profession of faith

299

was present and in which good works were done, but in which most of the people had simply not been born again. They were taught "grace," but it was grace without conversion. As Proverbs says, "There is a generation that are pure in their own eyes, and yet are not washed from their filthiness" (Prov. 30:12).

In *The Cost of Discipleship* Bonhoeffer writes, "Cheap grace is the preaching of forgiveness without requiring repentance, baptism without church discipline, communion without confession, absolution without personal confession. Cheap grace is grace without discipleship, grace without the cross, grace without Jesus Christ, living and incarnate." *

This is precisely what we find in many large sectors of the so-called Church of Jesus Christ in our day. Several years ago Arthur W. Pink declared: "Never were there so many millions of nominal Christians on earth as there are today, and never was there such a small percentage of real ones. . . . We seriously doubt whether there has ever been a time in the history of this Christian era when there were such multitudes of deceived souls within the churches, who verily believe that all is well with their souls when in fact the wrath of God abideth on them." And then he added, "And we know of no single thing better calculated to undeceive them than a full and faithful exposition of these closing verses of our Lord's Sermon on the Mount." **

In the light of these truths, it is evident that Christ's words are a particularly pertinent warning to those who blithely believe a few doctrines, or who perform a smattering of so-called good works and yet have never entered into that kind of true commitment to Christ which results in increasingly costly obedience and in true discipleship.

FALSE CONFIDENCE

Does that describe you? Are you one who is correct in doctrine but who has never come to the point of knowing the Lord personally? If you are, the Lord Jesus Christ is speaking to you when He says, "Not every one that saith unto me, Lord, Lord, shall enter into the kingdom of heaven, but he that doeth the will of my Father, who is in heaven."

* Dietrich Bonhoeffer, *The Cost of Discipleship* (New York: The Macmillan Company, 1966), p. 47.

** Arthur W. Pink, *An Exposition of the Sermon on the Mount* (Grand Rapids: Baker Book House, 1969), pp. 377, 378.

What does that mean? Well, the address, "Lord, Lord," is actually a confession of faith. The word "Lord" (both in Hebrew and in Greek) is a word that denotes divinity. In the Old Testament, "Lord" is the word "Jehovah," a name for God. In the New Testament the word for "Lord" is *kurios*, by which citizens of the Roman Empire were required to confess the godhead of Caesar. Thus, Jesus says that there will be those in the history of the Church who will confess His divinity but who will never have entered into a true personal relationship with Him. Such persons will be found throughout the Church, and even, unfortunately, in its pulpits.

Someone will say, "Can that be? Can a man come out of seminary and still not be born again?" He certainly can. Moreover, a man can sit in the pews of a local church for years firmly believing that Christ is God, that He died on the cross, and even that He is coming back one day to judge the world, and yet never come to the place where he trusts that same Jesus Christ as his Savior.

That was the case with Luther. Luther was so concerned for his soul that he left his training in a secular occupation to enter the monastery of the Augustinian hermits in Erfurt, Germany. Erfurt's monastery was popular and respected. There Luther soon made good progress and was ordained to the priesthood. He studied Scripture, becoming a doctor of theology. He lectured on the Psalms, Romans, Galatians, Hebrews, and Titus. Now, if anyone had asked Luther at this point in his life, "Do you believe in the divinity of the Lord Jesus Christ?" he would have answered, "Of course, I do. I have always believed it." If you had asked him, "Do you believe that Jesus died on the cross and that He died for your sin?" he would have answered, "Yes," even though he did not then understand what that meant and was not born again. If you had asked, "Do you believe that Jesus Christ is coming back again to judge the world?", Luther would have answered, "Yes, I do, and I tremble at the thought."

Yet at this point in his life Luther did not know the Lord personally. Jesus was God, but not his God. Jesus was Lord, but not his Lord. Jesus was Savior, but not his Savior. Before the peace that he craved became his and before he could be used of God as the great Protestant reformer, he had to confront Jesus Christ Himself.

Because a man can believe certain Christian doctrines with his head and yet not be converted, there always will be counterfeit or nominal Christians in church circles. Some of them will be dangerous, for they will be planted there by the devil to deceive the unwary, like tares in fields of wheat. Others will only be self-deluded. Whatever the case, however, the world will be able to point to them and say, "Ah, look at those hypocrites; that's why I'm not a Christian." Do not be discouraged by that. Just be sure that you are not one of them. Ask the Lord to reveal the state of your own heart before Him and allow Him to lead you to the fullness of belief in Christ and commitment to Him.

GOOD WORKS

Doctrine is only the first area in which many persons find a false spiritual confidence. There is a second area also; that is works (v. 22). There will always be somebody to say, "It's not just that I believe these things and hear sermons about them, I really *serve* Christ. I prophesy in His name. I cast out demons. I do wonderful works." Now Jesus says that it is quite possible for a person to be baptized, to be confirmed, to take communion, to serve on a church board, even to be a missionary, and still never have been born again. So He says, "Examine your heart, you youthful reformers, you church members, you servants of the Church, you preachers. Are you born again?" The Bible says, "For by grace are ye saved through faith; and that not of yourselves, it is the gift of God — not of works, lest any man should boast" (Eph. 2:8, 9).

This latter verse does not mean that there are not to be good works in Christianity, for there certainly should be. However, good works have to be those that come forth out of the life of Jesus Christ within. That is why, for instance, in theology the phrase "faith and works" is used. Faith is not mere intellectual assent to certain doctrines, the kind of belief that Jesus warned about earlier. It is commitment, or personal trust. Thus the phrase means that there must be personal commitment, and then, growing out of that, there must be good works. These are the two oars of the ship that are meant to propel it forward. If only one oar is present, there will be trouble.

In one of the great battles that took place between the Greeks and the Persians just prior to the Greek Golden Age, there was an incident that perfectly illustrates this principle. The Persian fleet had sailed from the Bosporus out along the Macedonian coast and then down the edge of Greece to Attica. It finally met the Greek ships in the bay of Salamis just off Athens. The Greek ships were lighter and quicker; the Persian ships were cumbersome. So, in the battle that followed, the Greeks made short work of the Persians. In one particular encounter a Greek ship managed to sail close to a large Persian vessel and brush by its side. Because it had done this quickly, the Persian oarsmen did not have time to draw their oars in, although the Greeks did. The result was that the Greek ship broke off all of the oars on that side of the Persian vessel. Few on the Persian ship realized what had happened, and because the oarsmen on the other side continued rowing, the ship swung around in a circle leaving a fresh set of oars visible to the Greek captain. The Greeks then reversed their ship, trimmed off the other set of oars, and sank the enemy.

It must have been a humorous sight, the great ship going around in circles. But it is an illustration of what happens when there is faith without works or works without faith. Oh, we can generate a big storm with one oar. We can get attention. But we will just be going around in circles spiritually. Real Christianity is a personal relationship to Jesus Christ through faith resulting in a new life that goes forward and that is increasingly productive of good works.

BECOMING A CHRISTIAN

At this point you may be quite ready to say, "Yes, I acknowledge that the personal relationship you are talking about is necessary, and that I must have it. But how does Jesus become my Savior personally?" It is quite simple. To begin with you must stop what you are doing and listen carefully to His voice. It is quite easy to do the opposite. John R. W. Stott, minister of All Souls Church in London, writes in *Basic Christianity:* "It is tragically possible to turn a deaf ear to Him and to drown the insistent whisper of His appeal. Sometimes we hear His voice through the prickings of the conscience and sometimes through the gropings of the mind. Now it is a moral defeat, now an inexplicable spiritual hunger, now sickness or suffering or fear, through which we detect His pleading. We can listen to His call through a friend or a preacher or a book. When we hear, we must listen." *

Second, when He speaks to us we must acknowledge that the things He is saying, however difficult to accept, are true and that He alone has the answer to our problems. Jesus is kind, but He

* John R. W. Stott, *Basic Christianity* (Chicago: Inter-Varsity Press, 1968), p. 128.

does not pull punches. He will spell out the problem. Whatever form your sin may have taken, whether the sin of Abraham, or David, or the rich young ruler, or Paul — whatever it may be — He will reveal that sin to you. He will tell you why it is serious in His sight, why sin must be dealt with, and why the solution to the problem had to be His death on Calvary.

There was no other good enough
To pay the price of sin;
He only could unlock the gate
Of heaven, and let us in.

Finally, there must be an act by which you open the gate of your heart and admit Him. Or, to put it another way, you must pass through the narrow gate to salvation. This does not mean that you are responsible for your own salvation. If you do open the door, it is because He is there beforehand moving you to do it. And yet, from your own point of view, the act itself is absolutely indispensable.

C. S. Lewis, the great Christian apologist, writes of his own personal conversion: "I was going up Headington Hill on the top of a bus. Without words and (I think) almost without images, a fact about myself was somehow presented to me. I became aware that I was holding something at bay, or shutting something out. Or, if you like, that I was wearing some stiff clothing, like corsets, or even a suit of armor, as if I were a lobster. I felt myself being, there and then, given a free choice. I could open the door or keep it shut; I could unbuckle the armor or keep it on. Neither choice was presented as a duty; no threat or promise was attached to either, though I knew that to open the door or to take off the corset meant the incalculable. The choice appeared to be momentous but I was also strangely unemotional. I was moved by no desires or fears. In a sense I was not moved by anything. I chose to open, to unbuckle, to loosen the rein. I say, 'I chose,' yet it did not really seem possible to do the opposite."

Later, in his rooms at Magdalen College in Cambridge, Lewis made the final decision. "In the Trinity Term of 1929 I gave in, and admitted that God was God, and knelt and prayed: perhaps, that night, the most dejected and reluctant convert in all England." *

* C. S. Lewis, *Surprised by Joy* (New York: Harcourt, Brace & World, 1955), pp. 224, 228, 229.

It does not matter in the slightest whether you feel the dejection of Lewis, the peace of Luther, or the joy of countless others. What matters is the reality of your own personal commitment to Jesus. Are you a Christian? That is the question. Is it real? The answer to that question does not depend upon your intellectual beliefs ("Lord, Lord") or upon your good works ("Have we not prophesied in thy name?") but upon your relationship to the Lord Jesus. Have you ever asked Him to be your Savior? Have you ever said, "Lord Jesus Christ, I want you to enter my heart"? If you have never done that, then you must know that you are at the gate to salvation. If you have said that, then you can be assured that He has entered your life. For He has said, "Blessed are they who do hunger and thirst after righteousness; for they *shall be filled*" (Matt. 5:6). He says, "Him that cometh to me I will in no wise cast out" (John 6:37).

Chapter 43

The House on the Rock

(Matthew 7:24-27)

We come now to the last words of the Sermon on the Mount, in which Jesus Christ pictures the difference between those who hear His teachings and do them and those who hear His teachings and do not do them. He draws a picture we all know, a picture of a wise man, who builds his house upon a rock, and of a foolish man, who builds his house upon sand. Most of us have sung about this, in one hymn or another, since we were children.

FOUNDATIONS

Basically, it is a matter of foundations. Let me illustrate the importance of having a firm foundation for a building by means of this contrast. Toward the end of one summer, after having spent several months in Europe, I returned to the United States on a student ship that sailed to New York from Rotterdam. I thought when I boarded that it was probably the smallest ship allowed on the ocean. Perhaps I was right, for it was certainly slow and very light in high seas. We boarded it at night, and the next morning we were sure we could still see Holland. By the end of the third or fourth day we were just passing Land's End, England. All in all, the crossing took nine days.

The difficulty, however, was not only the length of time. The hurricane season had arrived, and a number of storms had managed to churn up the ocean midway between England and Newfoundland. We arrived at New York harbor after days of tossing about like a cork in a bathtub, and our first calm was the calm we felt as we entered the harbor in the middle of the night. Because I did not want to miss seeing the harbor, I spent most of the night on the deck, watching the ship slowly maneuver into place in the channel, drop anchor, and stop. Then I saw the gray spires of lower Manhattan emerge like mountains in the constantly bright-

306

ening light of dawn. I thought how firm they appeared and what a contrast they were to the way I had been spending the last nine days.

One summer several years later, my family and I visited Venice, where we received a very contrasting impression about foundations. We arrived about 12:30 at night. Cruising along peacefully under the warm Italian night sky, we took a motor launch down the Grand Canal to the Piazza San Marco, where our hotel was located. Venice is like New York in some respects. They are both great ports. They are financial centers. But I knew, even as I gazed at the great Venetian buildings, that Venice was slowly sinking into the waters of the Adriatic sea. The difference between Venice and New York is that Venice has no foundations such as New York has.

That is a bit whimsical, perhaps, but it illustrates in vivid, contemporary terms what Jesus is talking about in the Sermon on the Mount. Jesus says that a man builds a life the way designers build cities, and His point is that the factor that determines what will remain and what will not remain is the foundation. "Therefore," He says, "whosoever heareth these sayings of mine, and doeth them, I will liken him unto a wise man, who built his house upon a rock. And the rain descended, and the floods came, and the winds blew and beat upon that house, and it fell not; for it was founded upon a rock. And every one that heareth these sayings of mine, and doeth them not, shall be likened unto a foolish man, who built his house upon the sand. And the rain descended, and the floods came, and the winds blew and beat upon that house, and it fell; and great was the fall of it" (Matt. 7: 24-27).

In these closing words of His sermon, Jesus stressed the importance of an adequate foundation. What is your foundation? On what do you build?

CHRIST IS THE ROCK

That is a most profound question, and it is a good one to come to at the end of the Sermon on the Mount. For, you see, it is quite possible for a man to have heard all Jesus' teachings and to have said, "It is true. These are great sayings. They are the key to morality. I'll just go out and try a bit harder." But if you are thinking that way, you have missed the whole point of what Jesus is saying. He says, "I am not asking you to go out and try harder.

You will never be able to do it. To go out and try harder and to try to construct that kind of character in your own strength is like trying to build a mansion upon sand. Actually, you will only achieve that kind of character when you build on Me."

This is really the first and most important point of these verses. Jesus Christ is the foundation. He is the rock. I know, of course, that not all Scripture passages that use the word "rock" or "foundation" imply this, but certainly it is the only true sense in this passage. It is true that in 1 Timothy 6:17-19, Paul speaks of works as a good foundation: "Charge them that are rich in this age . . . that they do good . . . laying up in store for themselves a good foundation against the time to come." He also speaks of God's eternal decree in election as our foundation: "Nevertheless, the foundation of God standeth sure, having this seal, The Lord knoweth them that are his" (2 Tim. 2:19). But these are exceptions, and for each of these texts there are many more which apply the same imagery to Jesus Himself or (in the Old Testament) to the Messiah.

Thus, Isaiah writes, "Therefore thus saith the LORD God, Behold, I lay in Zion for a foundation a stone, a tested stone, a precious cornerstone, a sure foundation" (Isa. 28:16). Paul writes, "And [ye] are built upon the foundation of the apostles and prophets, Jesus Christ himself being the chief corner stone" (Eph. 2:20). Shortly after the Resurrection Peter told the Sanhedrin, the highest court of the Jews, "This is the stone which was set at nought of you builders, which is become the head of the corner" (Acts 4:11). He wrote in his first letter, "Behold, I lay in Zion a chief cornerstone, elect, precious; and he that believeth on him shall not be confounded. Unto you, therefore, who believe he is precious, but unto them who are disobedient, the stone which the builders disallowed, the same is made the head of the corner" (1 Peter 2:6, 7).

That is the true sense of Christ's teaching. He is saying, "If you want a construction that will last for this life and for eternity, build on me." Are you doing it? If so you can sing:

> My hope is built on nothing less
> Than Jesus' blood and righteousness;
> I dare not trust the sweetest frame,
> But wholly lean on Jesus' name.
>
> On Christ, the solid rock, I stand;
> All other ground is sinking sand.

Christianity is Jesus Christ. Thus, the life of blessing promised by Christianity must be constructed on Him.

THE HOUSE WILL STAND

The second important point to be seen in these verses is this: a life built upon Jesus Christ will stand. That is a simple point, of course, but we need to have it clear in our thinking and to get it planted deeply in our minds. A life built upon Jesus Christ will stand. It will stand even in the midst of the tribulations of this life or the judgments of eternity.

We are going to have tribulations. They are the common lot of man, but only the Christian who is building upon Christ and whose mind is captive to the will of God can triumph over them gloriously (Rom. 5:3). In the Book of Job there is a passage in which one of Job's comforters says, "Although affliction cometh not forth of the dust, neither doth trouble spring out of the ground, yet man is born unto trouble, as the sparks fly upward" (Job 5: 6, 7). The image is highly poetic. It tells us that each generation of men can be compared to a stack of cordwood that is placed upon the burning embers of the past. That is our destiny, to pass through fire and in due time to be released forever. Every child of Adam — you and I and countless millions of others — will experience sorrow, pain, suffering, disappointment, and eventually death.

What is the solution? Not escape certainly, for escape is impossible. The solution is to build upon a sure foundation. So Jesus says that although the rains will fall, the floods will rise, and the wind will blow, the life that is constructed upon Him will survive.

That is true. It was true for Job. It was true for Moses and David and Isaiah and Jeremiah and all the other great Old Testament figures. It was true for Peter, James, John, and Paul.

Let me give you a more contemporary illustration. Dr. Joseph Parker, a noted English preacher, who for many years proclaimed the Word of God in the great City Temple of London, tells in his autobiography that there was a time when he gave too much attention to the modern theories of his day. Men were undervaluing the Word of God, and he found himself, as he read their books and mingled in their meetings, losing his grip upon the great fundamental doctrine of salvation through the atoning blood of the Lord Jesus Christ. At this point there came into his life a great sorrow.

His wife, whom he loved deeply, became sick and died within a few hours. He was unable to share his grief with others, and walking through the empty rooms of his home with a breaking heart, he felt for some footing in the theories of his day and found none. "And then," he said, addressing a company of his Congregational brethren, "my brethren, in those hours of darkness, in those hours of my soul's anguish, when filled with doubt and trembling in fear, I bethought myself of the old gospel of redemption alone through the blood of Christ, the gospel that I had preached in those earlier days, and I put my foot down on that, and, my brethren, I found firm standing. I stand there today, and I shall die resting upon that blessed glorious truth of salvation alone through the precious blood of Christ." *

> *On Christ, the solid rock, I stand;*
> *All other ground is sinking sand.*

Precious Stones or Stubble

There is one last point here, and it is a point for Christians. What are you building, Christian? Oh, you are on the foundation all right. Christ is your Savior. But do you know that it is possible for Him to be your foundation and yet for you to go through life building things that are worthless and will not remain as fruit for eternity even though you will be saved personally? Listen to Paul, "Now if any man build upon this foundation [Jesus Christ] gold, silver, precious stones, wood, hay, stubble — every man's work shall be made manifest; for the day shall declare it, because it shall be revealed by fire; and the fire shall test every man's work of what sort it is. If any man's work abide which he hath built upon it, he shall receive a reward. If any man's work shall be burned, he shall suffer loss; but he himself shall be saved, yet as by fire" (1 Cor. 3:12-15).

I believe that there are really only two mistakes that a person can make here in regard to Christ's teaching. There is the error which says, "I need no foundation at all; I'll just drift." Many people are drifting today, especially the young. But the trouble with drifting is that you go downstream. Water always flows downstream. You can never drift into happiness. A drifter needs a foundation.

* From H. A. Ironside, *In the Heavenlies* (Neptune, N.J.: Loizeaux Brothers, 1937), pp. 56, 57.

There is also the error which, I suppose, is more generally committed by the older generation today. They say, "Yes, we all must build upon a firm foundation," but they do not see that it is possible to build wrongly upon the foundation. Thus, they do not enjoy true happiness or security either.

What are you building? The precious things of God? Or things that may dazzle now but will soon pass away into nothing? If it is the latter, you may find yourself on the day of judgment in the ridiculous position of Ozymandias, that legendary Persian king about whom Shelley wrote a poem. According to Shelley, the great statue of Ozymandias lay prone in the desert in the midst of thousands of square miles of rolling sand. The inscription said, "Look on my works, ye mighty, and despair."

What are you building upon the foundation that is given you by God? Are you living for yourself? It is entirely possible for Christians to do that. Or are you living for Him?

Quite a few years ago William Borden went to Yale University as an undergraduate and afterward became a missionary candidate planning to work in China. When he made his decision to invest his life in this service, many of his friends thought him foolish. He had come from a good family. He had wealth and influence. "Why are you going to throw away your life in some foreign country," they asked, "when you can have such an enjoyable and worthwhile life here?" But William Borden of Yale had heard the call of God. While in Egypt, on the way to China and even before he had much of a chance to do anything, he became sick. Soon it was evident to everyone including himself that he would die. At this point Borden could have said to himself, "What a waste. My friends were right. I could have stayed in New Haven." But Borden did not think this way. As he lay on his death bed in Egypt, he scribbled a farewell note to his friends that was in some sense his epitaph. The note said, "No reserve, no retreat, and no regrets."

How could Borden of Yale write such a statement? Simply because he had learned to build upon a firm foundation. And he was prepared, as we all should be prepared, to pass confidently into Christ's presence and to hear His warm welcome: "Well done, thou good and faithful servant. . . . Enter thou into the joy of thy Lord" (Matt. 25:21, 23).

Chapter 44

He Spoke With Authority

(Matthew 7:28, 29)

Everyone knows the difference between a person who speaks out of vast and accurate knowledge and a person who merely repeats what he has heard from others. The one is the voice of authority; the other is the voice of a parrot. The first is the sound of the fountain bubbling forth freshly from the ground; the second is the sound of an empty cistern.

There are times in history when there are none to speak with authority, and when that happens, there will always be some who, although they have no authority, nevertheless assume it. That was true in Christ's day. For five hundred years the Jews had been without a prophet, and, as a result, the scribes had emerged as apparent authorities because they had learned the Scriptures by rote. They were the recognized expositors of the law, and it was their duty to memorize the law, together with all the various opinions about it given by the most learned rabbis of the past. They were then to pass this knowledge on for the benefit of their contemporaries.

The Jews who heard Jesus of Nazareth preach the Sermon on the Mount had long been familiar with these authorities. But when they heard Jesus for the first time, they were at once impressed with the infinite distance that lay between His preaching and the teaching of the scribes. Jesus spoke *with* authority, while they spoke *from* the authorities. Or, as Alexander B. Bruce, in *The Expositor's Greek Testament,* says, "The scribes spake *by* authority, resting all they said on traditions of what had been said before. Jesus spake *with* authority, out of his own soul, with direct intuition of truth; and, therefore, to the answering soul of his hearers." *

---

* Alexander Balmain Bruce, *The Expositor's Greek Testament: I, The Synoptic Gospels,* ed. by W. Robertson Nicoll (Grand Rapids: Wm. B. Eerdmans, 1967), p. 136.

No doubt, this fact made a strong and lasting impression. Matthew, who records the Sermon, ends his account by drawing attention to it. He writes, "And it came to pass, when Jesus had ended these sayings, the people were astonished at his doctrine; for he taught them as one having authority, and not as the scribes" (Matt. 7:28, 29).

CHRIST'S PERSON

It is significant that when Jesus had finished speaking, His audience was apparently more impressed with His authority than with the content of the Sermon itself. There have been times in the past in my own studies of the Scriptures when I would have thought that this was not good. I am not sure that I feel that way anymore. To be sure, to have come to the fullness of faith in Jesus Christ as Savior and Lord would have been a far better reaction on the part of His hearers than the type of amazement that is recorded here. But certainly no one then was at the point where such a profession of faith was possible, not even the disciples. It was therefore far more important at this stage of Christ's ministry that their attention should be riveted to the Preacher of the Sermon Himself. He is the narrow gate at the end of the narrow way they were to follow. He is the rock upon which they were now to begin to build.

Thus, to be impressed with the authority of Jesus was not bad because it meant they were impressed with Him. And the Sermon on the Mount was not ineffective, even if it was not perfectly understood, as long as it fulfilled this function.

It is the same today. At the beginning of these studies, I pointed out that one important reason for studying the Sermon on the Mount was that, like all Scripture, it points us to the Lord Jesus Christ. The Preacher of the Sermon on the Mount *is* the Sermon on the Mount, and so by studying it we are brought into the most intimate contact with Him. There is much we may not understand. But this at least should happen: we should see Him. And thus, it is proper to glance upward to the Lord Jesus Christ once more and to reflect on the authority which was His then and is His now, the authority with which thesewords were spoken.

THE WORDS OF JESUS

We need to do this piecemeal. And we need to begin with the authority of Christ's words themselves, for it was these which first made an impression on Christ's hearers. Did His words have intrinsic authority? Certainly, they did, and anyone can see it. If a person will study the teachings of Jesus Christ, in this Sermon and throughout the gospels, he will soon see that they have an intuitive assurance and character that distinguish them from the words of all other men.

Christ's most startling revelation was Himself. As early as the Beatitudes, in His words about persecution, Jesus assumed that the persecution His hearers would experience would be persecution "for His sake," not for His teaching's sake but because of their relationship to Him. In the next section of the Sermon on the Mount, Jesus set Himself up as the authoritative expounder of the law. He repeatedly said, "Ye have heard that it was said by them of old, Thou shalt do so and so . . . but I say unto you," thereby placing Himself above the rabbis and scribes and doing so without the slightest apology, reserve, or qualification.

He said, "Think not that I am come to destroy the law, or the prophets; I am not come to destroy, but to fulfill." In other words, "I am the Messiah." In chapter six He instructs men how to give alms, how to pray, how to fast, how to avoid materialism and anxiety. In the final chapter He warns against anything that might turn attention from Himself and thus lead the wanderer into judgment. He ends by saying, "Therefore, whosoever heareth these sayings of mine, and doeth them, I will liken him unto a wise man, who built his house upon a rock. . . . And every one that heareth these sayings of mine, and doeth them not, shall be likened unto a foolish man, who built his house upon the sand" (Matt. 7: 24, 26).

These statements immediately distinguish Jesus from all other religious teachers. For, as John R. W. Stott observes, "They are self-effacing; He is self-advancing. They point away from themselves and say, 'That is the truth as far as I perceive it; follow that.' Jesus says, 'I am the truth; follow me.'" * Certainly, if any man ever spoke with authority, it was Jesus.

THE WORKS OF JESUS

But Jesus did not only speak with authority. He also acted with authority. And thus, His works serve to substantiate His claims. What were His works? By the time of the preaching of this Sermon,

---

* John R. W. Stott, *Basic Christianity* (Chicago: Inter-Varsity Press, 1968), p. 22.

according to Matthew 4:23-25, Jesus had already healed various types of sickness among the people and had cast out demons. They were yet to see lepers cured, the eyes of the blind opened, the dead raised to life, a storm stilled, water turned to wine, thousands fed from just a few shreds of lunch, and heaven opened. These works were meant to accredit Him by revealing the source of His teaching. We cannot study them candidly without coming to the conclusion reached by Nicodemus: "Rabbi, we know that thou art a teacher come from God; for no man can do these miracles that thou doest, except God be with him" (John 3:2).

As I say this, I am aware that there have been gigantic attempts in the world of scholarship to remove the supernatural element from the gospels. But I am also aware that all attempts have ended in total failure.

In the year 1768, in Germany, a historian named Hermann Samuel Reimarus died, leaving behind a manuscript that was to have far-reaching implications. The manuscript argued that, in dealing with the New Testament, historians must distinguish between the "aim" of Jesus and the "aim" of His disciples, by which he meant that there was a difference between the Jesus who actually lived and died and the Christ about whom the apostles were preaching. Faced with the choice between what he had come to consider two mutually exclusive positions, Reimarus chose the historical Jesus (stripped of all supernatural elements) and thereby launched a whole century of similar research. In this period in Germany Christianity was viewed by many scholars as the product of the early disciples who stole the corpse, proclaimed a bodily resurrection, and gathered followers.

Unfortunately, in seeking to find the historical Jesus, each of the scholars only succeeded in producing a Jesus in his own image, and it became increasingly apparent that in each case the supernatural had been eliminated at the whim of the historian and not at all on the basis of objective evidence. Thus, idealists found Christ to be the ideal man, rationalists saw Him as the great teacher of morality, socialists viewed Him as a friend of the poor and a revolutionary. The most popular theories of Jesus, those of David Friedrich Strauss and Ernest Renan, rejected most of the gospel material as mythology. And Bruno Bauer, who followed them, ended by denying that there had been a historical Jesus at all.

A person can hardly fail to be impressed even today at the immense amount of energy and talent that these German and French scholars have poured into the old quest for the historical Jesus. But in spite of their subtle imagination, genius, historical knowledge and literary skill, all their work came to nothing. They had attempted to eliminate Christ's miracles. But when their work was examined under the most careful critical analysis, it collapsed. By the beginning of this century, when Albert Schweitzer declared his moratorium on the liberal quest, the entire scholarly world recognized that the previous attempts had been failures.

Look at the miracles any way you will. The miracles in the gospels will stand the test of your scrutiny. Let any candid man read the life of Jesus with genuine attention and care, and he will soon acknowledge that the life presented there cannot have been imagined but must really have happened, that the teachings are real teachings, that the miracles are real miracles, that the teachings set forth in the gospels and the miracles that accompany them are inextricably interwoven. What is more, both of these reinforce Christ's authority. Reuben A. Torrey once wrote, "If Jesus lived and wrought substantially as the Gospels record, cleansing the lepers, opening the eyes of the blind, raising the dead, stilling the tempest with His word, feeding the 5,000 with the five small loaves and the two small fishes, then He bears unmistakable credentials as a teacher sent and endorsed by God." *

These two things, the words of Christ and the works of Christ, are joined by Jesus Himself in a comment in John's gospel upon those who had both seen and heard Him and who yet had not believed; "If I had not come and spoken unto them, they had not had sin; but now they have no cloak for their sin. . . . If I had not done among them the works which no other man did, they had not had sin; but now have they both seen and hated both me and my Father" (John 15:22, 24).

THE RESURRECTION

The final and, in many ways, the conclusive bulwark of the authority of Jesus Christ is His resurrection from the dead. At the time of the preaching of this Sermon, of course, Jesus had not died, let alone been raised from the dead. But we must remember that He was ending His sermon with an encouragement for His hearers to keep on as His disciples until they came to that point. And

---

* Reuben A. Torrey, *The Bible and Its Christ* (New York: Fleming H. Revell, 1906), p. 12.

whatever the cause may have been for them, for us the Resurrection is paramount. Did Jesus rise from the dead? If He did, then His authority is established. His teaching is established. His deity is established. And Christianity rests upon an impregnable foundation.

Did Jesus rise from the dead? It is an assertion demanding a Yes from every true believer and every honest historian. There are literally volumes of evidence for it. In the first place, there is the evidence of the sepulchre. It was found empty. The fact that it was empty is best proved by all lack of evidence that it was not. If it had not been empty, the Pharisees would have been quick to have shown the body in order to have refuted the early preaching of the apostles. The same is true also for the Roman authorities, for had they been in a position to have produced the body they, too, would have done so. If the disciples had stolen it — which was the first explanation of the Jewish authorities — they would have hardly been willing to die (as they later did) for what they knew to be a fraud. In the absence of any evidence to the contrary, it is only a sober act of small faith to accept the biblical explanation.

Second, there is the evidence of the graveclothes. When Peter and the beloved disciple (who was probably John) arrived at the tomb on that first Easter morning, the body of Jesus was gone, but — and this was the remarkable thing — the graveclothes had remained behind. They were wrapped as they had been when they were wound around the body. They were not unwound. The napkin which had been around the head was there also, in a place by itself. Yet, the body was gone. The only thing that could possibly account for this state of things was the passing of Jesus' body through the graveclothes just as it was later to pass through closed doors. In other words, there must have been not a resuscitation but a resurrection.

The third line of evidence is found in Christ's appearances, strengthened by the fact that He appeared to many different types of people, to different-sized groups of people, and under a wide variety of circumstances. This argument was so commanding that Paul appealed to it when writing to the Corinthians, showing that Jesus was "seen of Cephas, then of the twelve. After that, he was seen of above five hundred brethren at once, of whom the greater part remain unto this present time, but some are fallen asleep.

After that, he was seen of James; then, of all the apostles. And last of all he was seen of me also, as of one born out of due time" (1 Cor. 15:5-8).

Finally, the truth of the Resurrection is shown by the transformation of the disciples. Men who once had been cowardly and after the death of Jesus were abjectly despondent were then suddenly filled with joy, love, faith, power, and new confidence and were ready to lay down their lives for their Master. What can account for such an extreme transformation? Certainly there is no explanation short of the fact of the Resurrection and of their having seen the resurrected Lord.

THE COMMITMENT

What does all this mean to you personally? The people who heard the Lord Jesus Christ in Galilee on the occasion of His preaching of the Sermon on the Mount were "astonished at his doctrine; for he taught them as one having authority, and not as the scribes." And yet, it is not said that any who heard Him that day believed in His doctrine or committed themselves to Him. Unfortunately, it is possible to do the same thing in our far more hectic and perhaps more sophisticated century.

What is the most important message of this Sermon? Certainly, it is the Person of Jesus of Nazareth Himself, the Son of God, who spoke as no man has ever spoken before or since, who lived as He preached, and who then died and rose again that He might offer us a full and perfect salvation. Do you believe that? Have you committed your life to His care? If you will make that commitment, He will then do for you all that He has promised. He will make you blessed in the sense given to the word in the Beatitudes. He will make you the salt of the earth, a light in this dark world. He will interpret the Scriptures to you through the Holy Spirit. He will teach you to pray. He will carry you through all the cares and tumults of this life to an eternity of unbroken fellowship with Him.

Do you believe that? Today He is speaking to you. He is saying, "Come unto me, all ye that labor and are heavy laden, and I will give you rest" (Matt. 11:28). "Believe on Me." Let your own heart answer, "Never man spoke like this man" (John 7:46). "Yes, Lord, I want You to be my Savior."

Subject Index

Aaron, 39
"Abba," 195-197
Abraham, 68, 94, 95, 150, 195, 233
Achan, 245
Adonai, 203
Adultery, 105, 113; different from fornication, 136, 137
Alms, 178
America, 297
Ananias and Sapphira, 246, 247
Anger, 37, 105-111; cure for, 107-111; righteous, 107
Anxiety, 222, 252-257; groundless, 237; how to avoid it, 256, 257; reasons not to have it, 253-256
Apathy, 258
Aristotle, 36, 37, 193
Aristides, 176, 177
Asenath, wife of Joseph, 39
Assets and liabilities, 103, 104
Assurance, 228, 229
Augustine, St., 26, 42
Authority of Christ, 312-318

Barclay, William, 29, 37, 151, 222, 249, 270, 280, 283, 298
Barnhouse, Donald Grey, 20, 51, 54, 120, 142, 229, 230, 261, 269
Bauer, Bruno, 315
Bayly, Joseph, 58
Beatitudes, 15-69
Beethoven, Ludwig von, 279
Belshazzar, 206
Bible, see Word of God
Bible study, 243
Bible Study Hour, 56, 235
Bibliolatry, 84
Blaiklock, E. M., 47
Blessing for Christians, 14
Bliss, 17
Blood ritual, 16
Bonhoeffer, Dietrich, 300
Borden, William, 311
Brahms, 269
Bruce, Alexander B., 312
Buddhism, 280
Bultmann, Rudolf, 205
Bunyan, John, 235
Business, 31

Calvinism, 183, 184, 277
Calvin, John, 31
Campus Crusade for Christ, 296
Carey, William, 31
Ceremony, 109
Charity, 176-182
Children, of God, 273, 274
Character, assassination of, 107; Christian, 50
Chaucer, Geoffrey, 149
Children, must obey parents, 131
Child labor, 31
China, 155, 156
Cicero, 149
Christ Jesus, 14; answers the Sadducees, 89; authority of, 312-318; birth of, 76; came to fulfill Scripture, 84, 87; death of, 227; divinity of, 301; exposed sin, 60; fulfills Scripture, 91-97; gospel of, 269-271; Great Physician, 264; happiness of, 17, 18; heart of Christianity, 296; identity with, 65, 66; in the Christian, 167, 168; *is* the Sermon on the Mount, 14, 27, 313, 318; light of the world, 78-80; only sure foundation, 307, 308; only way to God, 287-291; praying through, 186, 187; reflects the Father, 27; rejoiced in suffering, 68; resurrection of, 316-318; return of, 41; self-advancing, 314; source of good, 286; temptation of, 87, 88, 235-237; thirst for by Christians, 75; view of the Scriptures, 84-90; wept, 32; will do all He has promised, 318; words of, 313, 314; works of, 314-316
Christian, becoming a, 291, 292, 303, 304; character of a, 50; child of God, 194-197, 273, 274; defined, 70, 71; identity of with Christ, 65, 66; love, 162-168; no rights for a, 155-161; obliged to walk in the light, 82, 83; perfection of a, 66, 67; thirst for Christ by a, 75; witness for Christ, 211
Christian marriage, 112-148
Christianity, nominal, 299-305
Christianity Today, 153
Christian life, cross bearing, 161; love

Scripture Index